PRIMAL LEGACY
Thinking for the 21st Century

Joseph Costa, Ph. D.

The Institute of Thought
BETTER LIFE BOOKS
1995

First Edition

A BETTER LIFE BOOK

Published by the Institute of Thought
312 S. Cedros #240
Solana Beach, CA 92075

Cover
design by Institute of Thought
computer graphics by Sharon Tate Soberon
and Ed Martin

Manufactured in the United States of America

Library of Congress No. 95-75390

Costa, Joseph, 1924-
    Primal Legacy - Thinking for the 21st Century
    "A Better Life Book"
    1. Spirituality   2. Psychology   3. Science
    4. Reincarnation   5. Channeling   6. Metaphysics   I. Title.

ISBN 1-883333-25-3

Contents

2 THE THINKING SYSTEMS OF PLANET, ANIMAL & HUMAN BEING

3 SCIENCE & CREATION

4 RELIGION & SPIRITUALITY

7 MALE/FEMALE GAME

8 CONSCIOUSNESS & ALTERED STATES

9 ILLNESS & WELLNESS

Reincarnation
Mass thought & consciousness
Balance
Freedom
Grounding

ACKNOWLEDGEMENTS

I owe my respect and gratitude to those who I refer to as 'masters on the other side' who insisted over the many years that I test and prove for myself all they helped me see and learn. I also wish to thank the many leaders in their fields today for what they have shared through their writings and lectures. In addition there are those closest to me, my friends, students and co-workers who helped in many ways, directly and indirectly, with the production of this book: Joan Currey, Ed Martin, Cathy Carey, Dolores Smith and Kris Mansell. Special thanks go to my associate Gisela Sommer for the many hours of editing and publishing this work. Last, and most of all, I wish to thank my best friend, partner and wife, Joni, who has seen me through my human frailties, often lifting me back up with her love.

PREFACE

I started writing this book when I was five years old, at least I started gathering the information I will share with you. It all happened in my bedroom night after night. A group of robe clad men taught me to play a game with colored lights; my bedroom ceiling would become a giant board of circuitry with flashing lights. This was in 1929 when such circuitry was a thing of the future.

I took particular notice of the big redbearded man. I guess I had a sense he would be trouble, and he was. Redbeard said, "Joseph can't do it!" and he repeated that statement. This made me nervous even though I knew he was wrong; I was already manipulating the lights to show me things like the where-about of my favorite uncle, Jesse, and other places and things I found exciting. Sensing my nervousness one of the men I knew as Matthew coaxed me to continue playing the game, to pick the right light to move so I could see more things. His smile was reassuring. I mentally tried to move the lights again, but nothing happened. Then 'Redbeard' repeated, "You see, Joseph can't do it."

I was angry and glared at him. I tried to make the lights work once more, but again I failed. I cried out in despair, "But I did it before!" Now my heart was pounding, because I suddenly realized my father might have heard my outburst. If he awakened I knew he would beat me for having all the men and lights in my room. Redbeard again said, "You see, Joseph can't do it."

Angrily I threw back the bed covers and slid off the bed facing Redbeard. He smiled at me. I became angrier because I knew he was making fun of me. I ran at him with my fists clenched and started pounding on him only to find he had disappeared and I ran into the dresser. I had passed right through him. Shocked, I turned toward the others to see them fading away and the light in the room diminishing.

I scrambled back into bed throwing the covers over my head. My hair felt like it was standing on end and my skin felt clammy. I started to sob aloud, thinking they would all feel sorry for me. I soon peeked out from under the covers, but the room was dark except for the faint glow of the street light coming through the window from the corner at Myrtle Street.

Matthew and the others came back in a few days but it took all of forty years before Redbeard returned. His greeting to me then was, "I have waited (all this time) for you to learn your lesson of arrogance, Joseph. You were being tested before I could go on with your other learnings. You failed that test when you struck out at me." Apparently I had learned that lesson, and he returned to teach me other things. I now know him as Joseph of Arimathea.

For years my old friends have come and gone, and most of the time their information seemed of little meaning, although, during World War II, as a GI in Europe, they steered me through many perilous situations, and it seems they were always available to help me in my business and personal life.

Years later I came to the realization that the light games were a way of teaching me about thinking systems and thought particles; but it wasn't until the 1970s that the teachings of those old masters started to fall into place. Coincidentally, that was the time I met my present wife, Joni. We fell in love and married. After the honeymoon was over our faults became evident, and we both considered separation. Neither of us wanted to fail another marriage, so we made a six-month pact to devote all our time to finding the answers to the 'secrets' to relating. After five months of intensive but fruitless searching, during meditation one Sunday, we both received a psychic message in the form of a mental voice that said, "Get the book *All About Angels*." We searched everywhere for it for a week without success. That following Sunday, while meditating, we again received a psychic message, "The book is in your local 7-11 store." The book was there, I bought it and we read it voraciously. Two weeks later another book was recommended that we could not find, and a week after that we were told where to find it in a neighboring community book store. Joni and I felt we were finally getting somewhere in our search.

The book episodes were followed by a visit from my old childhood 'friends' who said our request had been granted they were to teach us the secrets of all relationships. And our daily training began and would continue for more than twenty years. It not only included every level of balanced relationships and communication - vocal, mental, vibratory, religious, spiritual, social and more - in work and play, but specific training in all aspects of thought and thinking; the uses of thought by all things, including the planet, animals, humans, and other kinds of thinkers. The information has been in depth about languages, thought transference in and through this and other dimensions, altered states of consciousness, and moving through dimensions and various levels of what we call consciousness. The teachings involved understanding the science of particles and non-particles and their energies. I marvel at the patience of those masters, especially in view of my early belligerent behavior; I questioned and had to verify everything they said until I was certain in my thinking of its validity.

As a child, my education was limited to the seventh grade. It wasn't until later in my life, my formal education continued. After some successful and not so successful business ventures, I chose psychology as a profession. I attained a hypnosis certificate in 1957 followed by a doctorate in transpersonal psychology. To me, there are no accidents in life, and I see now how I have gradually evolved into my life purpose from the experience as a five-year old who was learning to manipulate the ceiling diagrams to a 70 year old who is teaching classes and seminars, writing and sharing what I've learned.

I write this information in the first person sense as though I am the originator of this paradigm of 'thought and thinking'. I do this without apology except that I ask the indulgence of my peers for the manner of presentation. It is done for two reasons: 1) Much of the information is scientifically untested, and this is not a research paper but meant for general reading and 2) if written as though it were fact, the reader may feel challenged to prove or disprove the concepts. Many of the concepts I share come from my years of 'psychic research' work through altered states of consciousness via my own meditation process or having been guided into these states by 'inner' masters for the purpose of examining various levels of thinking.

This book is titled *PRIMAL LEGACY: Thinking for the 21st Century* because it is about our inheritance since our beginning when the soul and the animal joined together. It is about how to think and how to find purpose as a human and spirit being.

There are many paths to the truths of life and each person must eventually find theirs. Here I share my story, my path, and truths I discovered in over 70 years of searching. When we find our way we are obliged to leave footprints so that others might use them to find their way. I have been graced with guidance from the inner, those who have gone before. This guidance is available to all of us, it is a gift already given to us that we must learn to develop and use in our search for meaning.

Since those memorable Sunday afternoon meditations when Joni and I both heard the same voices telling us about the books in the 7-11 convenient store and other book stores, there has seldom a week gone by that we have not communicated with our guidance. By using special excercises taught us by the masters we have learned to balance both our yin and yang powers and together create an optimum energy for clear channeling. This took many weeks of practice. When we finally succeeded and the messages were consistent in clearness, using Joni as the voice, there was great rejoicing by the masters.

Throughout the years we communicated on a daily basis and recently mostly on Sundays. The learning continues, and occasionally I ask something of them that I feel is important to have specific input on. Such was the occasion in reference to this book as it was about to be completed and ready to go to print. In discussing the preface with a master I asked how I might address you, the reader, and prepare you for reading this work about the path of the soul here on this planet. I was advised to tell you it is about purpose.

Here is an excerpt of our conversation:

Me: "I am close to the completion of the book. Is there something more I should be putting in it?"

Guide: "Put forth that which is you with the understanding that, 'This is my gift to the human experience, this is how I do the human experience.' It is not to say, if you do as I do you shall be like me, for no one is you, all are as they are. It is the exchanging of what you are that is the gift you give."

Me: "What specifically can I point out that might be most important to those who read it?"

Guide: "Man's greatest need is to find purpose in an unpurposeful world. Is this not the greatest question you are asked, 'help me find my purpose, I need a purpose,' my friend? Man needs a purpose! Is your book the fulfiller of man's needs? Can you give man a purpose or the understanding to find purpose?"

Me: "Yes. In this book there are ways to find purpose."

Guide: "Then is that not what you give?"

Me: "That is what I give."

Guide: "Is this not a planet where needs are filled? Is this not what it is about?"

Me: "This is true."

Guide: "Man does not have a need to be, shall we say, a masterful human being. Do you understand what I say? To lift himself above all others, that is not man's greatest need. Man's greatest need is to - in his heart - feel the purpose of living in an experience crowed with pain and sorrow. Man needs to find reasoning within the pain and sorrow. Man needs to know. Man needs to know, for he is losing faith in all and slowly becoming the animal. Is this not true, is this not what is happening? Is not man going back to his primitive nature of animal? What is the difference between an animal and a human being?"

Me: "The soul and the mind."

Guide: "A human being has purpose above and beyond the feeding and the procreating of the species. Is this not true?"

Me: "Yes, this is true."

Guide : "Then is this not what you put forth in your book - in words that man can truly understand and say, 'Aha, I have purpose! I have purpose!'"

Me: "Is the title sufficient, or should I have purpose in the title?"

Guide: "Stress in your opening - and it can be on cover if you choose - that man's greatest need is to find purpose in the human experience. Say what is the need for that is what man will respond to."

Me: "I shall do that and thank you."

Guide: "Man is lost, my friend. Man is lost. His entertainment is violent; his thoughts are violent; his deeds are violent. And woman is sorrow; her demeanor is sadness; her thinking is pity; her actions are remorseful, for she is not listened to nor part of the balance. For man's struggle has grown much too animalistic for woman to try to balance. You may state this in the beginning of the book to set the tone for man to find that which he seeks and woman to understand her sorrow, her sorrow."

Me: "I thank you for that."

Guide: "You are most welcome."

The ideas in this book are simple and are meant to show that life on earth is simple. It is my hope that what I have written will entice you to explore the path of simplicity to the attainment of ultimate joy and a better life.

Joseph Costa, Ph.D.

1

The Soul
the Mind
& the Animal Brain

INTRODUCTION

The first thought I wish to share with you is this: I am an advocate of the soul experience as being an aspect of our existence. You will find the soul referred to throughout the book. I refer to the soul in the context of what the soul is doing here and how it goes about doing it through the thinking of the person. I have approached the subject from different angles to assure it is stated clearly to facilitate understanding. In the relating of my personal experiences and those of others, the reader may find some of them hard to accept, but it is my feeling that the concepts will be readily understood once the principles of thought and thinking are grasped.

This paradigm of thought and thinking presents ways of looking at science and the behavior of human beings in an enlightening way. The 'principles' of this new paradigm cover every aspect of the human experience. They tie together, in simple, common sense, all the modalities used, including scientific laws, human behavior on every level, everyday activities of relating, working, healing, and how and why we think as we do.

We begin with gaining an understanding that the universe is composed of thought particles and non-particles and their energies; therefor planet earth and all that is within or upon it is of the same composition of thought particles. Consider that the essence and make-up from the first non-particle on up to the largest particle of matter is thought itself. Human thinking, or consciousness, is a sea of thought particles and thought non-particles which pour through the human and other thinking systems of creatures in the planetary sphere. This is the paradigm of thought. Let us follow it further.

Impressed by its many attributes, we have had a romance with the human animal for thousands of years. The Olympics show off the physical body, the space program and computers show off the brain. These are remarkable representations of the human animal, but they fall far short of explaining who and what we really are. With all our material and physical accomplishments, we are still left with a feeling of emptiness. The higher we climb in social acceptance, the more we feel something is missing from our lives. Our happy states are short and few between because we know there is more to life.

The more to life is what this book is about. To have fulfillment in life, we have to unearth our true selves and become aware of who we truly are and where we are. As to what we are, we each are gifted with a body which is the symbol of who we are. We are gifted with a mind which is separate but connected to our body, the soul-mind, not the nondescript mind we half believe we are using when we think. *soul-mind*

The soul-mind surrounds you like a giant ball or bubble (fig. 1). Your physical body is at the center of the ball, connected to it at the pit of your stomach. Imagine yourself in this ball you cannot see, its outer edge six feet from the pit of your stomach in every direction.

The soul-mind functions as a thinking system entirely separate from the one in your brain. Its thinking ability far exceeds our present comprehension. You have heard the two voices which seem to be in your head, always at odds with one another? Sometimes we call one our intuition, the inner voice, or, perhaps, our conscience? This is the thinking system that whispers messages in your ear, the voice of the soul-mind. When you have eaten your fill, and the desert is offered, and your brain says, "My, how delicious that looks, I'll have a piece of that chocolate cake!" it is the soul-mind which says, "Don't eat it." The soul-mind alway takes the position that there is another way to think about things. The soul-mind holds the truth of what is most beneficial for our growth and understanding. *our higher self*

As to where we are in the dimension we are in and how we project

19

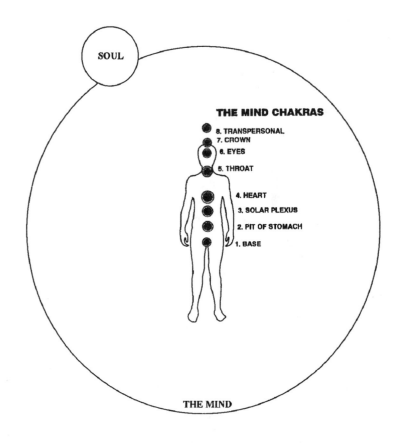

Fig. 1. The soul-mind thinking system.

our lives, requires clarification, because that deals directly with what we are calling 'raising consciousness.' It is just as important to understand about dimensions as it is about thinking systems; both are keys to this paradigm and the consciousness raising we all desire.

Our studies of science lead us to believe we are living in the third dimension. We are taught that the third dimension simply means being able to see depth or thickness; it means much more than this simple deduction. If you become aware of exactly how you look at things, you will realize you usually see things two dimensionally.

When we look at anything we are in the habit of automatically

20

focusing on that particular surface and the picture we get is two dimensional. If we expand the viewing and eliminate the direct focus we then see three dimensionally. However, if we take conscious notice of what we do when we change our visual focus, we simply focus on what is around the object we first focused on. This is again two dimensional viewing. Almost all the time we are viewing this world two dimensionally.

Try this. Compare looking at someone in a room two dimensionally and then with three dimensional viewing. Focus on a person and then notice how s/he stands out from the background. That person even 'stands out' as if s/he were in front of everything. This is so even though there may be a desk or chair between you and that person. This is two dimensional viewing. Now try this. While observing that same person, allow your eyes to 'unfocus' and take in everything in the room just as clearly as you do when you focus on only one thing. With practice you can see the desk or chair in front of the person as clearly as you see the person or even what is behind the person and not lose broader focus of the other objects in the scene. This is the beginning of seeing three-dimensionally.

3-D

We have the ability to view three dimensionally and then if we choose to we can narrow our focus. However, today we focus first (two dimensionally), and then, some of us, do some three dimensional viewing, but rarely. We may go through the whole day not having entered the third dimension once from a viewing perspective.

In addition to this observation of the two ways of seeing there is the third dimensional approach with all the other senses involved, hearing, feeling, smelling, etc. We have little appreciation or ability of how to use all the senses as they are supposed to be used at this stage in evolution.

WHAT THE BOOK IS ABOUT

What you are about to read is a journey into this new paradigm of thought and thinking, a new model of a three dimensional universe and its thinking systems; mind, brain, planetary, animal And human.

For scientific readers, it may seem that what I present here supports the idea of mechanistic science or particle philosophy, and I wish to point out the differences between hard science particle theory and what I am sharing. Mechanistic science has a biological foundation, however, if we consider quantum science, we discover that there is a factor of the particle and non-particle in quantum physics that makes the particle something other than a hard science basic biological material building block. Particles, or non-particles, in the pre-origin of matter phase have a living essence that makes their behavior unpredictable. This alters the idea that one plus one must equal two.

Science has already traced non-particles in the colliders while recording behavior of what has been labeled as the quark (a suspected particle). It is at the quark level that the influence of the observer (scientist) begins to have measurable effect on the outcome of the research. As non-particles diminish in size their behavior is more easily influenced by the observer. At the level of the pure non-thought particle (pure, meaning not previously used by human thinking), human influence keeps the non-particle in chaos. Weight (mass) is added to the non-thought particle as it is attracted toward manifestation through human thought influence, then it slows and becomes more predictable and eventually observable as the particle.

Throughout this work I refer to thought particles as the basis or basic building blocks of thinking and manifestation. I use the word particle to imply a basic principle. Particle implies a part of something, and this is how I use it. When one examines the thought non-particle one sees a non-particle energy form, however, this is not easily explained or described, and for that purpose I simply state 'thought particle'.

Many mechanistic scientists insist that there is no soul and that life is a simple formula of evolving matter. I mention this because I want to make the point that the foremost thinkers who are bound to the mechanistic theory have no more foundation of proof of their evolution theories than the believer of the creation theory has proof of the soul. This very point is made clearly, but unwittingly, by one of the leaders of science, Francis Crick, who claims to be a non-believer of the soul. Crick is a winner of a Nobel Prize (DNA) and author of *The Astonishing Hypothesis*. While expounding on his no "soul' theory in that writing, he states, "We simply don't have all the answers yet". This statement is an admission of no foundation of his 'no soul' thesis and the theory of evolution.

Francis Crick is a great scientist, however, he is only that for the left brain element of humanity. I say this respectfully to point out a dilemma of humankind; and that is humankind's past inability to realize that right brain subjective thinking (reality as personally perceived) is as important to the mental and physical growth of the human being as is left brain objective (intellectual/materialistic) thinking. Subjective thinking has its own foundations and can be as scientific as non-subjective (critical/intellectual) thinking.

When we examine the history of great thinkers of the world we discover that some of them originally gave the world personal subjective theories. Those subjective theories became the keys to paradigms or formulae embraced by hard science. An example of this would be Einstein's heuristic formula of quantum physics. He presented the right brain subjective possibility, and others in hard science, using his information, confirmed the mechanistic logic of his thesis. It is interesting that many hard science scientists of today still avoid or disallow Einstein's mc^2 formula which is not implemented today as it could be, because the average scientist is not able to work with it due to left brain training.

Even though scientists are using subjective research in the examining of the quark, it is not recognized that they are actually doing subjective research. Due to the lack of scientific expansion into methods of subjective research, the world is behind in mental evolution. Unknown to science, human beings are struggling to fully enter the third dimension as an aspect of the evolving universe. It is becoming increasingly necessary for humans to understand how the thinking mechanisms of the planet and its creatures work. Through this knowledge we can understand third dimensional living.

INDIVIDUAL OR COLLECTIVE HUMAN BEING

Although there seem to be various kinds of societies on earth, from the so-called primitive to the highly 'advanced' intellectual, we find that all are an expression of the single human unit. This means that by examining the thinking structure of any human being anywhere, we find the formula for behavior of individuals and societies everywhere. When we examine the thinking systems of the human being we find that all humans process thinking in the same way and have the same impression of what thinking is. Most people read the words 'thought and thinking' and say to themselves, "Oh yes, we all do that!" When

I follow up and ask someone, "What is thought and where are you getting it from?" there is usually a blank look on the face of that person. Although thinking has been an accepted practice there has been very little success achieved by scientists or educators to answer the questions of where thought comes from or what it is.

When planet earth learning first began, we, as souls, came into this earth experience with a far greater understanding of who we were than what we believe of ourselves today. We knew we came here as light beings, and we had more memory of our past available to us than we have now. As the thinking of human beings densified with distorted energy on thought particles, our ability to use thinking in a balanced way changed. Ultimately, we accumulated a 'veil', shutting down our ability to draw on the simplest of past memories. Since then we have been compounding our confusion and complicating life.

Today, we all have egos which serve to tell us how great we are, no matter what. This false view of ourselves is what hides the truth of ourselves. It is an interesting enigma: on the one hand we like to think that we are far more advanced than our caveman ancestors were and we brag about going to the moon and such, yet, on the other hand, close examination of our behavior today reveals how easy it is for us to kill one another and destroy that which is in our way. This kind of evidence gives one cause to think we are still grossly primitive; certainly we do not act much more advanced than what we imagine the caveman might have been like. What has changed in us is the human animal brain. The human animal brain has developed a false ego which works constantly to suppress thought and beliefs that might in some way take power away from ourselves individually.

Because there is a planetary synchronicity of thought systems, the human mass experience, in its totality, has a mass ego. Although we are individuals, we are also a mass of thinkers and are subject to the false ideas of the mass ego.

As an example of this idea of the mass ego overdoing things, let us consider that schooling today leads us to believe that we are already in the third dimension. We are mentally accepting our level of reality as being the third dimension. Actually, if we examine mass thinking closely enough, we will realize that we mentally think in terms of the second dimension. We have not yet transitioned fully into the third dimension. As we shall see here, we have much to do to find ourselves

24

truly in the third dimension.

In 1992, the International Transpersonal Association (ITA), held their annual congress in Europe, in the city of Prague. The focus of this conference was on consciousness raising. People such as Barbara Marx Hubbard lectured on the needs of the planet and the need of human beings to come together in oneness. The problems of the planet were emphasized at this conference; such problems being the suffering caused by the extremes of mechanistic behavior of societies and governments. The hope expressed for the salvation of humankind and the planet was in the obvious consciousness raising the human species seems to be phasing into. There was a desire at the conference to help accelerate world consciousness raising. It was pointed out that old paradigms had run their course, creating chaos and a chemically polluted planet, and the answers must be found in a new paradigm.

A paradigm is a philosophy, but more than that, it is a thought form, a formula of thoughts for projecting life. We might say the last paradigm that the world accepted as a world truth was the mechanistic view as science presented it. It is a paradigm that has exceeded its role and needs changing or adjustment.

At this conference in Prague social scientists were propounding ideas about a new way to think and live, a way which would save the earth from the biological poisoning and destruction set in motion by mechanistic ideas. Most of the speakers talked about the need for humankind to look to the inner or spiritual side of life for the new paradigm that would serve to rectify the human way of living.

One of the interesting presentations made in Prague was the idea that humans are evolving, and that the new superhuman being is forming. This idea was emphasized by statements that the coming superhuman would not only have the intellectual knowledge of a genius, it would be a physical model like the best the Olympics could produce the evolving consciousness raising of the human being would result in the arrival of the superhuman. This superhuman would then solve all the problems of humankind and the planet. Sounds like a Disney fairy tale? It is! Human beings don't evolve in such a manner. If we are to depend on evolution to save the planet for us, we can just forget it. Evolution does not necessarily mean things become superior to what they were. It simply means there is adjustment. It could mean there is more awareness in us, however, it could also mean there is less.

As a matter of fact, the human consciousness has digressed in the last few thousand years, turning humans into narrow intellectual thinkers. Consciousness raising does not mean developing more brain power, as many might suggest. Consciousness raising is the act of expansion of belief systems, both individually and collectively. Consciousness raising will reveal to us that the super human being has been here for eons of time.

When we once believed the earth was the center of our universe, the earth did not correct that idea by trading places with the sun the human being changed its belief of where the center is. When the idea about the earth changed from flat to round, the earth did not change its shape the human being expanded its belief of the shape. Consciousness raising is simply the expansion of the belief systems which are used as parameters for thinking. We have the superhuman today we are the superhuman; we only need to examine ourselves by expanding existing beliefs to discover this.

Why haven't we 'discovered' ourselves before this time? The reason we have not found our true selves is simply because what manifests on this planet does so out of need. Need is the cause of all things coming into existence in this dimension. In the past, that dire need was for intellectual knowledge. Today there is a dire need for the balancing of thought.

I have said earlier that consciousness is thinking. The next question is: What is thought? Let me begin to explain what thought is by stating that your mind is not in your brain. We do not create thought, we use it. Human beings have a mind separate from the skull brain. We have several mechanisms or systems for processing thought besides that of the skull brain. We have several thinking systems that use streams of thought particles which come to us from the planetary sphere. soul mind vs skull brain

What we call conscious thinking are thought forms made up of conglomerates of thought particles. Each thought particle carries various levels of yin and yang (see YIN & YANG) energies. The field of attraction set up by our desires, emotions and thoughts dictates which thought particles we will attract for our use. We have specific mechanisms for attracting varieties of thought particles, mechanisms for processing them, and mechanisms for expelling thought particles from our thought system. Thoughts are expelled either into material

26

reality or the non-material mass thought fields of the planet.

We are designed to attract thought particles in a steady, unbreakable stream from the planetary sphere. This process is supposed to function in harmony with the natural thought systems of the planet which is a living, thinking, entity itself. Thinking is automatic for all creatures with a thinking system. All species of animal, including the human animal, are served thoughts through streams especially suited to the specific brain or thinking mechanism of that specie. There is only one creature that can use thought streams of other species, and that is the human being. Unlike all other animals, the human animal, through its soul-mind system, is the only one which can interfere with the natural streams of thought particles the planet is sending forth to thinking mechanisms of other animals.

There is a dire need today to understand what thoughts can do. Humankind thinks of pollution in the biological sense, and it is true that we have created a dangerous level of chemical distortion throughout the earth globe. However, there is a much greater danger existing from a much more powerful pollution. We have poisoned the very source of the structure of our reality. We have polluted the quality of thought particles which create the material earth and all material things. The streams of thought particles which we use to think with in this dimension are becoming so destructive in content that it is distorting the cellular structure of the planet as well as of the human physical body.

As a living, intelligent organism, the planet has regularly used destructive forces to diminish the level of human anger and greed in the mass thought streams. Volcanoes, hurricanes, earthquakes, lightening and other natural disasters periodically cleanse and modify the quality of thought particles that make up the thought reality.

An example of this destructive cleansing force was the 1992 hurricane Andrew in Florida which created more devastation than we have witnessed before from a hurricane. Yet, it had its better earth purposes. Consider the result this hurricane had on the quality of thinking of the masses who suddenly found themselves expressing through the use of thought energies great empathy and care for others. This infusion of quality thought particles into the thought streams served to offset some of the masses of negative, polluted thought particles which were dangerously unbalancing the planet. The earth, by choosing to unleash this force on humanity, regained some of the positive thought force it needed to sustain its balance. The earth is a material form created out of balanced thought particles and sustains its illusion through the ongoing process of balancing energy influences (thought).

There are always mass mental changes in motion which could make the planet untenable and bring emotional and physical pain to many. All changes, social or physical, affect the health of the planet as well as the human being. Whether it is a hurricane like Andrew, which devastated south Florida, or a single case of child abuse, all destructive forces have their cause in the thinking processes of both the planet and human being.

When human beings do not excercise choice of thoughts, they automatically attract average mass thought from the planet according to their state of emotions. The average mass thought today has great negative force in it. This is the reason why masses of angry people will do things that ordinarily they would not do. The looting and vandalizing during the Los Angeles riots in September of 1993 is an example of this. The need is here to understand the effects of thinking by the individual through mass thought.

After the riots, the host on a Los Angeles TV talk show was asking a psychiatrist if there might be any truth to the idea that mass hysteria was at fault for the ugly behavior of people in the Los Angeles riots. The host made the point that attorneys were trying to show their clients were not in command of their behavior, they pleaded that some kind of hysteria had control of the defendants' minds, and that was the cause of their destructive behavior. The psychiatrist answered that such an idea was nonsense and that there was no such thing as mass hysteria. He added that human beings are fully capable and responsible for making decisions in the conscious state. I disagree with this psychiatrist who is not aware of how thought systems work on this planet.

In the section on MASS THOUGHT I explain why and how thoughts were delivered into the thinking systems of those people who were caught up in the energies of the Los Angeles riots. All of us who were connected (energy wise) to the riots contributed to the thoughts entering the thinking systems of the rioters. This is true even though we might be thousands of miles away watching the riots on TV.

28

Of course, the fact that others contribute through their thinking to someone committing aggressive acts does not excuse the aggressors, it is still the individual's responsibility to control emotions and choose thoughts and actions wisely. The time has come for us to become aware of the influence of the thinking of others on our individual behavior and how we affect others when we think.

Humanity must once again shift forward in thinking (consciousness). We have phased through many confining beliefs over the ages, including those that said the earth was flat and the brain was in the heart. We have come to the time of having to move from a primitive automatic use of thought to understanding thought and its role in human reality.

By raising the quality of our thinking we help humanity make changes in mass thought. Through understanding thought and thinking the human being can come into a balanced consciousness raising. If this can be accomplished we can cleanse the planetary sphere of much of the polluted thought particles which are responsible for destructive diseases and earth changing forces.

Many great leaders and speakers are trying to make sense of what is occurring today on this planet. Typical of forerunners who are trying to give understanding as to what is happening in the world is Richard Tarnas, author of *The Passion Of The Western Mind*. Tarnas shares with us his look at tracing the development of western civilization. His book deals with human life in many areas: philosophy, myth, science, history, physics and others. He makes an assumption that the western person has experienced a historical evolution which has reached a 'dark night of the soul' or crisis state. His book is well done, but it is not the content of his work which gives me cause to refer to it. It is the title of his book which I want to talk about. The title Tarnas used for his work is important because it points up one of many misconceptions of the word 'mind'.

I am writing here about the thinking systems of human beings and the planet, and a major aspect of the thinking systems is the mind. In his title, Tarnas uses 'mind' as a noun, a thing which feels passion. The studies I have done reveal that the real mind, which is different from the brain, does not have passion. Tarnas refers to the consciousness of the collective western people of the planet; therefore, he is referring to western thinking (consciousness), not the western mind.

the mind does not have passion 29

In this work, I am presenting the need for educators, scientists and other 'watchdogs' of the human language to clarify the confusion about mind, brain, consciousness and similar words used in discussing aspects of thinking. The word 'mind' is used in our language in many ways, for example, "mind your own business," and "what is on your mind?" In these statements, mind is a verb and a noun. Where there is confusion, there is misunderstanding; the misunderstanding is in what the mind really is. I wish to clear our language and thinking from this confusion with the information I am sharing about the two different human thinking systems: the physical animal with its physical brain, and the soul with its non-physical mind.

I am asking you, the reader, to permit yourself to be open to what I have to share about the 'mind'. Tarnas and others are simply applying the word mind as most do. The dictionary itself is not clear as to the meaning of mind. It is understandable that the dictionary confuses language where it is referring to thought and thinking as there has been little investigating done into the processes of thought particles and how thinking systems use them or what the mind might be.

When I first learned about the soul-mind, I considered substituting a new word for mind because of its wide usage. After much consideration I decided against using another word for the mind since it would only add to the existing confusion.

The word mind has been used interchangeably with brain, think, thinking, thought, consciousness, unconsciousness, and other words to the extent that all these are also confused in their usage. "Mind what you say," really means, "think about what you say." There are many variations in the use of the word 'mind', however, it is generally used in the context of having to do with thinking. This is so whether it is used as a noun or a verb.

Imagine that the mind is a mechanism separate from the skull brain which functions as the brain of the soul has a different role in the human experience than does the brain in the skull. Although few people have seen the soul-mind, I ask that you be open to finding out what the soul-mind might be. The soul-mind is not measurable in the hard scientific sense; as a thought processing mechanism it deals with thoughts on the subjective or quantum level. If you can be open to examining this writing with the idea that there might well be a mind separate from the human brain, then you have the opportunity to

30

expand your understanding of many things which were difficult to grasp in the past. This is true for layman or scientist. In using a concept of the mind that is shared here you can apply the idea of a separate mind to many unanswered questions and receive greater understanding of human behavior and of those things which have not been explained by other formulae or paradigm.

When it is understood that the human being consists of two distinct beings, an animal with a brain and soul having a mind, one can see there is much more to the psychology of the person. The human animal has a brain which is designed to function in the material dimension, and the soul has a mind (a separate thinking mechanism) designed to manage subjective non-material thinking.

Others in the past have touched on mass thought, including Carl Jung with his idea of the Collective Unconscious. Jung's writings about the Collective Unconscious (which I label mass thought) originated in the archetypes of Platonic ideas. I personally believe he centered on that particular aspect (archetypes) of mass thought and overlooked the other dimensions of the Collective Unconscious. I would refer to Jung's Collective Unconscious as one part of mass thought, the archetypal . There are many more aspects of the planetary mass thought fields than the archetypal. Consider that mass thought encompasses all the thought particles of the planet which are conscious and unconscious, fixed or unfixed, manifested or not manifested and all brains receive thoughts from mass thought.

WHAT WE ARE

Human beings are a composite of two entities. We have an animal body with a brain patterned similarly to all earth animals. We are also souls with individual minds (brain of the soul), which we refer to as 'inner being'. Figure 1 shows the three aspects of the total human being: the human animal by itself, the soul and its mind with its chakras by itself and the two joined as the total human being.

To understand our thinking processes we need to know our thought relationship to the earth. But first we must consider what the earth is. The earth is a living, pulsating, intelligent entity made of

31

thought which is ever manifesting in a universe created of thought particles. As a thinking creature in the thought universe, the earth sustains its illusion using thought particles. It is made of thought particles which materialize and dematerialize in a balanced process. All that exists in it, on it and about the earth is made of thought particles. This includes all matter and non-matter, water, ground, air, animals and humans.

The earth feeds mass thought into all creatures as part of the living process. It sends creatures with thinking systems thought streams needed by them for energizing their bodies and for use in foraging, sexual activity, rearing of young and other basic needs. Each of the earth's brain functioning species feed on their own streams of thought particles. Particles process through brains and through the material bodies' magnetic energy lines. Thought particles used by earth creatures pass back into the earth structure in a circulating feeding process which nourishes the illusion called earth.

What I am presenting is verifiable, using subjective research. It is easily examined by psychics trained to see particles and non-particles. Science is rapidly reaching the point of discovering this 'inner' world through instruments. It is only a matter of time before what is presented here is verified through quantum science research.

The human animal was designed to exist on the earth as other animals and creatures do, using thought particles that pass through its brain and its physical body. As with other earth animals, thought particles used by the human animal are returned to the planet to sustain the whole. No creature can function or sustain life without having thought particles fed to it by the planet. The human animal, like all animals, has its particular strata of thought particles which feed its brain and its magnetic body.

What is the difference between human animals and all other animals? If all there was to the human animal was its likeness to the other earth animals, it would never have choice of thought, appreciate a sunset, or try to figure out the meaning of life. The human animal would function and behave like any other earth species. The difference between humans and other animals is that when a Light Being (soul with its mind) arrives on this planet, it attaches itself to a human animal.

32

The soul cannot function in this material universe unless it expresses through a human animal brain. The only way it can participate in earth life is to connect to an animal designed to permit the soul-mind to use thought particles. By fixating to a human animal, the soul and its mind can be involved in the earth's thought processes and thereby function on the material level.

Why would the soul want to do this? The answer is quite simple. In the thought universe there are two opposing forces or kinds of primary thought energies. These are the positive (yang) energy and the negative (yin) energy. When these two energies are balanced, they create harmony. When a soul needs to refine its balance, it chooses to come to the thought dimension where imbalances are easily exaggerated. By involving itself in material thinking processes it can learn to balance itself into a greater harmony. The soul uses a human animal to become a human being that has the most likely chances of behaving in a manner which would serve the balancing attempts of the soul.

The union of soul-mind and human animal has gone through vast changes since the initial joining of the two, ages before ages. And the union has cycled through many material evolutionary stages again and again. A great problem exists today because of the inequities in the thinking between the skull brain and the soul-mind. The brain of the human animal has usurped too much of the soul-mind's role in the thinking processes. This imbalance of thinking between the two systems has a great disruptive influence on the thinking mechanisms of the planet and other creatures with brains. In summary, the human being is made up of an animal with a material brain and a Light Being soul with a mind, each having its own role in what it needs to think. Thinking is taking place on different levels when we use thought, and different thinking mechanisms are in process when we think.

There is considerable difference between animal brain thinking and soul-mind thinking. Each of these two thinking processes are used for different purposes, however, both influence the actions of the person. Rather than meld for the benefit of the whole, the brain usually rejects the mind influence.

Going to the heart of the problem between the human being and the planet, harm to the planet is caused by misuse of the earth's thought particles. This is done by the thinking of the individual and masses of people. Harm is done to the world simply by our lack of understanding the power of thought. Human beings are continually feeding back into the planet an excess of destructive thought energies. These energies are abusive vibrationally as well as denser in weight, causing an imbalance in the balancing of the planet to sustain its optimum movement in the universe.

THE LIGHT BEING/SOUL-MIND

The Light Being is a title used by masters of the 'other side' to describe the soul with its mind. Many people of different lands have reported that they have seen a brilliant ball of light surrounding human beings. Or they report they have seen a ball of light, and out of it appeared someone. Some people surround the self with white light. As a psychic I am able to see the Light Being which surrounds and permeates the human body of the animal. This is not an aura, it is the energy emitted by the soul-mind.

Like the brain, which has parts that serve different purposes, the mind of the soul contains parts that serve different thinking purposes. Some of these mind 'parts' are referred to by eastern adepts as chakras. With training one can learn to see the chakras of the soul-mind. The chakras appear to most who see them as energy centers aligned vertically in and with the human physical body, or looking like pulsating colored flower petals. At times the chakras appear to grow in area and expand, sometimes fusing with one another. At times, the combining of energies of the chakras merge and they become like one large brilliant ball. The chakras in the mind are mechanisms to attract thought. The more intense the thinking becomes, the more the chakras are 'turned on'.

When the chakras appear to be fusing into a ball of colored light, the thinking of the person has reached a very intense level, intense in the sense of balancing powers between physical kinds of thinking and spiritual thinking of the soul-mind.

Sometimes someone sees a soul-mind which is not bonded to a human physical body. On occasion someone observes chakras by them selves. They would appear as a vertical series of colored lights.

I recall an occasion when a friend called me very early one

morning in great excitement. He told me he had that very morning seen balls of light of various colors in his bedroom while he was in bed. He had suddenly found himself wide awake, aware that something was present, which made him tense and his hair stand on end. The lights were in a column, and when first seen, were in a corner of the bedroom. He said he could see them just over his wife's bare shoulder and arm. Momentarily unsure of being awake, he looked about the room and noticed the window showing the first light of morning. By then he could feel and hear his wife's breathing. Looking back at the lights, he was startled to realize they were moving toward the bed. He nudged his wife and called her name as anxiety rose within him. She had been sleeping facing the lights. When he disturbed her, she turned over to ask what he wanted. By then the lights were almost at the bed, and he was feeling an apprehension and wonder which prevented him from speaking. As his wife repeated her words, she raised on one elbow and he could see the lights very close behind her.

Finding his voice, he began to blurt out what he was seeing, and by the time she understood him and turned to look, the lights had faded away.

The two of them were understandably frightened and got out of bed and went into the living room. Shortly after that he called me to ask if I knew what it was he had seen. He told me they were reluctant to return to the bedroom to get dressed for work.

I explained to him that he had seen the chakras of a soul-mind, he asked me if I would contact his inner guides and find out what was taking place as he was worried that a family member might be in danger. I did psychically contact his guides and was told that one of them had materialized enough to reinforce his belief system about the possibility of him communicating with them, and that shortly he would be in full communication with one of his guides. They said they were doing this in answer to his asking for guidance in a crucial time in his life.

I relayed this information to my friend, and he admitted that previous to this experience he had doubted there was such thing as guides. His wife, however, had encouraged him to consider the possibility of contacting a guide. As a result of her belief he had been researching information on channeling with the intent of contacting his guides. Two months after seeing the chakras he began channeling,

and today he is teaching aspects of the present world consciousness raising with the assistance of a guide from the inner dimension

The soul-mind with its chakra system can be seen by anyone who asks from the heart. On occasion, if the asking is granted your own guide may appear in the mind and chakra form. How much or what one sees of a soul-mind, or the chakras, depends on the amount of thought particles that soul-mind (the guide) is processing when you make a communication. The more thought the soul-mind is able to get from the human being's brain process, the more influence it can exert over and on thAt person. The soul-mind can only manifest things in the material dimension by going through the brain of a human being. My friend's focus on trying to get through to a guide created enough energy for the guide to partially materialize.

As human beings we have taken our identity for granted, and usually that identity did not include being a soul as well as an animal. Most of us acknowledge that we are human beings, not just animals. Others see themselves as a person with maybe some religious background. There is a great difference between being religious and recognizing the self as the soul-mind, knowing what that means and projecting ones life through it. There is the need today to acknowledge the self as the total human being. This requires deliberately identifying the self as being the soul as well as the material person.

SOUL SPLITTING & ESSENCES OF THE BEING

Many people wonder if there are sister souls or twin souls. Based on my information from angels (masters or guides of the inner dimension) the answer is yes, there are twin souls. There are examples of soul splitting in the book *Secret Places of the Lion* by George Hunt Williamson. This writing is mostly about a cadre of special soul guides who have chosen to return again and again to help all mankind. These souls, and possibly some others, seem to have the power to split themselves to become involved in more than one life experience. In tribute to Williamson's work and to his 'leaving of footprints', I wish to honor his recent transition back to the other side.

A soul has a powerful essence with which it permeates the

vibration of the human being it is connected to. Because a soul 'splits' itself and becomes one with more than one human being does not mean this dilutes the essence of the soul. The essence of each split of the primary soul contains the cumulative essence and powers of all the soul experiences. Splitting is a way for a high soul to learn lessons faster. It also explains why several people can claim having been a famous person in past incarnations.

The essence of the Apostle Peter was and is the essence of the soul of that being. No matter how many times the soul of Peter has divided itself (if it has), all of the human beings who share the essence of the soul of Peter are of the essence of Peter, and therefore can say they were Peter in a past life.

Another way to look at soul splitting is through the understanding of 'no time, no space'. Based on the formula of no time and no space, all incarnations are being lived at once in the now. If one truly lives all one's incarnations at once, then the soul is very busy splitting itself to accomplish this. My understanding is that some souls have lived a hundred lives. If this is so it means the soul could have split itself several times.

BIRTH & THE GAME

Unlike animals which are born in seasons, the soul chooses its time for birth. Before joining with a human body, the soul-mind ordinarily chooses its mother and father, gender, ethnicity, as well as all the other powers it must deal with in entering the human experience. The choices are based on the expectation of the powers that are probable and inherent in the pending experience. There is a good reason for choosing the most suitable circumstances as there is a knowing by the soul-mind what it will attempt to learn in this dimension.

Most of us have the belief that the soul is perfect, and that it is the human being that is imperfect, 'sinful'. Consider that the human animal offers the soul an opportunity for growth. The soul is not perfect. It has the need for balance. If it were perfect it would not have ←— to go through this school of duality which is very well suited to learn the balancing of powers.

If the soul is young it might very well be described as hardly developed when it is venturing into its first few human physical incarnations. In that case the soul might choose a life that is basic, and survival itself may be the primary issue of the life. It might choose to be born to a starving black African mother. That soul will be aware that the newborn baby it will bond to will live only hours or days, possible starving to death. The soul making such a choice has many soul lessons yet to face and is jumping into life 'feet first' to learn as quickly as it can. On the other hand, a soul may be on its last bit of learning in the material dimension, and it will be very selective of the baby it bonds to, not wanting to get caught in a life where lessons become major experiences or where there is long suffering pain.

At times, there is a seeming contradiction to the matching of soul lessons and pending life experience, and a soul seems to be at odds with the chosen life. That person appears to be out of step or alienated from those around them, alienated in the sense that it does not accept what seems to be the obvious way of expressing life. This is the case, for example, with the person who is born one sex and begins life believing he/she is of the opposite sex. Confusion about sexual orientations most often has its cause in the soul not leaving the planetary vibration after its previous body expired. For example, a soul might be here to learn patience, and if the lesson of patience was not learned in that lifetime, it is not uncommon for the soul, after death, to immediately return into another human incarnation.

The normal practice of souls at the time for expiration of the body is to pass over to another dimension for the purpose of reviewing and 'digesting' the human learning they just experienced. After a period of self examination and perhaps some further learning in another dimension, a soul can choose an infant it desires to bond to for a new human life experience.

When first born, or reborn, the positions of the planets endow the infant with the essence of the powers of the universe. We call these astrological influences of that particular moment in time. In addition to universal powers, the ethnic and racial essences acquired at birth impart power and energies. Parents carry various physical genetic powers that will also be transferred to the new human being.

Of great importance to the soul is the choice of gender, male or female. This is primary in relation to the overall use of all the subtle powers. All these powers, including the yin or yang energies (see yin & yang) of the female or male, will serve to assist in the learning of soul lessons expected by the soul during the life.

Prior to the birth of the chosen infant the soul-mind reviews and evaluates all the factors involving the infant to be. After examining all the expected energies and powers as well as the people associated/related, and after evaluating if the life will offer the opportunities to face and learn the lessons desired, the soul either accepts the infant or not. If it chooses to not bond with the infant, there are many other soul-minds 'waiting in line' to accept the infant as suiting their need for lesson learning.

I am reminded of a series of events that I was involved in years ago. I had a close friendship with a man who had been recently married, and his wife and he were expecting a baby. This was a man I had known for years, and I respected him as a quiet, solid kind of character who spoke gently and wisely. A few days prior to the birth of their baby I was visited by a soul-mind and asked if I would take it upon myself to be of influence in the raising of the child as a friend of the father and as a favor to a spiritual brother.

After considerable discussion based on my reluctance to do something the father might consider presumptuous or meddling, I agreed that I would help the parents and the child whenever it was possible to do so. I had been reminded that the father had asked me to be godfather to the child and it would be my human duty anyway. When I asked why it would be necessary for the child to have my help, I was told that the concern was with the father, not the infant. The soul-mind informed me that the father was entering a psychological crisis, and the soul was concerned that the infant would not have the expected favorable early life. I personally felt that the father would be just fine and that the infant would have the benefit of a fine mother and father.

After the infant was born, the soul-mind came to me on three occasions to ask me to speak to the father about his yelling at the mother and resenting the birth of the infant. Each time, I called the father on the telephone under the pretense of discussing some work. Each time, I could hear the baby screaming in the background. I would talk to the father until his emotions calmed and the baby would stop crying. After the third time the father accused me of some connection to the infant and in a rage ended our relationship.

 After that last call the soul-mind appeared to me and advised me that the soul considered the circumstances of the infant as unacceptable to the learning it needed and would leave the infant permanently. It thanked me, and before it left I blurted out my concern of the infant being without a soul, and asked if it would now die. The soul-mind assured me that there were *many* souls willing to bond to the infant for their specific learning, and the infant would live. This was a case of an advanced soul trying to protect its choice of a life on this level.

 There are many, many souls with different needs for learning. Souls are not impressed with human positions or status. They choose the life only in relation to the lesson they are hoping to learn for the purpose of acquiring greater balance.

WHAT IS BEING HUMAN?

Being human is having respect for the human animal and its partner, the soul with its mind. The quickest route to failure in the human experience is either being too animalistic or too spiritual. If one is so enamored with the animal that all that is meaningful is satisfying the animal appetites, the life has no dignity or purpose. If one is so enamored with the spiritual life that all that is meaningful is the pursuit of the spirit, there is not enough regard for the material body. Without the body there can be no material experience for the soul with its mind. Without the soul-mind there is no purpose. It requires both to be a human being. Life is sustained by the drive of the animal body to perpetuate itself, along with the process of thinking through the mind which feeds the electromagnetic chemical processes that permits subjective reality to exist in the material reality.

SOUL-MIND AND THE INFANT

Beginning at birth, the infant receives streams of thought particles
(see MASS THOUGHT) from the planet which it starts processing as
soon as its thinking systems are functioning separately from the
mother's. With the taking of the first breath, the soul-mind fuses with
the infant, the the two thinking systems, one of the soul and one of the
animal body, begin working together. Immediately after birth the
soul-mind starts its process of managing thought for the brain. The
soul-mind edits the mass thought coming to the infant and channels if
to the brain according to the priorities of the soul's need for advancement.

In the early months the soul-mind is more involved in the
thinking process than the physical brain is. In the beginning there is
little need for thoughts of physical activity by the brain. The brain
needs programming with beliefs before there is much brain processing.

The average mother and father of the newborn usually search the
face of the infant for signs of recognition and acceptance. There is an
emotional need of the parents to see proof that the infant is all they
expect it to be and that it is theirs. At some point the infant appears to
be focusing and making facial expressions which, for the parents,
means the infant is seeing and accepting them. The parents believe that
the infant sees their facial features, but this is not the case.

During the first few weeks of adjusting to the human experience,
the infant sees mainly by using the mind. The brain of the infant is only
just beginning to build image references. To begin with the infant sees
mostly fusion and radiation of colors, mainly third dimensional. What
some people call the human aura is closest to what the infant sees. Part
of that color fusion and radiation is the life force emanation from the
body of the parent.

The first priority of the infant is the need to feed the adult life ←
force which the infant has a great deal of. We can say that because it
is a new creation the infant is fully charged with life force. The infant's ←
first human act is to immediately send forth life force to the adult that
is communicating with it. This is done automatically without thinking.

41

It has been explained to me by the masters that this is a gift of the infant's soul to the adult for giving life to it.

This act of the infant of feeding life force to the adult can be described thusly. Imagine the ray of life force as being similar to a ray of laser light. It is sent out to be absorbed by the target which is usually the parent, but could be another adult. If the adult is not open to receiving the life force energy ray, it automatically reflects off its target and streams back to its source which is the pit of the infant's stomach.

When the unaccepted energy comes back to the infant, its high level of life force causes a painful jolt of electric type power to strike the pit of the stomach of the infant. Often the reason for colic in an infant is the unwitting rejection of the life force by the adult boomeranging back to the infant. If the infant has no one bonding with it on a mutual acceptance level, then the life force is not projected and causes discomfort in the pit of the stomach. This can be the case when parents are too involved in their own life to fully accept the infant.

Colic pain does not necessarily mean the parent has deliberately rejected the infant. There may be no intended rejection on the part of the parent. What often occurs is that the parent is not open to receiving from the infant. The parent is normally not aware that the infant is trying to feed it life force. This can occur simply by the parent not wanting to hear the cry of the infant when it calls for its milk. Or a parent may be so involved giving to the infant that it does not receive from the infant. Many parents who are stressed in their life try to shut out the calls of the newborn.

I recall being asked by one mother why her baby was in such pain with colic. Knowing the father was extremely busy in his work and seemed to never stop thinking about it, I told the mother to do the following: "Pour him a warm bath when he comes home from work. Fix him a soothing drink. When he is settled into the bath tub simply put the naked baby in his arms and walk away." In this case the baby cried at first, and I had warned her that would be the case, telling her to ignore the cry from either baby or father. She followed my suggestions and soon she was amazed to hear the father playing with the baby who then stopped crying. Soon the baby was making happy sounds. That was the end of the colic and the beginning of a happy ritual between father and baby.

What happened was that the infant was aware of the need of the father for life force, and it projected the life force to the father. The father had acknowledged the presence of the baby in the family but was not involved at the psychic or love level. In other words, the love was not reciprocated between father and child. This rejection of the infant caused a rejection of the life force stream coming from the baby.

THE HUMAN ANIMAL AND ITS BRAIN: THE EXPERIMENT

Science heeds the theory that human beings evolved out of primal slime. After this idea had become thoroughly fixed in the belief systems of the human being other theories were added to the evolutionary idea, including the theory of an evolving consciousness. What science has tried to establish is that the human being developed out of primal slime cells, and one day it began to think for itself, and as time passed and the body evolved, the thinking ability expanded.

Unlike hard science thinkers, creationists like to believe that human beings were created as a material form patterned after the creator's form. This creationist concept serves the different religions and their teachings depicting humans as a special creation, separate from the animals. Both ideas have substance, but are not quite what the beginning may have really been like. My training and understanding of creation is that the 'creator' (whatever it may be) made the human animal using the laws of the planet, keeping within the principles of evolution.

Some might ask, what of the fossils of early man that have been found which reflect evolutionary phases? In the sense of earth time it appears that man has not been here very long since the fossils go back a questionable two million years. It takes very little intelligence when examining what has been dug up as representing 'evolving man' to discover the great discrepancies of the so-called evolving human being.

What has been dug up as evidence of evolving humans reflects the limited range of the thinking of science in that area. Since the law of attraction determines what manifests in reality, what has appeared as fossils matches the cumulative (mass) thought expectation of those who dig for fossils. When science opens its cumulative belief systems and expands its parameters of where the human being might truly have started, records (fossils) will be exposed to represent and support that.

When we examine the need the creator had in the beginning for a material animal with which its 'children' (souls) could learn lessons, it seems appropriate that a human type animal was in order. Having decided that a human animal was needed, it was natural for the creator to examine all animals, and taking special parts from many, it made the first human animal. The result was an animal with many well developed features, what someone might call a perfect animal, capable of multiple functions in the sense of managing a planetary existence. This new animal was primarily a herd animal as there would be many souls coming to the planet, and the herd animal was ideal for such migrations. The human herd animal was created and became ready for the human experience or experiment.

The material body of the human animal is essentially like the body of any other animal. It has a chemo-electric pulse rate originally designed to match the pulse rate of the planet. Like all animals, the human animal was designed to mentally function using planetary thought streams that are aligned with herd animals. Planetary mass thought fed the human animal brain as it fed the brains of all other animals.

In its original design, the human animal brain had the specific function of caring for the material animal and projecting thought particles sent to it by the planet.

The human animal's thinking process was simple and served its basic needs to effect survival and propagation. It had a forebrain to use memory, a primal brain to manage the physical structure, and a midbrain to integrate the simple processes of planet-fed thought particles and magnetic/electric forces. If not interfered with by the intellectual manipulations of the forebrain, the primal brain would keep the human body eternally healthy. This is the role of the primal brain, it is programmed to keep the physical body in balanced health. What does disturb the ongoing material balance of perfection in the body are the thought interferences placed upon it by other parts of the brain.

Like any other animal, the human animal with its brain functioned and evolved on the basis of need. Its motivation in the beginning was survival of the body and survival of the species. Prior to the connection of the soul's mind, it lacked free choice and all of the attributes of the mind which drives human beings to do the things that separate them from all other animals. Having no need to think about non-material things, it could live as simply as any other animal.

In the beginning all of the human animal's behavior was determined by thought the planet sent it. If somehow this human animal propagated too rapidly and caused overpopulation, the planet would deal with it as it does with all animals. It would contrive either a plague or some natural force to curb or cut back the human animal herds to acceptable numbers. The human animal is a herd animal and its existence was managed as any other herd animal was managed before the appearance of the soul and its mind. However, the human animal was created for a greater purpose than that of an ordinary animal. It was created to function in the third dimension which was beginning to evolve in the material universe (see DIMENSIONS). When the first soul-minds bonded with the human animals and the partnership was originated, the human animals were not prepared for what would happen to their normal daily existence.

THE ANIMAL BRAIN

The human being is divided down the middle for specific reasons. The body is designed to use all its senses in a manner similar to the process of eyesight. Information from one side converges toward the other side, and this makes it possible to measure where something is when the two sides meet. Every sense functions this way. The right side of the body has its chemo-electric magnetic sensing fields and the left side of the body has its fields. It is the merging of the information in these fields that makes it possible to measure the reality we create. If one side is dominant, the human reality is going to be distorted and will be trying to effect harmony out of mismeasurement.

Today, the average person and the scientist believe that all thinking goes on inside the skull. When Robert Schwartz at the Prague conference mentioned that when the man leaned close to Peter, the autistic, and asked, "how is it in there?" most of the audience listening to his story thought that in there meant inside the skull. For Peter it meant something else, 'in there' meant inside the soul-mind ball which surrounds the human physical body.

Thinking processed inside the soul-mind takes place all around and permeating the body. It is done at a non-material and non-particle level. As planetary thought streams flow to the human being, the soul-mind intercepts those thoughts. It edits and sorts them according to its needs for learning and rearranges them for use by the appropriate thought processing systems of the body. The soul-mind does this intercepting and editing to try to influence the brain into using what it (the mind) wants it to think.

For most people one side of the brain system is overdeveloped. If the left brain is developed far in excess of the right brain, or visa versa, the life is constantly out of balance. When we examine the present scientific mechanistic paradigm we use as criteria for learning today, we can see how the left brain of most of humanity became dominant, thereby distorting the original human reality. It is the left brain which manages the literal aspects of life projection. As a mechanism the left brain now dominates the information feeding into the skull, and as a consequence, we are not in balance with our thinking abilities.

There is a tendency to belittle the human being and elevate the lesser animals. "Who are we to think we are superior?" is what is being said. Well - no other animal can do or be all the things the human being can do or be. The dolphin can swim much better than the human animal, but it cannot build a boat. As to which animal is the most compassionate, it is the human animal. Even though in her/his lack of understanding the human being can unwittingly destroy other animals, it is the human animal, through its empathy, which cares for hurt animals on a grand scale, not the other way around.

Regarding the intelligence of lesser animals like the chimps and others which command a large part of Carl Sagan's and Ann Druyen's book *Shadows Of Forgotten Ancestors*, I would like to venture a question, "How far would the chimp get toward solving the researcher's tests if the chimp did not have its simple thinking system interfered with by the thinking systems of the researchers?" Researchers unwittingly influence the animals simply because the human is capable of unconsciously accessing the lesser animal's thought streams.

Thought transference from human to animal is possible in a variety of ways. It is not difficult to access the thought streams of the animal one observes. Thought transference is possible without using conscious thinking. The following example will illustrate this. On a recent nature program on San Diego's KPBS public television, the camera captured on film a bird who was unable to reach a worm in a hole in a tree. After a period of pecking and being unable to reach the worm, the bird flew away. It came back shortly with a twig, which it poked into the hole with persistence and pried out the worm.

On the surface, it appeared as though this bird, in its frustration at not getting the worm, had thought about how it could reach it. The impression was that it had actually thought what was needed and what to use to get the job done. Remember that the bird uses thought that the planet sends it. Would the planet send it the thoughts to use the twig? Not likely!

As I have mentioned, the human being has the mental power to encroach in other thinking systems. How? In this case we know a human being was watching that bird try to reach the worm. At some point, the human watcher emotionally placed himself in the position he thought the bird was in, that of frustration for not being able to reach its food. Focused on the birds efforts, the human being became frustrated for the bird and imagined the solution, probably even saying, "Why doesn't that bird stick a twig in there and get that worm!" Emotion supplies the energy needed in the projection and attracting of thought particles. The emotions of empathy and frustration projected the answer into the thought stream entering the bird, and the bird responded by acting out the thoughts transferred to it by the human being.

There is the question of how a bird's brain could understand the language of the human brain. Transference of thought from human to animal is a natural aspect of the ingenious soul-mind capability of communication. That capability contains the ability to understand any kind of thought language, interpret it and direct it where needed.

The human brain does access the lesser animal brains and this is why some people feel that their pets seem almost human, or have souls. Although soul-minds have the capability of examining all animal bodies, they bond only with human animals. Any activity of an animal that has seemingly human attributes is caused by a human brain having previously psychically influenced that animal brain. There are some individuals who do exercise the ability to interact mentally with the brains of animals. These people seem endowed with some special ability, however, that ability is common to all human brains.

THE SOUL & ITS MIND

Most of us believe in the soul; we may not see it but we have a knowing that it is with us. The soul has its own thinking apparatus, and this part of the soul is called the mind. Most people are not aware of the difference between mind and brain and they use the words interchangeably. They will often be referring to the brain and say mind. The reason for this confusion is that science has not found the limitations of the brain or the mind. Since the two thinking systems overlap it makes it difficult for science to differentiate between the two.

The following are examples to illustrate this point. When some one offers to help you 'expand your mind power', what they usually mean is that they will help you use your brain more effectively. The mind does not need to be expanded, it already knows all there is to know. It is the brain that has the limitations. Similarly, the phrase to 'reprogram your mind for success' shows the misconception of what the mind is. What is reprogrammed is our belief system.

Prior to now there has not been a great *need* (note this word) to know the difference between brain and mind. The two words, brain and mind, have been interchanged because we were not ready or evolved enough to know the difference. As a mass of human beings we are now reaching the aware position in evolution of having exhausted the understanding and limitations of the second dimension and mechanistic thinking. The *need* is upon us now to move completely into the third dimension (see DIMENSIONS), and this requires our consciousness (thinking) to escalate into quantum thinking. The entire planet is destabilized and suffering the consequences of excessive intellectual left brain usage of thoughts by the human being. The need is to balance our actions with more mind inspired thinking.

48

Unlike the brain which has many, many limitations, the mind of the soul has only one limitation: the brain. The mind can only project thought particles to the brain in the hope that the brain will use them. It is in the brain that the edited thought given it by the mind is mediated and willed into the planetary illusion to create its material reality. More often than not, the mind thinking is changed and stripped of soul intent and an edited version is selected and used by the human animal brain. In this dimension the brain has the final word. It chooses whether to listen to the 'still small voice' of the soul-mind or follow the impulses of habits, beliefs and planetary influences.

The mind is capable of using thought in ways which make the greatest of all computers appear as insignificant toys. In the mind is the record of all that was, is and is expected to be; past, present and future in this reality. The mind of the soul can process thought particles that the animal brain cannot process. The mind of the soul can access any thought particle ever expressed by any thinker that ever existed (see MASS THOUGHT).

The mind is the brain of the soul. Both, soul and mind, are on a wave length level which is not the same as that of the brain of the human animal. The level that the soul-mind functions from is non-material, where space and time do not exist; unlike the human brain that does exist in the level of space and time. It is possible to see the soul, and many people experience and perceive their soul during altered states such as meditation as a brilliant gold light. The soul is always moving around the perimeter of the mind, a twelve foot sphere of white light.

The soul knows it comes into this thought universe for the purpose of refining its balance, balance its forces and powers, one might say. With this intention, and prior to connecting with a human animal, it examines all the thought related to a particular fetus in a human mother. It examines the DNA, the psychic essences, and any other probable aspect of the fetus which reflects power and energy that might affect the future life of the person. There are many aspects (clues) that give the soul-mind an idea of the probable path the infant will walk through life, what obstacles it may encounter, what opportunities will unfold. It is through duality and conflict that the soul will attempt to achieve balance. It is aware that the infant is coming into a world structured with belief systems that dictate the behavior and future of the human being. After it has carefully examined the astrological influences, the nationalities involved, the energies of the spot on the planet where the birth is taking place, and much more, the soul makes a decision to join or not join the coming infant. If the infant and its pending promises hold to the desired formula for resolving lessons of the soul, the soul-mind will connect and bond.

The soul-mind at times surrounds the material field of the fetus, testing it periodically and examining the parents and other pending influences. Occasionally, the soul will leave the fetus, but at the moment of birth of the fetus, the soul-mind surrounds the newborn human with the intention of bonding to it.

At birth, when the fetus sucks in oxygen and infuses the animal body with life force and becomes an infant, the soul-mind affixes itself to the infant at the center of its body. For a short time after that the soul can detach from the infant, but very rapidly there is a point reached where the soul-mind must stay fixed to the human body.

From the time of birth, the soul-mind intercepts the thought streams the planet is sending the human infant. The mind edits the streams of thought particles and feeds them into the animal thinking system in the order which serves the needs of the soul for soul lesson purposes. These thinking processes are subjective and what we call sub-conscious. There is considerable thinking going on in the thinking systems of the infant, but it is of a kind different from what adults call thinking.

WORKINGS OF THE SOUL-MIND

The primary goal of the soul-mind is the continuous balancing of its powers and energies. This is done by the soul-mind's editing and processing of thought before the human brain uses it. The ideal situation for this balancing effort is for the soul-mind to have 50% of thinking under its guidance and for the brain to have 50% of the thinking under its control. This would provide for half of the thinking to be what we call spiritual and the other half to be thinking devoted to the material life.

Unfortunately, at this time in evolution, the skull brain has over

90% of the control over the thinking. Because the soul-mind has so little of its suggested thinking accepted by the brain, the person's thinking and actions are usually controlled by mass thought processes. When a person does not actually choose thinking, the planetary mass thought automatically 'feeds' him/her the average thought. The 'feeding' is in accord with the emotional temperature of the person.

This condition of 90% or more thinking being controlled by the brain is the norm for most adults. At birth, however, the situation is reversed. The infant's brain has little intellectual input and is virgin in its thinking (tabular rasa). This permits the soul-mind to process most of the thinking, but usually this only lasts a few weeks, sometimes months. The soul-mind's first effort at managing the infant's thinking has its limitations.

There are basic laws of energies that the infant must deal with right from the start. One of these laws is the need for energy feeding from infant to adult. This energy feeding process is a fundamental law of the planet and its creatures. As humans age they hold less life force in their bodies. Babies are born fully charged with life force and are generating it in pure form. They are designed to automatically feed life force to adults. This is not a choice, it is a basic law that must be acted on by the infant.

Because babies have so much life force, people feel drawn to them and always try to coax a smile from a baby when they see one. It is the joy of watching a baby play or smile that fills the recipient with energy like the filling of a low battery that has been drained.

As an aside, if one were to measure the world's population as to life force energy content, one would find that as populations age there is an automatic increase in births to sustain the life force energy balance between young and aged.

SOUL LESSONS

The soul enters this dimension and melds with a human being for the purpose of balancing its (the soul's) powers. This is what we call 'getting our soul lessons'. The powers the soul is attempting to balance manifest in the human life as energies, traits, habits, essences, psychic forces, etc. and are expressed through the human being's behaviors.

Prior to coming here and choosing to experience the human event, the soul has awareness of its weaknesses and it wants to meld with a human body that will live in an environment and set of circumstances which is likely to provide an opportunity of soul lesson resolution. The power lesson of the soul might translate in the human being as arrogance, for instance. Humanly, we use the word arrogance to describe a human behavior, however, for the soul it means power. That human behavior called arrogance translates into too much of a certain power being expressed. The life chosen by the soul may present conditions which force the being to face and recognize its arrogance and learn to change it into harmonious behavior or balanced energy.

As the human being it is difficult to see within the self that which is the soul lesson. We are the last to see our weaknesses. If you are arrogant, as I was most of my life, you are not aware of the arrogance. We cloak the arrogance under different descriptions of what we are doing.

Souls, before coming here, usually choose three soul lessons, hoping to resolve at least one of them during the life time. For a period of several years the first lesson is worked on for resolution. Failing or accomplishing that, the second lesson is presented. Failing or accomplishing the second lesson, the soul attempts to resolve the third one. In my case, my first lesson, that of arrogance, took me forty-four years to resolve. I was told that most people in any one life do not learn even one of their chosen lessons

It is my understanding that there are twelve primary soul lessons here on earth. Students often ask me to tell them what these lessons are and I am reluctant to point them out. Part of the answer to resolving our soul lessons is to search out our habits, traits and beliefs.

Everyone should begin their search for their soul lessons without influence from another. It involves their reason for being here and has to do with choice and free will to discover and learn in their own time, using experience gained from living life. I therefore share information about soul lessons in generalities and this is what I am presenting here.

The manner in which we face the doing of life tells a great deal about how much balance we have. Once again, when I say balance, I am referring to balancing our powers. It is through our powers that we face the doing of life.

A major clue toward discovering your abuse of power is to discover whether you live life always looking to the future and ignoring the past, or whether if you are always looking to the past and are ignoring the future. The words 'looking to' are no different than the words 'living in'. If you are constantly looking to the past, you are living in the past and are recreating events of the past to repeat themselves in the future. If you are constantly looking to the future, you are living in the future without enjoying the journey through life or learning from past mistakes. Either, living in the past or living in the future, is an abuse of powers and certainly is not balance.

Balance requires living in the now, having the wisdom to understand the past, and at the same time understand how to create the future.

If the person is caught in always living in the past or always living in the future, the soul lessons are not being dealt with. If we are not fully living in the now we need to examine our traits, habits and beliefs to discover what is keeping us too much in the past or in the future. We need to always monitor ourselves to be sure we are living in the now, while understanding the past and making our 'asking' of the future.

The soul-mind is always working to bring us to the point of balance in our human and spiritual life. In as much as the soul-mind can only accomplish its needs by coming through our confining egos (left brain) we need to make the effort to listen to it (the soul-mind) when it speaks to us. It speaks to us in several ways: it gives us messages in dreams to work with and always whispers to us in the 'wee small voice' of the inner.

From a mental perspective it is important to consider how to project our life experience forward. Living in the now correctly means being balanced in what we think about by expanding our awareness and belief systems in a way that stretches our thinking to encompass the past and the present. By fully accepting the past we can draw from it the wisdom to venture into the future. Melding thoughts of experience in the past with conscious choices about our future, we are free to live in the now, ever expanding our way.

WORKINGS OF THE HEART

When I refer to the 'heart' of man or woman I am not talking about the pump in the chest. The heart I refer to is the center of the human being. Therein, at the center, lie the seeds or mystery of the human expression. It is not a material place, but rather the center of the essence of the whole person. It is this center, or heart, which is referred to when we hear the time worn expression, 'know thyself!' When we know what is in the heart, all of that which is in the heart, we will 'know the self' and have learned that which the soul has come here to learn.

The heart also holds the lessons of the soul. Lessons are the situations the soul-mind creates and attracts in order to learn to balance and harmonize its powers. For one person this could be learning not to control others, for another the lesson may be greed.

What is in the heart must come forth. What does not come forth will bring chaos to the person. With all the power we have as the manifesting human being, if what we desire to attain is not truly in our heart, we must fail in manifesting our real desire. However, if our desire is in harmony with what is in the heart, we cannot fail to manifest the things of the heart. People will often say, 'I want this or that', but in their heart they really want something else. What they say with their mouth is not what is in their heart. It is in the heart that the soul has set that which it needs to fulfill while in the human experience.

THE HIGHER SELF

The term Higher Self is used by many in different ways. It is an aspect of the soul-mind. It is often used to mean the wise part of the person, a guiding aspect of the person, an aspect of the god self. The Higher Self is for the soul what the ego is for the brain. It has the power to create visions, dreams, telepathic messaging and inner voice projection, and more. The primary role of the Higher Self is to influence the human being to make decisions in favor of soul growth balance. For this end it edits and delivers thoughts to the brain that are in keeping with the learning of lessons by the soul while considering the level of spiritual growth the person has attained.

One can communicate with one's own Higher Self through divining methods and meditations of different sorts. As an aspect of the soul, it cannot interfere with the choices made by the ego, nor can it use willing forces of the brain to override the choices of the ego. However, It has the ability to withdraw soul influence if the person is exposed to danger that might cause the body to be destroyed.

The Higher Self can be looked upon as the greater part of ourselves in the sense that we have lesser ego identities which are usually concealed from others and at times come forth as alternate personalities. We often confuse the Higher Self with being our most virtuous self, and this is misleading. Just as we often unknowingly liken it to our most moral aspect. The Higher Self, as an aspect of our non-judgmental soul, has no need of morality. It understands that morality is in the eye of the beholder and is an aspect of the ego, just as it understands that there is no good or bad. It does not measure one against another. The Higher Self functions on a level which is beyond taking sides or taking issue with anything. It simply projects the thoughts in a manner which will best serve the soul experience in this dimension as it works to create balance. The Higher Self knows it probably will not have a great deal of immediate success in gaining soul learning in a physical body, however, it is content to take the time the human being needs to learn that which it wants for the soul.

WORKINGS OF THE SKULL BRAIN

To be able to understand the human skull brain we must release all past ideas of what it is or might be. Earlier I compared it to a system of muscles which expands and contracts like a pump. This is how the skull brain functions, thought particles are pumped through it. The primary role of all skull brains, in all animals, including the human animal, is to process the incoming thoughts from the planet. In humans a portion of the thinking serves the animal aspect of the person. This is thinking that has to do with the physical care and physical projection of the person such as eating, sleeping, working, propagating, shopping and other things that have to do with the body being physical.

What kind of activity does not have to do with material animal thinking? Those things we normally consider as being subjective. Imagination, religion, fantasy, planning, phenomena are examples of subjective thinking. Subjective thinking is the realm of the soul-mind, not the brain. Although subjective thinking must pass through the skull brain mechanism, such thinking has its origin in the editing process of the soul-mind.

The skull brain has three main physical parts: the forebrain, the midbrain and the hind brain. The brain is divided, front to rear, into two halves, left and right hemispheres. The left hemisphere processes linear, material thinking. It is the seat of the intellect and the belief system that has been acquired since birth. The right hemisphere processes subjective, non-material thoughts. It is the door to the soul-mind.

A person who has gained wisdom and spiritual maturity, uses both hemispheres and thinks in a balanced manner. This usually results in a healthy, prosperous material and spiritual life. Due to ages of excessive use of linear thinking (left hemisphere), caused to a great extent by pursuit of mechanistic scientific principles, the skull brain is not usually balanced and is limited and stilted. The ideal processing of the skull brain would be for it to serve a balance of needs that are put upon it by the animal, the heart, and the mind.

The idea most people have that thinking takes place only inside the skull is misleading. Most thinking is done on the subconscious level within the soul-mind surrounding the physical body. The mind edits the thought before it gets to the skull brain. The skull brain then processes the thoughts and evaluates them against information of the body. After processing the subjective thoughts of the soul-mind with the needs of the body, the brain makes a choice and the mid-brain sends forth (wills) matter-forming thoughts.

Because the left brain hemisphere is usually dominant in the thinking process, what is willed is most often that which is desired by intellectual ideas. These desires are directly connected to the formulated belief systems and as a consequence what is willed is nothing more than habit thinking or trait thinking. Habit and trait thinking have little or no power and usually serve to attract energy that will nurture and feed the habit or the trait. Most of the subjective thinking the soul-mind is trying to have the skull brain will forth, is unused and expelled back

56

into the mass thought fields.

The two brain hemispheres are designed to function in unison, but the left hemisphere has been more active over generations making the average person overdeveloped in the left brain. Unless the brain halves are balanced, the brain does not function at its optimum efficiency. This over development of the left brain half limits the creative ability of the average person.

THE BRAIN PRINT

The human thinking systems are complex and involve much more than what is going on inside the skull. Most of our mental processes occur outside the skull. An example is the cellular energy field which surrounds and permeates the body.

All aspects of our thinking system having to do with the material human experience I call the brain print. This includes all body connected memory since the present physical life began, all memory available through the cellular energy field, all belief systems created since birth, all data recorded by the seven senses, including the fear and change senses, and any other information connected to the skull brain, including mass thought.

THE MIND PRINT

The mind print has to do with our non-physical thinking system, all knowledge present in the twelve foot diameter 'mind ball' at any given moment which is referred to as 'the inner'. When people talk about the 'inner dimension' of the person or the 'wee small voice' within, they are talking about the mind. People who are in trance, or meditate, or are hypnotized, or psychic, usually are in the mind, meaning that they have withdrawn their conscious awareness within. Meditators often report feeling like they are within a ball, surrounded by white light. Again, this is the state of having gone mentally within the mind ball.

Within the mind are the eight primary mind chakras which are designed to attract thought particles from the planetary sphere (see fig. 1). Also contained in the mind are all dimensions of experiences of the being the being is unconsciously working on, all the incarnations of the being, past present and future. Every ego the being has ever been (multiple personalities) is stored within the mind.

A person having visions or reliving past life experiences, or future experiences, either through meditation or hypnotic trance, is mentally within the mind ball. Intellectually, we imagine that the universe (out there) is vast and endless, however, the inner universe of the mind is vast and beyond intellectual concepts.

It is important to make a comparison between the ability of the mind with its mind print and the ability of the brain with its brain print at any given moment. This is for the purpose of revealing the vast difference between the information available to the mind which is not normally available to the brain. I like to use the example of a bic pen. In a lecture I will hold up a white bic pen and ask the audience to tell me all about the pen. The answers are usually limited to: "It is round and about six inches long, it is white with a black tip, it has the letters 'bic' on it, and it is used for writing; it is obviously a pen." These are the answers the skull brain is able to perceive through the sense of vision.

I then explain to the audience that their perception is limited and ask them if each were allowed to hold the pen, would they be able to tell me more about it. They normally say they could tell nothing more about the pen. At this point I tell them that if they were able to use psychometry, the ability to access the thinking of their own mind (not brain) through the balanced used of all their senses, they would be able to tell much more about the pen. If a psychometrist held the pen and examined it with all the senses s/he would say things like: "This pen does not belong to the speaker, it belongs to a woman whose name is Mary. She has two children. Her husband was killed in a plane crash. She lives in Oregon now. As for the pen - it was assembled in Chicago from plastics made in Akron and metal that came from a mine in Colorado. It was packed by a girl in Chicago. Oh - for a moment the woman in Oregon thought about using it as a weapon to stab herself in the left hand out of anger and frustration."

All this information would come from the soul-mind. Most people would refer to the unconscious as the source of this information.

In a way they would be correct because the earlier pen information came from the ordinary conscious state. For every conscious thought the brain becomes aware of and expresses about the pen there were at least six thousand combinations of other thoughts about the pen that the mind was processing at the same time.

The mind print at any one given time contains thousands more thoughts, about whatever the focus or attention is on, than the skull brain uses consciously. A trained mystic can access those thoughts and make them conscious. This is the case with the psychometrist who seems to have more access to information than the average person. The mind is also the area of thinking the psychic ventures into when attempting to find a lost person. The mind print contains vast levels of information about anything one of the human senses has focused on. All things carry a historic print of the essence of the thing and in addition that essence contains the essence of anyone who has been connected to the thing; the thing could be a pen, a shoe, a ring. The more emotion emitted in the presence of the item, the greater the amount of information it contains.

CHAKRAS AS THOUGHT ATTRACTORS

I wish to make the distinction again between the basic method the planet uses for feeding thought to the animal, and the method the mind has designed for use of thought by the human being. The animal is fed thought directly into the skull brain by the planetary streams. The mind of the human being has altered that method for the human animal, providing a system of thought processes which serves the soul. The soul-mind intercepts the thoughts coming to the person from mass thought fields.

The mind has for its use eight mind chakras and impeller/expeller mechanism (body brain)which attracts and expels the thoughts from and to the planetary sphere. The impeller and expeller is at the center of the mind ball (fig. 2). This is also at the center of the human physical body, the pit of the stomach. The mind and the animal are connected in the pit of the stomach area also, which is the reason one at times feels a psychic/physical blow there. The feeling is caused when a major jolt of different thoughts floods into the center. Sensitive persons will often receive a nauseous feeling in the pit of the stomach at the very moment a person close to them is involved in a tragic event. This feeling is caused by the accelerated action of the thought mechanism, the impeller/expeller, having received the message of the tragedy in the form of powerful negative thoughts.

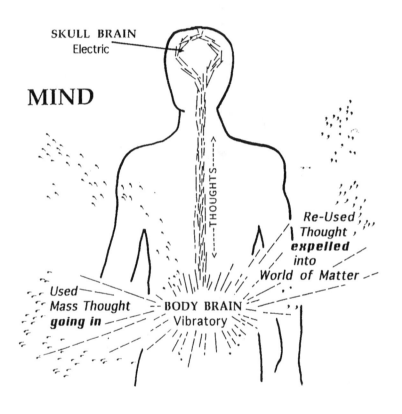

Fig. 2. Thought processing today

The role of the primary eight chakras is to attract different kinds of thought into the mind. Because we are thinking constantly at many levels, these attractors are functioning continuously.

Chakra, a word adopted from the east, means center. A chakra is often referred to as an energy center, and with good reason. Some yogis and adepts talk about seeing a chakra pulsate and vortex, comparing it to some kind of energy flower. What they are seeing is the action of thought particles being attracted by the particular chakra as the particles transition into the mind ball. They are seeing the result of the attraction of thought taking place.

I mentioned that there are eight mind chakras. It is rare that a yogi, adept or master sees the eighth chakra. The eighth chakra, approximately nine inches above the head, attracts thought particles which are not of the material creating energy. This chakra connects all humans beings as one.

Chakras are aligned vertically in the mind ball, and as a consequence they seem to be aligned with the human body, and on one level they are. Following is a brief description of the chakras, numbered beginning with the bottom one on up to the 8th one above the skull. As well as listing their location, I will include the basic type of thought each chakra attracts from the planetary thought streams:

#1 chakra is in the area of the base of the spine. It is referred to as the *base chakra* and attracts primarily thoughts that are body and earth related such as propagation and survival.

#2 chakra is in the area of the pit of the stomach. It is referred to as the *pit of the stomach chakra* and attracts primarily thoughts that are materialistic, emotional, sexual and combative.

#3 chakra is in the area of the solar plexus. It is referred to as the *solar plexus chakra* and attracts primarily thoughts which are energy related such as Yin and Yang, right and left brain projection, positive and negative forces.

#4 chakra is in the area of the heart. It is referred to as the *heart chakra* and primarily attracts thoughts which are monitoring, have desire and balance.

#5 chakra is in the area of the throat. It is referred to as the *throat chakra* and attracts thoughts related to communication and bridging (third party psychic connections).

#6 chakra is in the area of the eyes. It is referred to as the *eye chakra* and attracts thoughts primarily related to manifesting from the mental to the physical.

#7 chakra is in the area of the crown of the skull. It is referred to as the *crown chakra* and attracts thoughts primarily related to enlightenment and wisdom.

#8 chakra is approximately nine inches above the top of the skull. It is referred to as the *transpersonal chakra* and attracts thoughts which connects all soul-minds.

When in action, the chakras pulsate and vortex, attracting their specific thought quality, expanding as the particular thinking increases. They can radiate to a level where they dominate the entire space of the mind ball. For the most part, the action of the chakras varies as thought changes. It is only during certain thinking circumstances that one chakra dominates most of the thinking area; a case of severe depression might be one example. Another might be the instance of a person becoming obsessed, such as with thoughts of physical sexual experiences or thoughts of intense destruction.

The use of mind chakras as thought attractors is different in males and females because of the preference of use of thought by each sex. Fig. 3 shows the mind chakras and the physical energies (yin/yang). From the heart upward body and mind are shaded in one energy pattern, below that it is shaded in another energy pattern. This is to reflect the yin and yang influences on thought. The female, being of yin energy, usually does her thinking using the chakras above the heart. The male, being of yang energy, primarily uses the lower chakras for most of his thinking. Both sexes will at times use all the chakras; but the general rule is that the female is in the upper chakras, and the male is in the lower ones. This dynamic of chakra usage explains why the males and females behave differently from a physical/sexual perspective.

The male uses primarily the lower two chakras, meaning that most of the thinking is combative, physical, having to do with creating, destroying and propagation. The female is primarily in the fifth, sixth and seventh chakras for her thinking, and this has to do with the non-material aspects of life. Relating this to sexual behavior, one can readily see why the male may have to coax the female into physical sexual activity, and why the female generally needs foreplay, before she can be physically orgasmic. Since orgasms happen through the lower chakras, and the female is usually not in that mental range, the male has to bring her down to those chakras where he already is functioning by nature.

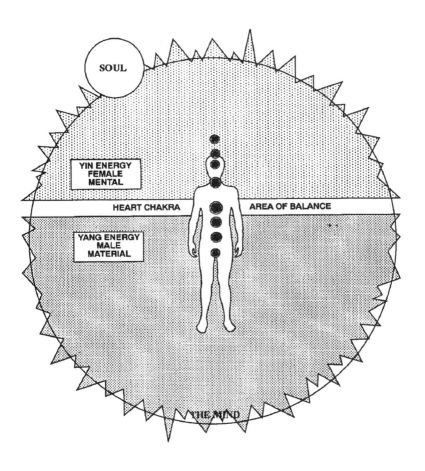

Fig. 3. Mind chakras & yin/yang energies

There is a widespread practice among many people in the meta-physical field of balancing the chakras. Some refer to the practice as "opening" the chakras. These well meaning teachers suggest various procedures for 'opening' the chakras, beginning with the base chakra and moving upward to the crown chakra. Their objective appears to be balancing of the body. This kind of manipulation is of no use to the mind chakras which open and close in direct relation to the kinds of thought being used and attracted by the person's mental activity and level of emotion. There are many energy centers (chakras) all over the body which do respond to the energy manipulation of another, but not the primary chakras that have to do with the thinking mechanisms. The eight mind chakras function independently of one another in the sense that each has its own level or streams of thought particles they attract.

RIGHT BRAIN HEMISPHERE

Research has revealed that the right brain has to do primarily with non-linear thinking, intuition and artful creative expression. It is the physical part of the human animal thinking system that is most closely connected to the soul-mind. The right brain is not normally aggressive and it manages what in eastern philosophies is called yin force. People who are artistic, and people who are spiritual seekers, often find themselves using the right brain hemisphere for most of their mental activity. Females are more often in the right brain then in the left. The right brain now functions as the doorway to the inner, the mind. Those who meditate are usually focusing on eliminating left brain influence.

Right brain thinking is a multi-dimensional activity. It expresses itself through metaphors and symbols. You could say that dreams are the language of the right brain. The right brain has a fairly small role in the managing of the human ego expression. Today the right brain is being suppressed by the domination of an overly trained intellectual left brain. This is an aberration in the human growth process. The stilting of mental expression of the right hemisphere has resulted in the human being falling behind in the understanding of third dimensional thinking.

LEFT BRAIN HEMISPHERE

The left brain is the seat of the intellect, it is the opposite of the right brain in that it is aggressive, dogmatic, as well as linear in its thinking processes. It is not directly connected to the doorway of the soul-mind and depends on ego and belief systems to manage its control over the human being's behavior. It is the left brain of the human animal's thinking system which has the dominant position at this time in evolution/history.

Prior to the time of the Israelites, the right brain had control of the thinking process of the human brain. At that time yin power was the dominant thinking energy on the planet. As I have noted elsewhere, need is the driving force which propels change on the planet, and there was a need for yang force to escalate in order to balance the planet's mass thought and its energies.

When we examine the trend of western history from the time when the Israelites began, we can see that as the male expression gained back some control, the left brain became more dominant. The result was a trend toward mechanistic thinking. The left brain thrives on mechanistic thinking. Today the world is dominated by the left brain and we can see its handy work in the social and physical machines it has created.

Having a left brain dominance results in a tendency to be two dimensional and not readily able to observe things in a third dimensional perspective. This limits the ability of the total brain to exercise its complete functions.

Thought particles being fed into the brain by the soul-mind are edited by the degree of intelligence of the left brain rather than the intelligence of the balanced brain.

Usually the left brain is dominating the flow of thought from the mind into the midbrain which is responsible for balancing the incoming thoughts. Consequently the mind thoughts from the right brain are denied any input into the life experience. The right brain has some input, but only to the degree the left brain wants to include it in supporting its left brain choice of thoughts. The average day of the male is spent in the condition just described.

We see the left brain being dominant in many areas but primarily in the area of education. This stilted application in the academic world keeps the human being at a level of consciousness which is not in keeping with the true needs of the planet and universe, the true need being that of harmony between right and left brain thinking.

RIGHT & LEFT BRAIN BALANCE

The optimal functioning of the human brain would be the condition where the two brain halves have equal share in examining reality from the material and non-material perspective and are balancing the information. This would give the soul-mind an opportunity to have an equal input on the behavior of the person. In this situation the animal aspect of the human being would have its proper and healthy share of mind input on how to behave, project and look at life. If the right and left brain hemispheres are balanced, the soul-mind can effect its input of spiritual thought through the right brain as a regular part of the living process.

Unfortunately this balance of the two halves is far from taking place. Educational institutions today emphasize left brain development quite exclusively. As a result of such academic conditioning, most human beings are automatically examining everything from a left brain perspective. One might argue that the present state of brain processing is an evolutionary stage of the human being, but that would be ignoring that there have been periods of human existence when the right brain had much more input than it has today.

When the intellect is exercised excessively and linear thinking influences the belief systems of the individual, the left brain gains even greater control over the quality of thought attracted for use from mass thought. As a consequence of this left brain belief limitation, the brain also increases its level of fear of more things. This results in the brain becoming even more confined in its beliefs. Consequently, right brain ideas going to the left brain generate fear in the person and cause the brain to shy away from the right brain thinking. However, there are situations in which the left brain will allow right brain input, but only if there appears to be no real threat to the belief systems.

The following excercise is an example that demonstrates how the left brain often allows some right brain input, but then reacts and stops the right brain from going a little further in its processes. Examine brain balancer (fig. 4). Place the diagram a few feet away. Be sure it is upright and perpendicular to the eye line. Focus on the center and allow your peripheral sight to notice all the lines. At some point you will notice that the lines begin to form angles that shift and change into different patterns. This is the result of the right brain beginning to examine the diagram. Stay focused and then slowly count backwards from ten to one. The pattern changes should begin to accelerate. Continued examination with the right brain hemisphere will cause the diagram to appear as though it were oscillating and three dimensional, like a wire cage, floating and turning. The right brain has now about equal influence with the left brain in examining the diagram. Also at this point there may be a tendency to feel uneasy or a slight loss of equilibrium. As the feeling grows, the left brain will begin to assert itself to get back to its original two dimensional perspective of the diagram. Often at this point, the left brain will refuse to observe the diagram any longer and cause the head to turn away from it to reestablish its control and attain a comfortable level of equilibrium.

Fig. 4. Brain balancing diagram

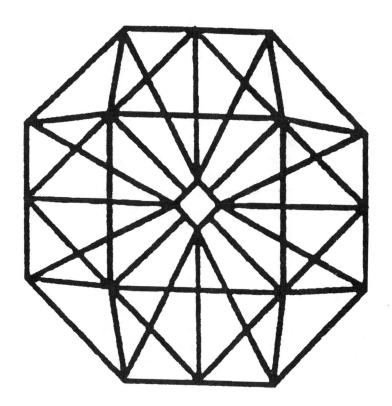

The left brain sees only straight lines and a two dimensional shape; the right brain adds the illusion of the third dimensional perspective.

This little exercise brings up the age old fear in the brain of any shift in thinking toward right brain input. At times the brain's fear of right brain input will cause the individual to do that which gives him/her the feeling of escaping. Many forms of addiction, drugs, tobacco, alcohol and others have their roots in the need of the person to dull the brain to free it from constant left brain control.

In this age, planetary mass thought is overloaded with thought particles carrying left brain yang energy. The yang energy is assimilated by the thought particles which have processed through human brains. These thought particles then return to the planetary sphere, causing an overall imbalance of energy in the planet. We see this expressed in the increase of crime, wars and other violent acts among people everywhere.

Excessive yang energies in mass thought causes the planet to react to this overload of yang forces with natural disturbances such as lightning, tornadoes, hurricanes and earthquakes. It is important to understand this connection between human thinking and the planetary attempts to keep itself in a balance of energies and powers. If we observe this condition as a play between thoughts on a world mass level, we can get some appreciation for why the planet is referred to as an illusion. There is a deliberate effort on the part of the entity called Earth to constantly meld thoughts to stabilize its material form. This balance is interfered with by extreme levels of yin or yang energies being fed into the illusion by the human thinking systems. If the human being does not take direct responsibility for the quality of thinking being done by it, the planet suffers 'pollution' on the mass thought particle level. This is what is behind consciousness raising: to clean up mass thought and return to a more perfect yin/yang balance.

RIGHT & LEFT BRAIN AND SOCIETY

When we observe human behavior as a mass, we can see far eastern people as right brained or yin oriented and western people as left brained or yang oriented. In the east more importance is placed on

68

spiritual, non-material ideals. The manifested life of the easterner reflects this. Life is lived with less dependency on material possessions or what we in the west call material life style. In the west thinking is primarily left brained, focusing on material ideas and literal material thoughts, a mass belief that more material is better. The manifested life of the westerner reflects this thinking. Life is lived with dependency on material possessions or things which serve us.

We in the west see the east in great lack of the material things we expect and take for granted. The east sees the west as dependant on material goods and technology. This they believe interferes with life and takes one away from inner and more meaningful living. Wise ones of east and west know that the answer is to live a balanced life, in the center between the extremes of left brain and right brain thinking.

When we examine the world, we see evidence for the need for those of the west to move toward the ideas of the east and for those of the east to move toward those of the west. In the west we see this attempt in the form of many westerners practicing eastern meditations to acquire some of the ways of the east. The practice of meditation is about as far as the average westerner goes toward eastern behavior; as a rule, we Westerners do not abandon our desire for things. There is little understanding for most westerners about eastern meditation, except there is the idea that by stilling the brain, one might become more balanced and consequently closer to God.

One can say that neither east or west has considered what right brain thinking is about, nor what left brain thinking is about. Balancing the two hemispheres is automatically accepted as the right thing to do if it is considered at all. Meditation is somehow supposed to help balance the two, but there is no program or exacting process anyone has offered to accomplish brain balancing through meditation.

The idea of brain balancing needs some interpretation. Science has done 'EEG' testing of the brain with the idea of measuring the level of electric impulses in the brain. This testing is designed to determine the level of electricity and the presumption is that if one side of the brain has the same level of electricity as the other, then the brain is in balance. This is misleading simply because the brain does not process thought equally in both hemispheres. At any given instant, one side of the brain is processing one type of thinking and the other side is processing different types of thinking. We have no machines at present which measure thinking processes in the brain on the basis of yin and yang content or whether the thoughts are feeding life force or draining life force. Using today's technology, there is no way of knowing what is being measured in the brain as to the thinking processes being balanced.

The practice of meditation by westerners has produced benefits such as stress relief. Psychic experiences have also been reported by meditators, but the benefits are often considered questionable by those who do not understand them. We already know that easterners have psychic experiences, but they appear to westerners to not have benefited them as a mass of people in regard to quality of life.

I see meditation efforts as a move toward balancing of the thinking mechanisms. Recognizing that a great portion of humanity is right brained and another great portion of humanity is left brained, and the seeming need for them to come together, we are witnessing the root feeling of the world's need for change of consciousness. If we recognize that the planet strives to maintain a balance of energies, it makes sense that if the eastern thinker is changing his use of thoughts by being influenced by western commercialism, then the westerner would need to adjust thinking accordingly. It follows that the extreme thinking processes of left and right brains, need to merge and balance.

When we talk about the world going through a major consciousness shift, this is what we are talking about; the balancing of right and left brain thinking. This balancing is accomplished not just by individuals trying to meditate, but by people as a mass changing the thinking streams we draw thoughts from. Through understanding what thought and thinking is, we can make this transition as a mass much more easily. If we do not change deliberately by choice, then it will be forced upon us by the planet itself. Change can be in the form of a swift transition or a long drawn out evolutionary birthing pain.

The consciousness birthing pains come in the form of nations at war, painfully learning how to balance freedom, and they also come in the form of diseases and plagues. This continues on until we learn how to correctly use thinking. For example: immune deficiency is a result of the misuse of thought streams and fields by the human thinking systems. The diminished quality of thinking creates a disturbance of the planetary feeding wave lengths and vibrations or sounds, and it is becoming more than human material bodies can manage.

70

If the planet is severely unbalanced in its energies, then the body of the individual person who has to use that planetary energy as life force receives a diluted energy. This may read like science fiction, but we must face the truth of our time which has been heralded by the discovery of quantum science. It no longer serves us to be ignorant of how we think or the fact that thought creates matter. Collectively all societies have a need to become enlightened about what thoughts are and how thinking influences their life and all human survival into the 21st century.

BRAIN & MIND PSYCHOLOGIES

When one understands that there are the two distinct systems of thought processes, the soul-mind and the brain, one can see the need for understanding their differences in psychology. Presently, much of the psychology of man has its roots in the brain aspect of the thinking of human beings. This is especially true of those aspects of the field of psychology which fall under the category of behaviorism. Humanistic psychologists have more awareness of the mind aspects of human behavior than do behaviorists.

The brain's primary interest is in getting all it can out of life for the physical experience. The mInd's interest is primary in conducting thought so that inner lessons, which some call spiritual lessons, are learned. There is a constant competition between the brain and the mind for the whole thought process of the human being. People working in the field of psychology should know whether it is brain thinking or mind thinking which is dominating the behavior patterns of a client.

PURPOSE

Purpose in the dictionary is defined as, 'an object or end to attain.' In the human experience as it is now for most people, that means, 'getting things'. In this society we are driven all our lives by the need to amass things. It does not take us long to learn and believe that quality of life is measured by how many things we control. By the time we are young adults and have received the left brain education available to us, our focus is out in front of us, centered on getting things and recognition which translates into things. The result of course is that we live in a society where everything is controlled, and those that control the 'thing' hold it up as valuable and therefore necessary for us to have. It follows that it is 'natural' to grow up believing that purpose translates into an object to attain.

Then there are those who see purpose as, "What should I do with my life?" They are asking the question as though there is some special vocation they are meant or destined for that has been hidden from them, and uncovering that vocation reveals their life purpose. Most people feel that this lack of knowing their purpose keeps them from having the things they need and desire and mainly the thing called money. They lament that they are penniless because they cannot find the purpose that would solve all their needs, especially the financial ones.

That ever demanding inner drive pushes one on, while purpose continues to elude us, no matter what the vocation or way of life; and this includes religious pursuits. The life training and education we receive has been very effective in keeping us focused on goal after goal which when attained seldom satisfies. We fail to see through the illusions we have created through left brain dominance. Our focus on commercialism is misleading us about our purpose and our true values.

Money is a good example of how we can be mislead. We fail to see that money is a principle of managing and living life and of itself money has no value. Yet we are conditioned to seek it by all means, and horde it when we are able to,and keep it from others who might want it. We have a fixation on what is called money, but the things called money are simply green paper and coins. This green paper has been touted as that which everyone must have and want. It is kept in vaults and under guard and in special building called banks and controlled by a certain special class of people who know they have control the lives of many with their 'money'.

We are fooled by money ideas to the extent that we do all we can to get it and conduct our whole life on how we can get more of it. We connect money to what we call purpose and if we cannot find a purpose that will give us money we feel we are less than those around us. The illusion is so strong that others feel we have no purpose unless we have the thing called money. We allow the idea of money to mislead us and confuse us about what purpose is.

Many times the question is asked in a way that sounds like the questioner feels as though God is withholding their purpose from them. As we attain and sometimes lose the things we pursue as goals and purpose we may begin to look to non-tangible goals when asking about our purpose. When someone asks me what their purpose in life might be I ask them if they are wanting me to tell them what their vocation should be. Then I ask them how long they have been looking for their purpose. After considerable thinking they usually say they have been looking for their purpose all their life. My next question is if we can presume that they have been after their purpose since they were born; they usually can admit that this is true. I then ask them if they can accept that they came here to do their purpose, and they answer yes.

Having accepted that they came here to do a purpose, I suggest then that their purpose might have to do with where they came from before they were born. This seems to make sense. The next question proposed is whether or not it makes any difference to the All-and-All or God ('where' they came from) if they became a butcher, baker or doctor? The true answer is that it makes no difference what we choose to do after we come here provided we do what makes us happy, and we do it as the best human being we can be.

Why is the true answer that simple? Because we are here to do what the soul came here to do and that is to learn to balance the self and be in harmony with all things.

We might ask ourselves, if purpose is that simple why do we struggle so hard to find our purpose? The answer is simple also; we have soul lessons to learn and that requires us to be happy. Yet at the same time our left brain is intrigued and influenced by those 'things' that we are 'supposed' to have to keep up the illusion that life is more complex than what it appears to be.

I have mentioned before that the soul is not impressed with position and rank, its only concern is that we learn to balance with whoever is in our life. This is why I sometimes say that you may be a queen in Europe in one life and a starving child in Africa in the next.

To the soul it is all the same. Humanly we value and judge position and possession, but these are not of lasting value. What is lasting is what we would escribe as having character and strength and we can find that in a palace or a jail cell. Ultimately, when we get close to being balanced, our human life will flow in harmony and things we need will come to us.

2

The Thinking Systems
of Planet, Animal
& Human Being

THE HUMAN BEING THINKING SYSTEMS

The basic process of how the brain uses thought is the same for the human animal as it is for any animal. The earth feeds thought particles to the skull brain and body. The skull brain uses thought particles and returns them to the earth's sphere. The body uses thought particles and they are returned to the material earth.

In the human animal, the thinking system is simple. Although there are cellular memory fields around the body which are involved in thinking processes, essentially the skull brain does most of the material oriented thought processing. The forebrain in the skull processes sense and memory information, and the hindbrain, if left to its own means, manages the physical structure, maintaining the physical form and keeping it in perfection.

Unlike other animals, the human animal has a mind which is a sophisticated thought processing system. This soul-mind system is designed to intercept and edit the earth's mass thought particles before the brain can use them. The soul-mind edits the thought particles and thought forms in relation to soul lessons it wants the human animal brain to think about. After processing the thought streams, the soul-mind then delivers the edited version to the skull brain for use in the material world.

Because the skull brain had to make adjustments over eons of time to the subjective input of the soul-mind, the brain now in turn edits the thoughts that come to it from the soul-mind. It is during this process that the dual thinking system (brain & mind) of the human being clashes. This reflects as that 'inner' argument we seem to have all the time the argument about whether or not we should do something. The final decision is under the control of the skull brain, the primitive animal brain; it has the last word, so to speak, in this third dimension.

When the soul-mind first began intercepting and feeding thought to the brain, the soul-mind was able to obtain the cooperation it needed from the brain. However, the differences between the needs of the two (brain and soul-mind) began to create problems. The animal brain was content to forage, propagate and survive. The soul-mind wanted to create illusory conditions which it could use as testing experiences for choice. The soul-mind would create unexpected imaginary situations for the animal.

Consider that in the beginning, as an animal, the creature had no fear; it had an instinct, as all animals do of the presence of predators. Without fear it would depend on its natural instincts to protect its survival, but it did not originally know any human mental fear. With the joining of the soul-mind, the human animal also became a mental being, acting on choices rather than entirely on instinct. As the primitive instinct diminished, the human being became more vulnerable to predators. After a period of integrating the subjective thinking, the mental changes resulted in predators endangering the human being's existence. This was due partly to the subjective conditioning; the human being did not know if what it looked at was a real animal or an illusion. To solve this problem, the mind of the soul integrated into the thinking processes a vibratory condition which today we call fear, and the sixth sense was born.

The soul-mind must connect to a human animal to function in this dimension and for this reason alone it is concerned with the physical survival of the animal. Because of this concern the soul-mind automatically withdraws soul demands from the animal brain when the physical survival is threatened, meaning that in a life threatening situation, such as war, famine, etc., the human being is left to its animal instincts to assure survival of the body. This is the evolutionary process the human animal was going through in its initial stages of integrating thinking between the animal and the soul-mind.

One other sense was created into the thinking system of the human being to accommodate the soul-mind's needs, which I call the change sense. Part of the early behavior of the animal was its instinctive herd urge to be passive and not progressive. For a long period after being joined by the soul-mind, the human being retained its instinctive herd animal behavior of slow-moving placidity. Because of the need for more action in the life experience, the soul-mind then integrated a change sense into the mental structure. This seventh sense activates whenever the human being refuses to be progressive for extended periods of time. It is the change sense which, when activated, forces the individual to readjust itself mentally and physically, forcing it to keep moving forward.

At this time in evolution the skull brain is dominating the expression of the human being. Unlike the autistic person who is dominated by the right brain and the soul-mind, most human beings are dominated by the skull brain (i.e. left brain). The optimum situation would be a balance between a healthy skull brain thinking process and the soul-mind thinking, a melding between what we call the inner and the outer.

THE INTERFERING INTELLECT

The human being conducts its life with two thinking systems. One is the soul-mind system which intercepts all thoughts being fed to the human being by the planet. The other is the brain in the skull of the material human animal which functions as all animal brains function. The ideal process of thinking would be that the thoughts used by the individual would be edited by the soul-mind and given over to the skull brain for use in the waking life. The use of thoughts would be balanced, meaning the animal nature would have 50% of the decisions about what thoughts to use, and the soul would have 50% say about what thoughts to use. This would create a balance of life projection between the physical needs and the soul needs.

As it is now, the skull brain, in its primitiveness, controls over 90% of what thoughts are being used. It does much of this by relying on old beliefs, old habits and anxiety provoking traits. In any case, the soul-mind has little input in the daily process of life. What is most dangerous about this condition is that the ego has become stronger as intellect has expanded. The intellectual aspect of the brain (left brain logic and reason) has egotistically promoted itself to such an extent that it cripples the natural functioning of the skull brain. In not contenting itself with managing the normal material needs of the human experience, the brain has ventured into controlling aspects of the behavior which are of the realm of the mind, the non-material or spiritual needs of the soul.

This unbalanced use of the human being thinking processes is having disastrous effects on the planet and the human experience especially in regard to male/female and family relations. Mass thought, today, is heavily laced with left brained (yang) energy, and any person losing control over his/her emotions falls victim to those streams of violent thoughts flooding their thinking.

In the circumstance where the parent seriously abuses the child, the parent has lost control of the thinking process, and actions being taken are directed by mass thought. The parent who strikes out in blind fury at the defenseless infant certainly would not commit such an act if s/he were using thought attracted by choice.

When the parent has reached an emotional disturbance level (emotional temperature) the brain reacts to defend the physical system and phases into an automatic thought feeding process with the planet. The planet then feeds thoughts into the skull brain mechanism designed to immediately destroy that which is perceived as threatening the body. This mass thought is acted on during a semi-trance state which blocks out the right brain and the wisdom thinking from the soul-mind and interferes with the balanced reasoning process which would interpret the action as harmful to everyone.

I used abuse of the child to emphasize a type of thinking and behavior fed by indiscriminate mass thought particles coming to the parent. This is the same kind of thing that happens to the adult who is acting harmfully toward another adult, or children who kill their own friends or parents seemingly in 'cold blood'. The brain, in this excessive behavior pattern, does not consider anything about the person it wishes to defend itself from. All the safeguards are blocked, and primitive survival thoughts which mass thought is overloaded with at this time, is being fed into the brain. There is no concern for morals or laws of any kind. The primary motivation is to get release from the emotional temperature level which is destructive to the body's cellular structure.

This defensive action is on the increase throughout the globe. People's bodies are being heavily polluted with negative energy thought particles today, and the level of chosen thought control is diminishing rapidly.

The failure to be selective about thoughts has a disastrous effect on most couples. As the confusion among the sexes grows, the pollution of thought particles increases, creating volatile relationships. The average worker who comes home after a stressful day finds it easy to 'dump' anger on the partner. Anger can have been suppressed all day, as it is not appropriate to economic survival to show anger on the job. At home, with a partner, the worker 'feels' safe in releasing anger, and so this becomes the thing to do. This particular mode to release tensions worked for couples, to some degree, in the past, but it has reached its mass limitations. Today, with the thought streams polluted with so much negative energies, releasing anger at a partner, or anyone else in the family, can result in physical harm and even death.

How can we improve a relationship and moderate the amount of intellect used in thinking? First we must understand that thought must be chosen at all times, as that is what we are supposed to be doing here. Second, it has become very important to understand who we are as human beings. There are many ways to discover the self. We can examine our country of origin for clues to inherent traits which might feed the intellectual process. We can look at our astrology sign to discover some aspects or reasons for too much right brain or left brain input. We can begin to take note of the things that cause us emotional disturbances, such as anger, anxiety, jealousy, suspicion, possessiveness, control and other traits. Understanding the self, being aware of and guarding against our weaknesses, helps us to choose our thinking rather than become victim to mass thought.

TWO KINDS OF THINKING

In our misunderstanding of what is going on in the thinking processes, we believe that when we think, we know that we are thinking. We take it for granted that we are aware of all the thoughts we process. Many (usually intellectuals) will argue that they remember everything they think and insist they know what they have been thinking about. We have multitudes of thoughts processing through us that we are unaware of.

There is a continuous stream of thoughts fed into our thinking systems from the planet's mass thought. This goes on whether we are awake or asleep. It is what keeps our bodies manifested in material form. Without it we would die. The thoughts we are aware of in our thinking are those which we are actually projecting at that moment of thinking. All the other thoughts either support our aware thoughts, or they pass through our system, feeding energies to different aspects of our material and non material bodies.

Some people refer to the two kinds of thinking as conscious and subconscious, and this idea has some merit. These two states of thinking are going on all the time and at the same time. The conscious thinking is the aware thinking, and the subconscious thinking is what is going on in the soul-mind. The soul-mind is always sending the brain thought it wishes to express, and at times the soul-mind will manage to get some mind thoughts through the brain when it is distracted. During this play between the two states there is the constant feeding of mass thought by the planet in and through the thinking systems of the person.

The brain ordinarily has the final say in what comes through its part of the thinking systems and is projected-acted out in the physical world. Speaking in religious terms, we could say that the brain is the veil that needs to be lifted. The brain, which is the doorway to the material world of thinking, is steeped in beliefs, habits and traits. Because of these conditioned aspects of the left brain, most of the thinking which we are aware of is simply repetition. There is a great difference between repetitious thinking and chosen thinking. The repetitious thinking is an automatic process that is fueled by mass thought impulses from the planetary thought fields. The thinking done when making choices disrupts the habitual automatic processes and causes new creative thoughts to be attracted for use.

I can not stress enough the difference between choosing your thinking and automatically attracting thought based on old repetitive habits. All of the acts done by people who seemingly 'thoughtlessly' maim and kill someone in what appears as an uncontrolled, mentally deranged act, has its roots in getting unwittingly stuck in using mass thought. Often times, such destructive thinking is not something that person had done in the past. But by not actually controlling his/her thinking, the mass killer or destructive human being has become susceptible to mass thought influences. These influences are often set in motion by a lack of life force in the body which is temporarily replenished by the adrenalin rush of the violence committed.

TWO PRIMARY DYNAMICS OF THINKING

I have discussed the human as a composite of the human animal with its brain and the soul with its mind. When we look at what is basic to each, we find two primal motivating factors at the roots of human behavior. The primary motivating force of the human animal is the need to propagate/survive. The primary force of the soul is the need to bond with another human being for lesson learning and balancing powers. These two kinds of needs are influencing the thinking.

For most people, at some time in their life, propagation is no longer a part of the life, and there is no longer a need to make babies. When the realization of no need for propagation becomes established it often creates emotional confusion in the person, not simple confusion, but deep confusion. On the surface there is no need for sex. Perhaps one is too old or has lost reproductive organs, yet there is still a deep urge and desire to do it. That deep desire has its roots in the need to survive and also in a basic need of the planet for life force energy, requiring more male and female babies.

The time when people stop creating babies in midlife, is what we call midlife crisis. It is a time similar to the crisis during puberty - another identity crisis. This is a great opportunity for the soul-mind to get the human animal to reconsider beliefs and old ideas and do some 'soul growth'.

The soul-mind's primary need is for spiritual growth. Spiritual growth happens during times of change and through interaction with other people, especially in what we call committed relationships. The need of the soul-mind for bonding, and the need of the animal to propagate has found ultimate fulfillment in marriage, a union of the male and female. In literature this is referred to as the 'sacred bond', and as such is considered to be the ultimate union.

BELIEF SYSTEMS

At birth the brain is *tabular rasa* - a clean slate (John Locke). From the moment we are born, the brain receives sensory input of many kinds, both pleasant and unpleasant. Based on this input of information the brain decides what is good or bad, safe or unsafe to think, say and do. Parents, schools, churches and political systems we live under all build and shape our belief system. Belief systems are left-brain oriented formulas for thinking that set boundaries in which to function. Without belief systems, we would not know our limitations and would find ourselves exposed to danger constantly. Having a specific system of beliefs allows the thinking process to function within an acceptable structure. Such a belief structure creates and provides parameters for how far one can extend the self safely.

Some beliefs are based on subjective knowledge, such as we find in religious teachings. Some beliefs are based on scientific facts, such as how fast the human being can run, for example. Most beliefs are set in our thinking through experience. Having a built-in reference system of beliefs (boundaries) allows the animal brain to feel it is in familiar and safe territory. The left brain knows the limits of its beliefs about various things and can think within these confines without exposing weaknesses, thereby protecting the life experience and what we call the ego.

Previously, I mentioned that in the beginning the human herd animal was just that, a simple animal who had no belief structures. It functioned on instinct and had few basic needs. When the mind first began injecting thought, the human animal became disturbed. It had no idea of what was happening to it. It would suddenly stop eating and find itself having unfamiliar thoughts and attempting to do strange things. This would be similar to us suddenly getting the thought that we could reach up and touch the moon. This disturbed the human animal causing it confusion and endangering its life expression. The soul-mind realized that it needed to provide the human animal brain with the ability to discriminate between 'real' and 'unreal' thinking processes and to make it aware it could do more than eat, sleep, propagate and avoid death. It devised a simple belief training process, which permitted the human brain to perform a certain amount of intellectual thinking. This is a process any researcher can train an animal to do (Pavlov's conditioning process). This worked, as the human animal could quickly adjust to such conditioning. It helped the human brain to develop reference processes, or belief systems, to keep from becoming nervous about its own behavior in response to the soul-mind's demands.

Unlike other primitive animals, the human animal was influenced by the soul-mind to make choices about its thinking, and the soul-mind fed it all kinds of simple belief conditioning for this purpose. After some time the human animal began to see the advantage of using the intellectual thought patterns to expand its basic desires of eating, sleeping, propagating and surviving. It began using the intellectual thoughts to expand its own ways.

Today we have many interconnected beliefs, all to cause us to feel secure in our behavior. Whereas the left brain is designed to stay within the beliefs when it processes thought, the right brain is willing to extend itself and test the limits of the belief. The soul-mind itself would be comfortable without limitations. However, it knows the human being needs belief structure in order to simply survive.

Driven by desires and the personal change sense, the individual today seeks expansion of his/her abilities. Expanding of the belief system is done by testing life and reaping understanding. This allows the human being to move out of a confining left brain intellectual bondage. When we become an observer and expander of beliefs, wisdom is acquired. 'Expanding of beliefs' is another term for 'raising of consciousness'.

Whenever someone tries to define reality, I am reminded of the statement, "Beauty is in the eye of the beholder". This means that everyone has their own idea of reality, just as everyone has their own idea of beauty. In addition, just as beauty is a part of mass thought so also are other aspects of reality. Mass thought conditioning is the reality by which most people experience the world. We each are equipped with our own belief of reality and we each are part of mass reality.

I described how beliefs are assimilated and built during life. I have also noted that some beliefs have to do with essences we are imbued with before birth which influence our thinking and the way we look at life. Beliefs formed during the first few years of childhood play a powerful role in our development and our ideas of reality.

Ethnicity is an example of an essence affecting the formation of belief systems. Some ethnic traits have an energy which is conforming. If we have an early childhood developmental process which is supportive and non-confrontational, we usually find it natural to meld into the mass reality of our social structure. Other ethnic traits are confrontational. If our early years are abusive and confrontational and we don't know what to believe, we often conflict with the social reality. By not having a belief structure which we can depend upon as common with everyone, we react based on our essence beliefs.

If we examine the human being as a user of thoughts we find that we are all sharing the thought particles used to do our thinking with. The black African uses the same thought particles to think with that have been used by the white Norseman and visa versa. What is different about the African and the Norseman is the belief structures of each. Although they individually develop their belief structures, they do so with thoughts used by other human beings. They also build their belief structures using the same kind of thought mechanisms. All humans construct their individual belief systems the same way.

Imagine the structure of belief systems being in the shape of a pyramid. The peak of the pyramid is the ego which is the composite of all the beliefs, and also projects the beliefs into the third dimension. The base layer of pyramid blocks contain the essences of the soul-mind (soul lessons, past/present/future), the essence of physical genetics, the essence of the personality (ethnicity, etc.), the essence of the cellular memory constructs (growth/death, etc) and others.

The middle and upper layers of the pyramid blocks contain our beliefs fashioned from our present life training, school, TV, family, marriage, etc. It contains our money consciousness, social and political views, attitudes toward fellow humans, the opposite sex and our selves. How we experience reality depends on what information we have accumulated in our pyramid blocks and how we interpret the information.

Today there is a great search for the meaning of consciousness and a desire to raise consciousness. Through expanding our beliefs by making deliberate adjustment to past beliefs, and broadening our capacity to understand more, we become more free and make great strides in our ability to stay balanced in life. This is an essential part of our consciousness raising - to expand ones beliefs to encompass and accept the reality of all there is, the being one with all.

EASTERN PHILOSOPHY AND KARMA

There are differences between western and eastern thinking. In both western and eastern thinking the human ego projects its ideas based on the beliefs accumulated in the left brain. The beliefs of the westerner are rooted on material goals and the left brain. The beliefs of the easterner are based in non-material goals, however, their beliefs, like those of the esterner, are also left brain limitations.

Leaders in the western psychology field believe there is a mystique about the east; the believe that easterners somehow have an advantage over westerners in achieving enlightenment. Connected to this is the idea that if westerners think eastern thoughts and adopt eastern philosophies they can attain enlightenment sooner. Westerners are going on pilgrimage trips to the far east, because that is supposed to increase ones measure of spirituality and/or enlightenment. Those who have returned from the east convey a more peaceful demeanor.

Practicing meditations is also widely believed to result in enlightenment. However, one cannot simply erase beliefs through meditation. Beliefs are building blocks of the ego, and simply covering beliefs over with a meditation does not alter them, they will seep through and affect the behavior eventually.

Enlightenment is the gradual process of expanding beliefs to understand all there is to understand in our dimension, expanding our belief system to include everything, without judging anything and to learn the lessons we came to learn on earth. Spirituality is the balanced use of thought, balanced in terms of inner and outer, mind and brain, physical and non-material.

Many westerners who become involved in eastern meditations accept other aspects of the east along with the meditations. Karma is an example of this; it has become a household word in the West. There are several interpretations of karma, but if considered in the sense that it involves punishment of the self, by the self, it is no different than western beliefs in a vengeful God who insists on payment for wrongs done to others.

To simply accept eastern practices as the path to spirituality is misguided. Easterners seek enlightenment as a basic philosophy, yet when we examine the condition of the common person we find that the Easterner is no further along in enlightenment than the Westerner is in spirituality. The answer to enlightenment/spirituality is not in trading one set of religious or spiritual beliefs for another. By expanding our beliefs to include ideas of east and west we become more balanced in our thinking.

3

Science
& Creation

THE UNIVERSE AND DIMENSIONS

Some people believe there is a human spiritual evolution headed for the fourth dimension now. Often they are referring to some who are experiencing different psychic states of consciousness, alluding to being in some advanced state. This idea is simply a misunderstanding between psychic abilities of that person and what a dimension is. Planet earth and all that we refer to as an aspect of this existence takes place only in the third dimension. Humanly there are no other dimensions here but the third dimension. The mental abilities of the human being at this stage of development are not able to understand what the fourth dimension might be. All of us on earth have chosen to come here to learn to balance our powers in a third dimensional framework. The human body and the brain are the vehicle in the third dimension, designed for the third dimension.

As a specie we are in a very primitive stage of third dimensional mental development. Are we really functioning as third dimension beings or are we functioning primarily in what could be called a second dimensional consciousness? With our present formats of scientific testing we can easily measure what would be optimal third dimensional use of all the senses. We have not done this because we are only now reaching a level of thinking that makes it possible to understand fully what exactly third dimensional sensing is.

At this time in evolution we are humanly performing primarily at a two dimensional level. One can readily observe this phenomena by noticing that when we look at something we see it as a flat surface first. This is so if we are looking at a newspaper or at a scene. We focus on that which we look at and exclude the whole of what we are observing. Sometimes we will slowly observe the obvious difference in distance or shadow, but not usually at first. This is second dimensional viewing followed by a partial three dimensional shift.

If we desire to see things in a three dimensional manner we have to make a deliberate effort to do this, we do not automatically see or think three dimensionally. If we examine the senses we use for seeing and measuring we can admit that we are designed to be three dimensional in all aspects of our thinking and sensing. If we are designed to function three dimensionally why is it we are not doing it? We are surprised when tricked into seeing three dimensionally by looking at computer generated 3-D pictures. We are reading reports of coming designs in televisions which will very nearly replicate three dimensional viewing, and we are impressed by this possibility. Why are we still thinking two dimensionally at this stage of evolution and science is not making mention of this?

I point up this fact that although we are in the third dimension we are functioning mainly in the second dimension because this is further evidence that the human brain is held back from functioning at its normal potential. That normal potential today is the ability of thinking in third dimensional processes. The interference in this is the confinement of human thinking in left brain paradigms. Educators and scientists, failing to see the situation, are forcing two dimensional patterning upon our brains.

Two dimensional left brain created laws, rules and paradigms reflect the level of awareness being expressed by humanity today. We base these man created laws on what we call science. Although these paradigms may have some basis in the true reality, they are limiting. As an example consider the edge of the universe. The average individual is not concerned with the edge of the universe. We see the edge of the universe as the outer limit of our own personal world. On the other hand, science, using its paradigms and laws, searches for the limits of the universe. Unlike the person who is involved in the play between inner measuring of life and outer manifestations of the inner, science continues to try to measure only the outer manifestation.

Reality encompasses all that the individual or the mass can think. This is so for the true reality of the individual or the false reality of the paradigm. When we apply this law of thought to the scientific question of where does the universe end, we have our answer: it ends where the scientist last looked for it. So long as science continues to look for the end or edge of the universe it will not find it. The reason is obvious, if science continues to use its paradigm or idea of the past as the source of information as to where the end is, science will continue to expand the universe simply by looking for it. Science does not find the future, it simply measures the past and the future responds to the measuring.

In as much as we find ourselves in a third dimensional universe and reality, why are we so engrossed in looking at everything with two dimensional vision and examining everything with two dimensional thinking? This has a lot to do with being mostly left brained in our thinking. The fact that we use predominantly one side of the brain by itself instead of both sides in balance is evidence of how far removed our thinking is from being fully third dimensional.

Presently, as a specie, we are barely moving out of the second dimension. When we are leaving the second dimension and are merging into the third dimension we are experiencing a consciousness shift. This means that we go through a period of adjustment in which we are using our senses in a mixture of second and third dimensional thinking.

Science states that we are in the third dimension, but the truth is, humanly we are consciously fading out of the second dimension and are phasing into third dimensional aspects. We are facing a distortion of what we call reality because human thinking has not mentally shifted into the third dimension.

This change in dimensional thinking is another aspect of what we mean when we state that we are undergoing some kind of forced raising of consciousness. This is also what is behind a great deal of the world changes that are happening now physically and psychologically. We should have moved well into the third dimension by now, but the mass human experience is not meeting that demand of the universe at this time.

It is the misuse of the planet's thought particles by the collective thinking of human beings which interferes with the dimensional shift of human thinking. We are in the third dimension, but the consciousness of human beings is slowly emerging out of the second dimension.

We hear lectures about the destructive state of the consciousness of human beings and the unbalanced ecological conditions of the planet as though they were two separate factors. They are not separate at all. Consciousness is a planetary condition which includes ecology and all things of this reality. The planet itself thinks, as do all creatures or entities in this dimension, and the condition of the mass consciousness is the responsibility of all thinkers. However there is a primary consciousness responsibility which lies in the hands of the planet itself. The planet has priority on the condition of all consciousness, or levels of thinking and thought projection. Human beings have usurped the primary influence on all matter with their unbalanced thinking. However, the planet can and will take back that position if the human influence persists in not fitting into the third dimensional consciousness.

If the thinking system of the individual were in balance and in harmony then most of what we would see would be third dimensional images, this without special glasses and instruments. If the right and left brain were being used in harmony, rather than one side being over conditioned, the average brain would pulse at the approximate level of the present pulse rate of the planet, and the total brain would function in a balanced manner. Thinking would not be as it is today, automatic and habitual, it would be selective, consciously using choice in all things. These are necessary optimum factors of the individual's thinking system for functioning in the third dimension.

If we ask the question why we are not further along into the third dimension, the answer is that we have become entrenched in left brain usage of thinking. Most of our early years are spent in developing the left hemisphere of the brain which is the primary user of two dimensional thinking. We have extended left brain usage about as far as we can as a mass of consciousness. There is an excessive amount of thoughts bearing left brain energies and forces. It is this left hemisphere pressure on the total planetary consciousness which is forcing the planet to intervene in the human thinking processes. As a consequence of human mental interference, we are experiencing mass mental anguish and material chaos perpetrated by the planet in an effort to stabilize the dimensional shift.

The push to raise consciousness is the push to bring us more in harmony, individually and collectively, with the third dimension. The mass thought being fed to individuals by the planet today reflects a demand on the planet's part to force the thinking systems of individuals to move toward the center of the third dimension patterns. This influencing of thought into the thinking systems of the human being by the planetary intelligence plays a major role today in the chaotic grasp for freedom throughout the globe.

This major energy change, called the consciousness raising process, creates psychological mass fear. An intense left brained, intellectual shift toward controlling things through monetary means has compounded the rift between planet and human being consciousness. This threatens many old beliefs and gives cause to conflicts between many ethnic groups. What appears as a move toward isolation of ethnic groups is actually a reflection of a panic that makes economic survival primary today. In this present world condition fear and panic have their roots in left brain oriented intellectual determinism.

If the consciousness shift is successful before the panic and fear becomes mass anarchy we could have our 'thousand years of peace'. This will only be a reality if we, as a collective mass of thinkers, balance the left brain with the right brain. If this is done then we will have transitioned into the third dimension and will 'see' all things from a more synergistic (3-D) perspective.

A word of caution about seeing three dimensionally: people who experience three dimensional vision are intrigued by the images they see. They also go through a stage of disorientation as they experiment with the viewing process. They tell of an oscillation of the images and a change in the viewing perspective when focusing on an object. With practice the disorientation will cease and permit greater perspective of what is being viewed.

Three dimensional viewing is a learning process and requires guidance at this stage of human evolution. In the near future more and more individuals will automatically begin seeing three dimensionally without being aware of why their vision has changed. Untrained health technicians will unwittingly interpret and diagnose the visual changes as being symptoms of illness rather than mental advancement. It is important to the welfare of the public that information about three dimensional viewing becomes part of the training health professionals undergo.

The dictionary defines evolution as a 'process of change in a certain direction'. This explains the basic idea, but it does not mean what many people believe evolution to be. Most of us have the idea that evolution is simply a biological process of selection, but that is not the whole story. We are also led to believe that we are superior to other animals, particularly other primates, because we have evolved, bit by material bit, into a 'higher' thinking animal, the idea being that we now think more involved thoughts because our brain parts are more advanced or developed.

When we examine the idea of evolution being a change in one direction and look more closely at its root idea which means 'unrolling' or 'unfolding'. Evolution does not necessarily mean getting better, it means change that is directive. Humankind is misled by the mechanistic paradigm which says you can only see direction if you can measure it materially. Since there is no research formula for measuring anything from the inner or subjective mental range, it is presumed by science that the inner does not evolve. This is the basis for discounting a creation theory.

As I have pointed out the inner does evolve. We cannot discuss evolution without discussing creation. In order to intelligently discuss material evolution, we must have a starting place. Science has not found the beginning of evolution and consequently it has no solid foundation for the principle of evolution. Science is actually at the same place as the creationist. At some point, when relating the story of evolution and trying to give it a beginning, science drifts into subjectivity and gives a theorized principle for the beginning of evolution; this is no different than the creationist principle. Neither evolution or creation can prove their existence as a principle from the material perspective, as there is no material foundation for either.

Both creation and evolution insist they have facts, but in reality both attempt to prove their points subjectively. Humankind has in effect accepted the mechanistic paradigm as part of evolution which is not proof but acceptance of an unknown foundation of principle. The thought systems of science voted and accepted that the God of creation is a 'big bang'. It takes little intelligence to see there is no difference in either paradigm, evolution or creation, both are God principles as both have a subjective unproven beginning.

To fully grasp the principle of thought as the creator of reality and human beings as the thinkers, one must be able to think without the restrictions of what we call literal proofs. Literal proofs are those which the left brain has so craftily designed as the origin of order, such as the mechanistic paradigm.

The creative thinker who believes in a greater source than the self can serve her/himself by understanding the theories of evolution and the mechanistic paradigm as being systems of thinking. Both systems, as we use them today are, limiting. Evolution says, "The beginner of the mechanistic paradigm was the big bang." Creation says, "The beginner of the universe was God's work".

We can see the influence of thinking on evolution by observing lower animals imitating other animals' shapes or colors for their own advantage. We often see them undertaking some form of behavior which appears as an act of ingenuity on the part of the creature. Evolutionists interpret this as learned behavior. The next question is, who taught the creature to do this? We might say that it taught itself by virtue of necessity but when we examine the creative behavior we have to admit that there are a lot of factors involved in the behavior. When we hear a scientist say that the creature changed because of an accident, we are hearing him say that the event was a subjective accidental experience.

Study of animal behaviors often reveal sudden exceptions to the established pattern. Who or what taught the creature to make such a shift? Above, where I gave the example of the researcher influencing the bird to use a stick to get the worm, we see the example of human thinking influencing a bird. The planet is very much involved in directing thought needed by creatures. It does this to keep the planetary balance it desires. This delivery of needed thinking to all creatures is an ongoing process which appears to have some connection to evolution biologically, but in fact the biological appearance is nothing more than the effect of the mental influence of the planet or human beings on the thinking system of the creature involve.

Hard science is well rooted in the thinking processes of all individuals. It is this way because hard science's kinds of thoughts (2 plus 2 equals 4) have been used over and over again and are now a major part of the mass thought fields. A basic rule hard science follows is the idea that if a process can be replicated, it 'belongs', or is reality. If it cannot be replicated, it is subjective and therefore under suspicion of 'not belonging', having no place in reality.

The human being itself is a subjective factor of existence. We can hardly accept the human physical being as a proven factor in material existence, since according to hard science, we are not exactly replicable. Those who live their lives measure life using a limited measure which in itself can not be proven, understand only a part of the third dimension.

When the quantum factor appeared on the scene, it was heralded as a great achievement of science. It was also immediately rejected by many in science, and they still suspect its validity. What has happened is that a certain accepted area of beliefs (the theory of replication) suddenly was threatened. Once more, those who have belief systems rooted in left brain intellect rose up to defend the old beliefs.

After some time of testing, quantum science is still suspect to many scientists. Hard science, as a concept, serves the objective human experience but fails when it is applied to the subjective reality.

The third dimension consists of subjective and objective realities, and many in science are beginning to come to this realization. There are efforts now to find formulas for measuring the subjective reality. It is quantum science which serves the human subjective reality. This becomes obvious when it is acknowledged that in research or in testing the researcher or tester influences the outcome. Quantum science contains the premise that the researcher influences the facts being used in testing. Subjective experience can not eliminate the human factor, this fact holds that research in that area should be done through quantum science formulas.

Humanly this opens a big 'can of worms', meaning that many

hard science followers will be disturbed. Subjective research is not in the realm of hard scientists. This causes great political/social disturbance as it means a change of political power in science as well as a competition for monies. These two factors, power and money, have always been at the root of stymied human advancement. It would be good for humankind if scientists of both schools joined together to acknowledge their separateness and agreed to share the power and the money involved in the many different areas research serves.

NO TIME OR SPACE

No time or space means that all that occurs happens now. This includes all past lives and the events we visit in our past life journeys using the hypnogogic states. To understand no space or time imagine being in the center of a large ball (the soul-mind). All around the inside surface of the ball you can watch the movies of events of your 'time and space' lives. Focusing attention on any point of the surrounding globe, you can watch (be in) 1847 AD or 652 BC, etc.

When we come into physical human form we can consciously only experience one lifetime event because the human brain is not capable of processing and distinguishing more than one life at a time condition referred to in psychology as 'multiple personalities disorder'. However, we can experience no time and space by mentally traveling to many past lives in hypnosis to examine other times. We venture into no time and space when we sleep and dream. We can also sit in a brief silence and be unaware of time and space, not knowing if a moment or an hour has passed from the perspective of linear thinking.

When there was no need for time, time of the clock did not exist. As we developed a need to use time we invented the clock. When we had nowhere to go, space was irrelevant and meaningless and took up no space as memory. When we developed the need to be somewhere else and had to refer to where it was, we developed the concept of distance (space).

In the beginning, when we needed to be somewhere else at a certain part of the day we put time and space together and began to measure life. However, time and space are relative, they are an illusion in the sense that we create them with our thinking. We accept the constant ticking of the clock as being real time and reject the reality of time created by each individual subjectively when an hour of joy is not the same duration as an hour of pain.

4

Religion
& Spirituality

RELIGION AND FAITH

One cannot comment on beliefs without considering religions. I mentioned that beliefs are systems of accumulated thinking which the left brain uses as guideposts for what it can safely and reasonably think about. This means that the left brain can, through the process of reason ('one plus one equals two', or 'my jumping limitation is five feet'), figure out what 'makes sense' and is therefore safe and acceptable to think about. If the brain cannot reason something through and see a safe, understandable conclusion to what the thinking is about, then it decides it is not acceptable to think any further about that subject. The belief system sets the limitations of comfort in how far one can go in thinking about something. It sets the acceptability level of what one pursues in one's thinking.

Most people may have thoughts which are not acceptable morally, but they may pursue the thoughts to some extent. When the thinking reaches a point where the belief system becomes violated or extends into an area of not seeing a rational conclusion to the thinking, the belief system automatically disconnects further thinking on the subject. There are exceptions to this which I cover in the section MASS THOUGHT.

It is necessary to point out that religious thought requires use of the right brain. With religion comes information which cannot be verified by left brain logic. Mother Mary of the Christian religion

97

conceiving a child without sperm from a male, would be an example. The reasoning left brain does not understand this as it is not logical. In this instance the brain uses another kind of logic, and that is called faith, which is subjective.

In the end religious belief is upheld by the logical left brain because it has accepted the belief as a viable thought structure which it cannot deny. All religions are thought entities formed out of left brain beliefs. It is the left brain which built the religion in the beginning and a preponderance of the information making up the religion is logical, thereby making it acceptable.

Another important aspect of the belief system which fortifies the faith principal is the built-in need to be like others. There is security in being alike which is instinctual in the herd animal. This human animal trait gives energy to the grouping together with others in religious doctrines.

A religion sustains its believability through those aspects which the left brain cannot make sense of. Once the religion is set in mass thought and readily available to individuals who are emotionally susceptible to attracting mass thoughts, the child conceived by a virgin, for example, is not doubted. As a construct of the left brain, once the religion is established in the mass thought streams, it is fed automatically to anyone emotionally ready to receive it.

There is an energy that travels with the thought forms of a specific religious belief. This energy is built by virtue of like attracts like. Religious energy is cumulative and directed unconsciously. We see this energy displayed in what are called miracles. It is the energy which an individual attracts with their thinking that causes stigmata, pierced hands and body parts which bleed. The stigmata is an energy or thought form which envelopes the person who is susceptible to it and becomes imprinted with it. We see it in the saints whose bodies continue to bleed for several hundred years after death. The energy of the stigmata is nourished by the thoughts of those who worship and believe in the saint even though it is a hundred years after the death. The more of these phenomena manifest, the more power the religion builds in mass thought, and as a result there is further increase in the phenomena.

Religion serves a great portion of the mental range of the third dimension. Third dimension consciousness has a range of thinking having two extremes. On one end is the survivalist, he is really against religion and collective thinking of any kind. The second extreme, is one who is not against religion but has been in religion and has moved beyond its beliefs. Another way of referring to the extremes is, the first is entirely left brained, is two dimensional and is easily plagued by fear. The other has an optimum balance of left and right brain thinking, is at the peak of three dimensional expression and uses fear only as a warning sign.

Religion serves the middle of the consciousness range. When the person has moved beyond primitive superstition but is still a survivalist, s/he becomes religious. Religion is important to the stAbility of the belief system for an extended time. When a person moves beyond fears connected to religion, s/he moves into more right brain expression. After becoming an observer without measure and judgement of others, s/he moves into the non-survivalist stage of life. Beyond this point is the balancing of right and left brain usage and optimum expression in the third dimension. The final stage is being in all things but not of them, and therefore being free.

RELIGION TO SPIRITUALITY

Let us examine some reasons why there is a shift taking place from religion to spirituality. Westerners are abandoning the churches of their upbringing in great numbers. If there were one church losing followers, we might say that the policies of that church were losing the battle to keep members believing in it. What we have though is a mass wandering of seekers out of their original church into other churches and even other religions. No one church can be said to be failing; all the churches are experiencing this phenomenon.

This has to do with the consciousness raising on the planet. Many souls are now here who are learning their last lesson or two. They chose this time to reincarnate because it has advantages in the sense of lesson learning. When souls who are in the last stages of learning in the third dimension return *en masse* to this dimension, they not only learn more, they also contribute to the raising of the consciousness *en masse*. This means that thinking done by masses of more learned soul-minds who are on the earth plane again, stirs up the mass thought fields. This infusion of seeker thoughts into the mass thought fields causes unrest. People who would normally stay in some mental groove, such as a particular religious faith, now attract the thoughts of those seekers and they too begin to question what is going on around them. The consciousness raising pressure of the world contributes directly to the shift from faith in one religion to questioning of all religions.

Consciousness raising is reflected in the great leap the world is experiencing in communications. Between television, computers and telecommunications nothing on the planet can remain hidden for very long anymore. All over the world acts of aggression, fraud, and control by fear are immediately exposed for all to find out about. This communication explosion has also contributed to a massive increase in thinking about aggression, fraud and control through fear. Those thoughts are attracted in great numbers, and millions of brains manipulate the thoughts with every kind of solution and judgement, after which they are propelled back into the mass thought fields for others to use.

In the past, fear of involvement and pain made certain people mind their own business and look the other way so long as what was perpetrated on another did not touch them. This is how the Hitlers, the Savings and Loan controllers and other abusers could be in power. Now that mass thought is compounding the exposing and the punishing of perpetrators, everyone in public life is under scrutiny. This includes religions and their churches. Religious leaders are being exposed for deviations from accepted moral conduct.

More and more questioning thoughts about religions and churches are attracted into the individual consciousness. This threatens all individuals' religious beliefs. As these awareness thoughts are attracted, the entrenched religious belief weakens and the individual begins to look for another religion or another way.

The brain wants to retain beliefs it can depend on. When the mainstay of its beliefs, usually religion, comes under doubt, the brain seeks a replacement. This results in the brain examining other beliefs which might take the place of the one it had depended on for its past stability in thinking. In this way every religion serves a purpose as a stage of inner growth.

When we look at social evolution, we can see that religions serve the part of the person which is not entrenched in literal left brain progressive thinking, the part which searches beyond the confines of closed circuit thinking. We look upon the early stage of non-literal thinking as superstition. Superstitious thinking was ritualized to make it acceptable. Ritual became religion, religion became doctrine which held non-literal thoughts (subjective thinking) as holy. These stages all reflect the attempt to frame non-literal thinking into an acceptable belief which reached its pinnacle in formal religions.

Today masses of people are moving beyond formal religion, and thinking is making a deeper incursion into the subjective realm. The large undefined area, called spirituality, is that realm the brain has moved into as it feels its way away from religious doctrine as a safe belief. For most who have moved away from religion, spirituality is undefined. Spirituality is a vague area to the human thinking, but it provides a temporary mental harbor to the wandering and seeking brain. This is temporary only while the thinking masses move toward another level of beliefs which allows the subjective aspect of the human being to surface. As a mass, and urged on by the collective consciousness raising in the world, we all are daily expanding the movement into spirituality.

SPIRITUALITY

For the sake of making a point about spirituality, I sometimes ask my students what they think being spiritual might mean. One woman answered that it is the special feeling you get when you are in meditation or praying to God. I then asked her whether she meant that if a meditator sat in meditation every morning for four hours that person would be spiritual. She commented that she thought four hours a day was too much meditating and somehow that was not spiritual. When I asked if there was an optimum number of minutes one should spend in meditation to be spiritual, she decided that the question was leading her into confusion. I next asked her if one could be running, working or singing and be spiritual. She quickly said, "Yes, of course". I then asked if it was possible to be in meditation and not be spiritual, and she decided that it was possible to be in meditation and not be spiritual. She soon came to the realization that she was not really able to describe what it meant to be spiritual.

Her answers are typical of many who try to answer the question what being spiritual means. This is understandable because for most people the word spiritual has something to do with religion. This idea of spirituality being connected to religion has stood for a long time and except for small segments of society, such as spiritualist groups, its vagueness remains. Today, however, as consciousness raises, the meaning and the use of the term spirituality is moving to the forefront. As the need to understand thought and thinking emerges, spirituality needs to be understood also.

Spirituality is a mental state of harmony in which balanced thought particles are permeating the human material expression. It is a balanced state of the material forces of the outer, physical expression and the mental forces of the inner expression. When these two aspects of the human being, the animal and the soul-mind, are in harmony, then one is in a state of spirituality. This state is called nirvana or samadhi in eastern philosophies where its attainment is sought mostly through quiet contemplation. However, this state of harmony or bliss can be attained while doing any daily function, such as washing dishes; it is simply a matter of choosing your thoughts at all times. To choose your thinking is the greatest act of spirituality.

Some people make the comment that spirituality is like a driving or pushing inner force, a search for the beginning or where we came from. This feeling has several sources. We all have the memory of where we came from, a knowing of who we really are, and this is something we want to revive or recall. There is also the change sense which is designed to propel us forward. In addition there is the need to be fully in the third dimension, experiencing life in a balanced way that is in harmony with the dynamics of the third dimension. Then there is the need for race survival which pushes one on. Finally there is the source of thinking, the world mass thought that is constantly flooding our thinking systems, an ever present force which makes us think and makes decisions for us when we fail to choose our own thoughts. Choosing the thinking without being pushed or driven brings us closer to being enlightened. Acting on all these inner impulses in harmony with the material life is being spiritual.

SPIRITUALITY & SURVIVAL

Living a spiritual life is a choice and requires that we are constantly examining our thinking to make choices. Having made the choice to live spiritually is the same as inviting the soul-mind to be more involved in our living experience. The soul-mind, as a due matter of process, intercepts all thoughts coming to us from the planet and edits them before they go to the brain for use. When we choose a spiritual existence (not religious), the soul-mind uses the person's energies to attract into the experience what we call soul lessons. As we learn soul lessons and grow spiritually, the lessons are attracted more quickly.

If for some reason, we face a life or death situation, the soul-mind withdraws any influence and demand on our thinking, leaving us able to draw entirely on instinctive survival thoughts to protect our physical life. The soul-mind knows that without the body it cannot be here in the third dimension, learning its lessons. After the danger is gone and we have regained control of our existence and the desire for spiritual expression returns, the soul-mind continues to bring forth the soul lessons.

Every human being has a responsibility to the soul to put themselves first, above all things. This does not mean that we ignore the good of all. It means that in the case where we forfeit our own good for another's we are in effect taking that other person's life. Taking a person's life, 'doing for them what they are supposed to take care of' in the spiritual sense means that we are interfering with the karma of the other person. When we fix another person's life by taking on what is their responsibility, we get the karma intended for them, as the event usually has to do with their learning process and growth, and we have robbed them of an opportunity to grow.

MORALITY: GOOD OR BAD?

Simply stated, morality, like reality and beauty, is in the eye of the beholder. Morality is a system of rules, standards and beliefs that differs from society to society and changes over time. All governments and religious organizations set their own standards of behavior to promote socially acceptable intercourse on all levels and perpetuate their system of control over those they lead. Morality is based on principles of good or bad according to the society. It is in the interpretation of good or bad that human beings often become engulfed in confusion and conflict.

In order to be spiritual and infuse the being with healthy energies, there must be a balancing of the inner and the outer with the chosen way of living. This needs to happen in harmony with the energies of the planet. On the surface this may sound like a plea for utopia. What I am pointing out is that the planet itself is always acting on the need to create spiritual balance in itself. If the western mass of thinking persists in putting confused conflicting thoughts into the mass thought streams, the planet will react to adjust the energies on the greater level. This adjustment will result in the planet making the decision on what is good for the human experience.

As I have stated before, the planet uses natural forces such as floods and storms to balance the energies of the earth. If anger and aggression among human beings persist, the planet will act to create some natural event which will cause the human being to reconsider its unbalanced thinking and selfish separateness. I gave the example of hurricane Andrew in Florida to illustrate one way the planet does this so-called good which results in the collective human mass to reconsider its path.

From the soul-mind perspective there is no good or bad. The soul is not interested in morality, human love or pain; it only wants us to learn lessons. Morality should be looked upon as a code of behavior we are obliged to follow if we wish to live in balance (spiritually) in our chosen community. The brain's primitive understanding has formulated and holds to moral laws and rules which often are stringent and confining to individuals in groups. It is the nature of human beings to be creative, and so long as rules and laws of morality allow for individual creation, we as a species are doing well. When individual creativity and unfoldment are denied, morality is discarded for violence.

TRUTH

Whatever we believe and accept is our truth and becomes reality to us. Like good or bad, truth is also in the eye of the beholder. I have stated that each of us is the creator of our own life. We have attracted to us all the things, conditions and the people who appear in our lives based on our essence for the purpose of showing us something about ourselves. This idea is confusing to most because there is the experience of all human beings to consider. Because there are other people in our life, we allow ourselves to believe that they have control or influence over what we think and do. However, when we understand that they also attract into their life what they need for their learning, then we begin to see how individually we each create our lives.

Each person has his/her own truth. You may find that no matter what you do, the same thing happens to you over and over again. This is your personal truth, it applies to your own world only. You may have a wart on your hand which is there no matter what you do about it; this is one of your truths. Other people do not have this truth; they have their own. A personal truth is something you manifest over and over again. It may be a simple habit you act out, it may be a particular thought you have which you repeat in spite of yourself trying to not think it. On the surface you may not want the wart on your hand, but because you think and say that it is impossible to get rid of, you continue to manifest it. If you stopped believing in it, it would disappear.

Most people are unaware how powerful their thinking is. Intellectually, we, our ego, think we really do not want the wart, but it is not the ego which has the only say as to what manifests in our life. The wart is reflective of an unconscious thinking process which created the wart to tell us something about ourself. It has to do with our truths.

In addition to our own personal truths there are other people's truths we must deal with. Some people are trying to put their personal truths on others, and they spend considerable time doing this. An example of this are the newly married who presume that they now have influence over the other person, and one begins to try to change the other's personal beliefs and truths. When this happens there is usually conflict since most people are reluctant to change their beliefs or truths.

What is truth to one, may not be so for another. At the same time each of us influence everything everywhere with our thinking, no matter what we think. When we learn to expand our belief system to include all truths we grow in wisdom. In a physical sense there is no ultimate truth. The thinker, on a subjective level, influences the truth. Nothing observed is without influence from the observer. This was discovered through quantum physics. Paradigms are presumed to be truths in themselves, however, over time there has never been a paradigm which has not varied in principles even though the variances are minute. Truth varies depending on circumstances and is different to some degree for every person.

What one believes to be truth, without question, shall manifest in the life of the believer. This is how miraculous healings, or total remissions happens. People often say they believe something, but it is the ego which is speaking, and the belief is shallow and not centered enough to manifest. There are other factors which determine how soon a belief will manifest such as will and emotions, however, unless one cancels the belief, expressed manifestation is automatic. What you contain in your heart is what comes into your life and that is your truth.

5

Psychic Energies
& Powers

HUMAN POWERS

The human being has many powers. Understanding our own special personal powers gives support to the discovery of the self. There are inherent powers which we derive from our material lineage, and other powers that are an essence which are derived from the soul-mind. All these powers are being expressed on the conscious, awake level and the unconscious level.

If your heritage is German you are industrious, hardworking and dependable. This is a power handed down materially from generation to generation. It is an inherent power special to the German person.

An example of an essence would be the power from ones astrological sign, a power chosen by the soul-mind. If you are born under the Virgo sign, you have a discerning quality or essence. This ability to be more discerning than others is a power specific to the Virgo person.

Each nation has a vibratory essence of its own. Those who are within that nation are imbued, to some extent, with its power. If you are born in the vibration of the German nation, then you are imbued with the power to be a follower. As German born, you have the essence of the German thinking as a thought form and emanate the essence of that particular power. There are many more powers that are not materially specific to the being, but are powers available by virtue of your state of thinking.

Two primary powers available to the thinking of the human being are those of yin and yang. These powers are often referred to as female and male, giving the impression they are exclusively used by either the male or the female. This is misleading as women, although being primarily of yin power, do have some yang power. The opposite is so for men, who are primarily yang, but also have some yin power. A male can become involved almost totally in projecting his life using yin power. Through his thinking he can draw on yin power to project his life. In doing so he becomes that which he is projecting: his voice becomes female, his mannerisms become female, his desires become female, and his body begins to dematerialize the male form and materialize the female form. The female has the power to use yang energy in the same way.

When the mind considers bonding to a newborn infant, it considers the gender and the ratio of yin and yang power of that infant. It usually chooses an infant that can be expected to project its life in accordance with the gender it had at birth and the yin or yang power corresponding to that gender.

Yin and yang power has a major influence on the life projection of the human being. Immediately after birth, if the projected path of the infant changes radically for some unexpected reason, the mind may withdraw from the infant. One of the possible reasons for the withdrawal of the soul-mind might be that one of the parents changed their behavior patterns, causing an unexpected change in the potential psychological development of the infant and also the amount of yin or yang power the infant would have to project its experience. If there is cause for a soul-mind to vacate from an infant there are other soul-minds readily awaiting the opportunity to bond with the vacated infant.

Yin and yang energies are basic forces in the magnetic electric sense. A person using yin power is basically a negative energy force. When a person thinks using yang power s/he is a positive energy force. We can think of yin and yang forces as a kind of magnetic electric energy force the human being emanates mentally.

'Know thyself' has been the reminder from all the wise ones throughout history. Understanding who we are means understanding all our powers and essences and being able to use them in a balanced manner. This makes it possible for us to recognise and resolve our human lessons while at the same time the soul is able to learn to balance its powers. Certain spiritual groups refer to this process as self realization, enlightenment and liberation (freedom from ignorance). Many different paths are recommended by different groups for attaining this state. I am taking the best suited approach to western thinking, which is primarily an active inquiry into the self, while learning to incorporate methods of getting in touch with the inner as a guidance aspect.

LIFE FORCE

Everything in this universe must have life force in order to live or exist at this dimension. Life force is an energy that pervades the very universe in subtle form. I liken it to or pre-quark electricity which is a life giving essence. As an energy force, it is possible for it to be attracted, collected and projected. Certain geometrical forms readily attract and collect life force. Pyramids are optimum collectors of life force. The pyramid of Giza, for example, was especially designed for that purpose. All creatures are users of life force and have systems for attracting and processing it.

The planet itself attracts and uses life force. As a mental mechanism, it has the ability to project life force, and it does this by using thought particles as the transporters of life force. Thought particles, by virtue of their quality, collect and carry life force and other energies. Without a sustaining level of this life force energy any creature ceases to live and its form dematerializes.

Like all living things, the human being needs a sustaining level of life force. Having enough life force is like having enough electricity in the automobile to keep it running. Let us take the example of the automobile to get an analogy of what life force does in the human being. Let us assume that the auto has a twelve volt battery. This means the auto has twelve volts stored in its battery and the auto runs optimally on a continuous level of twelve volts. The motor can run, the lights will work, and the radio will play as long as the electric system is creating the twelve volts needed. It also has to have the twelve volts stored in the battery when it stops, so it can have the energy to start up again. If something is wrong with the creating and storing of electricity, the twelve volts may go down to a level where the lights get dim and the motor has trouble getting enough electricity to run. When the system fails to the extent that no voltage is stored, the car will have died and cannot start. If there is an electric short, then something drains the electricity from the battery, denying it the power to run or start. The human body functions exactly the same way.

The human body is designed to function on an optimum stored level of life force. It has an electric system which sustains that level of life force. We think of the heart and its system of veins and arteries as feeding oxygen and nutrients to the body, but that is only part of the function of the cardiovascular system. The heart and the blood vessels also generate electricity which is carried through an electric grid system in the human body. Life force is stored and used in the body just like electricity in the auto. What is different about the two is that the human being mentally influences the quality and level of life force. When we are in a joyful, free, expressing state, life force flows in and through our system, bathing it in optimum energy. When we are morose, closed and withdrawn, life force cannot enter the system, and the body is being depleted of its ability to sustain health.

It is the quality and content of the thought being chosen and attracted into and through our thinking systems that makes the difference. Understanding this process is vital to the human species today, and understanding that we control the quality and level of life force with the quality of our thinking has to do with the need to raise our consciousness. This is the case for the individual and the whole human species.

All creatures who receive thought particles from the planet, receive life force energy with those particles. The thought particles which are used to project the life feed and energize the life. All entities which have the mental power to project thought into the thought streams can interfere with the quality of life force carried on the thought particles. The planet thinks and projects streams of thought to all creatures; it can also influence the quality of life force it feeds them. It does this in relation to the need of the planet to balance itself in the whole earth expression.

Like the planet, the human being also has the power to influence thought particles going to any brain. This is an ability those who perform voodoo and other psychic practices are sometimes able to perform. Fortunately, at this stage of understanding, the average perform voodoo and other psychic practices are sometimes able to perform. Fortunately, at this stage of understanding, the average human being has not discovered how to do this deliberately.

If the life force level of a person who is constantly mentally punished and dominated by another person were analyzed, we would find it to be very low. If we were to examine the condition of their body cells, we would find the cells beginning to mutate for lack of life force. This is an example of one thinker being able to dominate the thinking of another to the extent that the life force level going to the abused person is meager.

There is the general idea that we get life force from eating, and that it is the source of our energy. The primary use the body makes of the food we eat is the replacing of chemical supplies. Because food is made up of thought particles it may contain some life force, but it would be minimal. The major source of life force energy is taken into the body through thinking certain kinds of thoughts (see LIFE FORCE & DEPRESSION). Depending on the quality of our thinking, we either attract thoughts that use up our life force or attract thoughts which bring us life force. A person who has a depleted life force level can feel the physical difference when life force energizes the body.

From a planetary perspective there is a cross feeding of life force amongst human beings. Infants and young children supply life force for adults, and especially the aging adult depends on this supply. The planet strives to maintain a balance of infants to aged people. If one were to examine this global cross feeding, one would note that infants are born in relation to the life force levels needed by the whole human population.

By virtue of the purity of thought which the infant uses, its life force has high energy content. On the other hand, because of the inept and often negative use of thought by old people, the life force content in their bodies is of a low quality. Up until the time of puberty, children are feeding adults life force. After puberty, for a few years, depending on the quality of life style, youths functions on their own ability to develop life force. As adults we draw on children as well as our own thoughts for life force to sustain the body. There are those who have no connection with children and they often have a low level of life force energy.

LOVE AS ENERGY

Love is often described by poets as the elixir of the gods. There is more truth in this statement than is realized. When one considers that each human being is the creator of their personal universe, the statement about love has significant meaning. We each are the god of our life by virtue of the fact that through our thinking we create all that exists in our life. Most of us see love as being an ethereal nondescript feeling. However, love has much more substance than a vague emotional feeling. It is actually life force in pure form. If we could ingest pure life force from pure thinking we would feel love.

Pure love is not dependant or influenced by giving, getting, controlling, possessing or any form of deliberate mental influence. It is a nourishing wave of life force flowing through the thinker who holds the level of pure thought out to others, permeating their material bodies. This process renews mutated body cells by reversing their energies.

The healing one receives from the 'laying on of hands', or from any part of a healer for that matter, is the transfer of love (life force). Most healers are not aware that it is love they are infusing the patient with. The reason why most of the healing energy comes from the hands is because mentally the healer is projecting the love only from the hands. Many paintings show the Christ with hands upwards, palms toward the viewer. This is the symbol of healing love being expressed.

Love, the true energy, is the expression of pure life force. As we can easily understand, most of the life force we receive is not pure, because there are few individuals who think purely. Most thought has been used and reused by humans over and over and is distorted and confused, and the amount of life force that transfers between people in the course of a communication is minimal.

YIN & YANG POWERS

I have mentioned before that the two primary powers in this

dimension are yin and yang. Every thought particle carries either yin or yang energy. Let us presume the first particle of this dimension was a pure thought particle. This first thought particle was made up of two basic electric energies, negative force and positive force. Imagine now that this first thought particle vortexed into the third dimension, and as it did, the particle split and there was a separation of the two energies. Now there were two particles of thought, one carried negative or yin force and the other carried positive or yang force; this is the origin of the concept of duality in illusion.

The basic energy emitting from the female form is yin, and the basic energy emitting from the male form is yang. The amount of yin in a predominantly yang form and vice versa will vary in accordance with several factors or powers of the total form, as there are other powers inherent with the form.

Let us apply this formula to a human baby which has just completed its forming. This baby would be 90% yang or 90% yin, and whatever is the dominant energy would be reflected in the gender of the form. There is a primary memory influence which determines what the gender will be from the planet itself. When necessary for planetary balancing, the planet determines what gender is needed. Yin and yang energies are the primary energies of influence in the third dimension and specifically on the creation of matter. The dominant mass of matter here is the planet itself. In the planet lies the memory of its own balance of forces. It reflects onto all things of matter that planetary balance, thereby influencing the gender of the unborn. It is that essence of memory which makes up the influencing factor on the gender of all animals including the human animal.

The mental systems of the human being are capable of using and projecting either yin or yang energies for expressing their existence. This is meant when we speak about the human being having choice. The female, who is 90% yin, is capable of mentally expressing all thought using either yin or yang energy. This is true for the male who is 90% yang; he can express himself totally using yang or yin energy.

Thoughts are drawn from the planetary mass thought fields. They come to us by virtue of the law of attraction. When we mentally project yin energy, we attract thought particles containing yin energy. What is significant to consider is that if you are a male with 90% yang energy and choose to continuously bathe your being with attracted yin energy thoughts, you are in effect rejecting your yang form. That which we mentally (on an unconscious level) reject, dies.

I believe that this unconscious rejection of the original form is the root cause of the AIDS disease. Although the disease is there for everyone, as are all diseases, we can statistically support the idea that this disease has its roots in the mental disturbance of the yin or yang powers. Disease is attracted by us mentally as is everything else in our experience.

YIN POWER & FEMALE

There is a tendency to confuse yin power with female power. However, yin power is not exclusive to the female, the male does have some yin power but usually, not in the measure the female has. The female has yin power as a natural inherent part of her expression as the balancer. Yin power has the quality of nurturing or feeding, of nesting or circling; it is an energy that holds things together. The female also has the yin quality of managing, guiding, and healing. The female, in naturally having yin energy, finds herself able to be harmonious with the psychic state of the soul-mind. This state is often referred to as intuitive.

In certain animal species, we can readily see the yin energy expressed in the behavior the female uses to attract the opposite sex. We often think of this as a reflection of the need for the species to reproduce itself, but it is more than that. This ability of yin energy to attract extends beyond the mate-to-mate sexual needs. There is a nurturing and 'feeding' done on the physical levels that is part of the attraction process. The yin mother nurses the child and soothes the male. Her 'nesting' behavior is best described as creating the place to which the male naturally goes to attain rest (relief).

Pure yin management is devoid of aggressive behavior and functions as the optimum way of doing business through use of the law of attraction. The female is the natural healer, holding in combination all the essences or qualities for total healing of wounds, physical and psychological. Through the yin energy of the female, it is possible for the male to connect to the soul-mind and heal psychologically.

YANG POWER & MALE

The female does have some yang power, however, it is the male which wields most of the yang power. Yang power has its essence or focus in its projection. Used by the male, yang power can be destructive. Used by the male, yang power can be constructive. Used by the male, yang power has a pushing/willing consistency that is creative. Used by the male, it is a projecting, ongoing force of energy. Where yin energy goes in circles, yang energy goes on a straight line.

We see this yang force in the average male when he forces material into form, physically constructing highways, skyscrapers, moving mountains; mentally building or destroying empires. We see it as the male blindly moving in a singular direction after he has lost the meaning of moving forward. We see it in the male dominating others and things around him, pushing in one direction, usually upwards or beyond in the psychological sense.

HEREDITY & GENDER

It appears to most that we simply come into this world as a boy or girl, and there is not much to consider about that. Then we go into life basically ignoring our pattern body. Without realizing it, we think and act indiscriminately expressing male energies and female energies, and we do not realize what we are doing to the cellular structure of the body. When we volley between expressing yin or yang forces we are confusing the body, and it does not know whether to respond by growing into male form or female form. By doing this we are disrupting our cellular structure.

Many have the misconception that to be balanced means to be using both our yin and yang energies in about the same measure. Men are encouraged to 'get in touch' with their yin (female) nature and women have been asserting their own yang (male) power for several decades now. I discuss the proper and most effective use of opposite powers in chapter 7 'MALE/FEMALE GAME'. At this point I wish to express that the improper use of opposite power by each gender is destructive to the cells of the body. Cells which are imprinted with yin energy will be confused and eventually mutate when continuously subjected to yang influence of the thinking process. The same is true of yang formed cells which are mentally changed by yin thoughts.

There are several factors which can influence the human being to alter its original gender orientation. The infant is born with an essence of gender memory in its cellular body fields. The person may have been female in many previous life experiences, and now the choice is male. Because of a strong memory of a past life essence of yin, there could be a tendency for the yin power to surface in the male child. This can be reinforced by a disappointed parent who wishes the child were a girl.

Another influence to changing one's gender has its roots in the primitive animal nature of the human being. Ancient memory sometimes dictates the need for a person to act out a dominant or submissive role around other people, a common behavior in animals who seek position or rank in the clan. This can be the cause for one male, for example, dominating another male, or the reverse; one male desiring to submit to another. This can be so for the female also.

In all situations of confusion of gender identity, we have the thoughts of the person contributing to a gender change. The more often a boy uses yin energy while thinking, the stronger the influence on the physical cellular fields of his body becomes. Cells will change their gender essence if bathed in enough thought particles of the opposite yin or yang force, and this results in body changes. What is imperative to understand about gender is that we are mental beings first. We have the mental powers to reject our gender and alter the molecular structure of the original gender body pattern.

As the soul-mind, before we come here, we examine the fetus and family, then we make the choice of bonding with a particular infant. One of the primary factors influencing our choice is gender. We select our gender before coming here. Once in the body, we have the 'veil' before us which hides our previous mental life from our developing ego. We do not remember why we chose the gender we have become. As we grow, we acquire a human psychological framework which distorts our inherent wisdom and our original intents. Confusing our gender role is one of those distortions. As the distorted idea of our gender is reinforced by the law of attraction, we become entrenched in choosing the behavior of the opposite gender of our original pattern. The original form is rejected and the physical body is forced to begin altering its molecular structure.

Why is the person who rejects their original gender pattern getting sick today? After all, we have been doing this role confusion for generations. The reason is simple: the whole world is in a very confused state, and this upsets all the energies of the world. All plants, animals and matter of any kind, has its content of yin or yang energy. All is thought, even rock, and with the combination of chemical pollution and psychological pollution, the whole earth ball of illusion or thought particles is out of balance. Therefore if we add to this overall confusion and unbalance our own thoughts of gender identity, we are placing an even greater burden on our cellular structure, and balancing becomes a problem for the body. There is an attempt on the part of the earth and those sensitive to it to raise the consciousness (thinking quality) and gain more harmony and balance physically and mentally for all. Raising consciousness has to do with us learning about the energies we use, and how to use them correctly, especially yin and yang.

GOSPEL TRUTH ESSENCE

Our 'gospel truth essence' is the essence of our individual soul and of the lessons with which we must project our life. Our essence cannot be changed, it stays with us throughout our life, one might call it our 'specialness', that which makes us different from all others. The gospel truth essence is our basic nature, and unlike truths of the belief system which can change as we grow and the beliefs change, our essence is a gospel truth, a truth which is unchangeable. 'Gospel' is used to make the point that it is a truth which is accepted mentally as infallible truth, different from common truth which is born out of beliefs.

There is an assumption in psychology that adjusting the belief of a person can result in improved mental health. This may be so, provided the changes in the belief system are not in conflict with the gospel truth essence of that person. The belief system contains all information acquired by the brain throughout the present. It forms in the brain as intellect is stored and can be influenced by other intellectual input.

Unlike the belief system, the gospel truth essence is similar to a genetic characteristic; it comes with us when we are born. It pervades the entire being, materially and mentally. It is not genetic, it is a residue of the soul experience and its acquired distortions: the things the soul is here to learn to balance. It is of mental origin, stamped on all aspects of the human being, animal and mental at the time of fusion of the soul-mind with the newborn. The human being is 'cloaked' in its gospel truth essence from birth to death. It is the basic mental formula with which the soul projects its experience in the material reality.

Efforts to alter the beliefs and behavior of a person while ignoring the gospel truth essence causes the person frustration. The frustration can result in explosive behavior and could lead to anger and violence that might be deadly or suicidal.

We can sometimes observe this explosive behavior in the child who is in a family where all the siblings are similar in behavior but the one. The others are conforming to the family structure and seem to be part of the cohesiveness of the family unit. However, the one child seems to be out of step with the family unit. Most likely the gospel essence nature of that child causes the child to refuse to conform to the family structure. Understanding the gospel essence nature of the child would permit an adjustment of the family structure to take place which would include the nature of that special child.

The difference between a child who is simply overextending the behavior patterns and getting into trouble because of it, and the child with a gospel essence problem is considerable. The child who simply has over-acting behavior and traits and is unruly will adjust through guidance or even punishment. The child who is acting out a gospel essence energy will reject guidance and ignore punishment no matter how severe.

I am reminded of a male child in a family of four boys and two girls. This child had a gospel essence lesson about arrogance. If he felt that he had done his share of the chores and the father insisted he do

118

work the others had not done he would refuse. When the father threatened him with punishment the child still refused. When the child was punished with a belt on his backside he still refused. The father slapped the boy in the face for standing before him and defying the order to do the work. The blow was hard enough to make the boy's nose bleed and knock him to the floor. The boy stood up straight before his father and said, "You can beat me all you want I did my share and that's all I am going to do!" Needless to say, the boy was struck even harder. The father was enraged and it was the mother interfering that saved the boy from severe harm. This was a case where the father and the son had the same gospel essence lesson of arrogance and the power of the essence would not let either give in to the other. This is a true story and that boy was me and the arrogance was mine. My lesson was to see through the ignorance of defying that which I could not control. My father has the same lesson. When he died years ago I was visited by a master and told my father had just transitioned. I was also told that my father was learning at that moment that he had failed to see through his arrogance. In addition I was told that I was in his experience to see the folly of my arrogance and did not learn from him, as he had not learned through what he faced in raising me. Minutes later I received the long distance call that told me my father had passed away.

By examining the nature of a person one can find clues to their gospel truth essence. When we say, 'That person has a very caring nature,' or, 's/he is hyperactive,' we are touching on the gospel essence.

The gospel truth essence is not readily observed because it is hidden. The average individual is conditioned from birth to develop beliefs and traits, and the gospel truth essence becomes buried in the assimilated ego identity. We often make statements about being true to the self; this self that we refer to is that gospel truth essence. The statement of being true to the self must be made with tongue in cheek as the gospel truth essence of the person often needs management. Our soul lessons often lie waiting in the 'heart' to be released and they are part of the gospel essence.

As an example consider the person who is a teacher of wisdom, garnished with great mental powers. The gospel truth essence of such a person is 'wisdom with great power'. The nature of the person could appear as that of "one of great knowledge". That person may be primarily expressing great mental power. If the power is allowed to dominate the wisdom, the person evolves into a no-nonsense, controlling entity, and the true essence is cloaked.

I take the position that anything we are or have, essence, trait, habit, or belief, known and unknown, is a power and energy source. Beliefs are powers, so is the gospel truth essence along with all the other gifts we endow ourselves with. Traits are sources of powers. When we understand the influence and extent of our use of such powers we can learn to manage them. Once our gospel truth essence is known, we are then able to manage it.

Our gospel truth essence is more readily found if we take the time to describe every aspect of ourselves. I would use the analogy of peeling the artichoke of its leaves to get to the heart (essence). As we would peel off leaves, we peel off any superficial habits, traits, beliefs, and examine anything that might be a part of our nature until we get down to the root, the place which feels most sensitive or vulnerable when exposed. This is the gospel truth of our being, the core from which we operate in life. That core has been developing from the very beginning of the soul's journey in this dimension of reality. It could be that multitudes of past lives have contributed to the forming of the present state of the gospel truth essence.

PERSONAL INHERENT POWERS

The only reason we, as souls, come here to earth is to learn to balance our powers. We call the process: learning soul lessons. When discovering the self, or more specifically, aspects of the self, it is important to accept the discoveries as positive and meaningful. No matter what we find out about the self, if we examine it carefully, we find it is a benefit or a self gift. It is a tragedy that more often than not, there is the automatic (mass thought) input or belief that what we discovered is negative.

In America we like to think of ourselves as Americans even if we are of a specific nationality such as Irish. There is a tendency to overlook the fact that our parents were Irish or Polish or Jewish and that we are still carrying this national trait as an aspect of our self. The truth of self discovery is that the nationality of your parents is a gift you gave to yourself. It is up to us to discover the power of this inherent trait and to use it wisely and with discrimination for our greatest good.

Before we bonded with a human body, the soul-mind considered that which we needed to learn as a soul. We chose parents who carried certain national influences in their inherent essence to accommodate our soul lesson needs. As example: if, as the mind of the soul, you knew you needed to function as a human being having an essence of uninvolved simplicity, you would have chosen to be born to Polish parents. If your need was to learn lessons about control, you would have chosen Jewish parent. A national trait is a power built into the essence of the material being. Being of Polish descent, there would be the tendency to simplify all things. It is no accident that the Polish nation was the first to reflect the need to throw off the complications of bondage put upon them by Communism and bring attention to the need to throw off repression. This trait of simplicity is a power which is easily overdone and can cause the individual to seem unsophisticated and even become the object of everyone's joke.

The Jewish inherent trait is control. The soul-mind might choose a Jewish life experience for the purpose of learning to balance control. Like people of every national trait, Jews have a need to express the inherent power they are born with. Their challenge, or lesson, is how to use power without controlling other human beings.

When we relate personal power traits to the overall human experience we get some understanding of the mass thought involvement of planet and soul. An example is the World War II experience. Here we can observe the acting out of roles of nations on a mass basis, and we can see the mass lesson for many souls, in this case the lessons of the Jew and the German. The Jews were controlled in such a complete manner that millions of them went to their destruction in lines, one after the other. That which we are, in this instance controlling, is attracted upon the self. This is a basic law for human behavior. Each Jew, individually and collectively, in the grip of the Germans became controlled to the extreme. This was the soul lesson for the Jews, not to be controlling, and the experience might be called a mass karmic debt.

The German national trait is to follow blindly. The German nation, as a whole, (and its individuals) blindly followed a leader to their own destruction. Germans brought upon themselves what the conquerors forced upon them. This was well exemplified by the results of the First World War upon the German nation. We are too close to the time of the Second World War to see all of its karmic effects on the German nation.

There is an automatic balancing process in operation which adjusts exaggerated nationality energies. Looking at these dynamics of national energies working to balance one another, we can readily see how the planet does control world social activity if it needs to. The planet's need to sustain its own balance causes it to intelligently interfere with human processes. In the sense of world and universal energies which influences planetary balances, there is always the greater force which will take precedence over the lesser force. In this example we see the planet's needs taking precedence over the careless forward stressing of the human idea of nationalism. It is not a matter of one nationality getting the better of the other or one being right and the other wrong, and it is not a process of evolution. It is simply an adjustment of universal synchronism, of energies seeking their levels of balance. The end result of the world adjustment following World War II is that many nationalities in the world received mass lessons on the effect of the abuse of ethnic powers. What brings balance to the whole is the empathy expressed for humanity by all. Unfortunately, humanity has a short memory and needs frequent reminders.

The personal powers inherent from the nationality essence are bestowed upon the self when coming to earth. Being of a nationality simply gives us notice of a trait we have, and when we ignore and misuse the inherent national power, it will result in us attracting a penalty.

When we examine the Jew, the German, the Poles and others, we often detect the inherent trait in their behavior patterns. In all cases, if the trait is not managed in moderation (balanced) in a relationship for example, the trait causes disharmony. If the behavior is such that the trait is a dominant factor and we ignore the need to modify the trait, it will reap upon us that which it perpetrates. If we are too controlling we may end up being controlled. If we are blind followers we may fall off a cliff.

I cannot repeat enough the necessity of seeing your chosen essences as powers. If you see them as being negative and yourself as the helpless victim, it means you are automatically trapped in the

122

power and will repeat the negative conditions you experience over and over again. The answer's to modifying the inherent power by understanding that it is a power and being deliberate in how it is used.

If we ignore the inherent power, it will run our life through the automatic attraction of mass thought. Instead of being in command of our life and knowing who we are, our traits will control us. List your signs and symbols: horscope, ethnicity, race, religion, birth environment, etc. Discover what these personal powers are, then understand the use of them and how they can benefit your life.

Every relationship serves a purpose, the purpose of knowing the self and growing spiritually. This is the primary reason the soul-mind bonded with the human body. Relationships can further the learning needed by the soul, and as mates, partners, friends we can help one another identify and manage our powers (while keeping in our thinking that we are another teacher). Make a list of your powers and discuss them in the light of the goals of the relationships you are in. Understand that each individual is the last to see their own powers manifesting as distorted behavior. Your relationships provide a mirror for the purpose of helping you see when yours are excessive. Examine where the powers conflict in the relationship and be aware of how they become impositions on others. Personal powers are often difficult to see in oneself. Ask those who know you for input about your behavior and examine that which is pointed out to you.

I am reminded of a group of therapists I spoke to about powers, ethnicity and inherent traits, and one woman mentioned that she had three nationalities in her background. She wondered how she could know which of the three nationalities she was most influenced by. I asked her which one she thought she reflected most. She answered that she thought she was more English than anything else. Since there were several of her friends present I asked her if we could ask their opinion. She agreed. I then asked the audience to call out what nationality they thought she expressed most. In unison they all chorused: 'German'. She was dumbfounded that they all felt such. There was no question that those who knew her, saw her as expressing German traits.

Children are adept at pointing out our excessive behaviors, and though they may not know anything about nationalities, if questioned, they will reveal to us the traits that are dominant in our behavior. These traits are clues to our powers and through them we can become more aware of how to conduct our life in a balanced manner. Used wisely, our powers will serve us well materially and in our soul lessons.

CHANGE SENSE

Human beings have altogether seven senses. Besides the obvious five physical senses we have a fear sense and a change sense. At the beginning of the human experience the human animal was content to be a slow moving herd animal. The soul's desire, however, was to express itself creatively, to be a creator with the All-in-All. To satisfy this creative need the human animal nature had to go beyond its animal needs. It had to learn to fulfill imaginary needs injected into its thinking system by the soul-mind. To ensure that there would be a driving force in the nature of the animal, the brain was reconditioned with a change sense mechanism which caused the body to feel the need to activate and move forward. This change sense is an aspect of the memory process. When it is necessary this mental mechanism produces a chemical or drug which is fed into the blood stream. This chemical works on the nervous system, creating the desire to keep the body moving physically. The imaginary needs triggers the mechanism in the brain to produce the change sense chemical which then forces the body to move, the initial idea being that if the body was forced to move it would move, in the direction of getting or doing the imaginary things.

Human beings have the mental ability to totally transform themselves and their physical condition and circumstances because of this change sense chemical which is always pushing for change once it is activated. This need to do more is an important energy for the human life experience. Once activated the change sense will force a change in the behavior.

If the individual is caught up in a false existence, for example, trying to keep up economically with the neighbors, the result will be a stressed life. The stressed life reflects in the physical condition of the body as an excess of acids in the bloodstream. Like any substance which is fired or burned, stress (too much thought usage) leaves ashes. These ashes are in the physical body on a level where they interfere with the cellular processes. Because of increased stress the ash level increases and the cell is less able to function as it was normally designed to do. This interference by the ash content in the system weakens the cellular structure and causes mutation of cells. Because of the level at which this action takes place the immune capability of the cell becomes diminished. This causes the physical system to be weakened and become susceptible to any number of diseases.

When the change sense is activated it naturally adds to the level of ash in the body, and there needs to be more care taken to ensure body eliminations are not interfered with. Drinking lots of water and being certain that all elimination is regular aides in care of the body when there is an increase in mental and physical activity.

The answer to alleviating this condition of excess stress and ash in the body is to educate and give understanding of what is occurring to the person. By giving understanding of what the individual is doing to the self the person can monitor their needs and behaviors more carefully. This would hopefully result in a shift in the quality of thinking as well as a drastic change in attitude and in the style of living one chooses. Life will be projected on the true needs of the individual who wants a flow rather than chaos in their life.

The change sense will oftentimes activate suddenly in masses of people who have been suppressed from moving forward creatively. We often hear about the wrath of people who have been pushed by collective mass thinking. The Los Angeles riots were a result of people, as a mass, trying to satisfy their need to move forward in life. Those who were involved in the riots were pushed into taking action by the brain change sense chemical working in their systems.

Day after day those people in the riots had been brainwashed by society through television and other media to improve their style of living. At some point the planet became involved and activated the riot as a collective force, feeding thoughts to all the brains involved to 'get what they needed'. This is what was behind the statements of rioters who, when interviewed, simply said that the things they took out of stores were theirs. The things were there, something told them they had a right to those things as human beings, and they simply brought them home.

If it was necessary to do violence, the doing of violence was automatic, not personally intended. The human being, for the most part, does not do its own thinking, and because of this the planetary streams of thought automatically supply the thoughts needed to project the life experience. The thoughts that come to the individual to use are delivered on the basis of the person's essence and level of emotional temperature. The planet fed the thoughts of 'righteous intent' into the brains involved, and they acted. The riots ended abruptly because the need to offset the driving intent caused by the infusion of change sense chemical into everyone's body who was involved in the riots was temporarily satiated.

It will now be easier for those who rioted to attract thinking that will cause them to repeat the riots on a greater scale if the root of the problem is not addressed for each individual. The root of the problem is the frustration of not being able to act as the motivating change sense chemical continues to create a demand for action.

The enormity of this condition now upon the human experience all over the world is difficult to imagine. It is a primary factor in the discontent of all human societies. As the need to exercise more activity to do the simple things of attaining sustenance accelerates, so does the amount of change sense chemical increase in the body. As the person and masses become more hyperactive and anxious, the change sense chemical level increases individually and collectively; it can be a vicious cycle.

Most people live on the thinking of the mass thought streams of the planet, and as a consequence they automatically become more intense and hyperactive. Not being aware of what is happening to them, they fail to question their way of life. As they attract and use more and more mass thoughts laden with the energy of intent to accelerate their activity, they feel compelled to drive ever forward. Advertising agencies, while peddling products for companies, take advantage of this natural automatic mechanism feeding the human being mass thinking. They repeat and repeat ads in a way that serves to hypnotize buyers into reacting to the advertising in spite of their intent to do otherwise.

When the content of ash level is high in the blood stream one may feel a light-headedness when moving about. Less continuous non-stop kinds of thinking, and drinking of more water than usual helps to offset this condition which I call natural chemical poisoning.

People who think for the self, and who examine their life and find themselves hyperactive, in a vicious cycle of trying to catch up with life, have a chance to change the level of chemical they have been generating in the brain. By reevaluating the life experience and making a decision to make their life less complicated, one can diminish the flow of chemical and ash from the brain. Deliberate choice to pace the self and see life as a flowing process of the laws of attraction, will result in the brain reverting to a natural processing which no longer requires injections of the change sense chemical.

CHANGE SENSE & MASSES

As human beings we cannot remain unproductive and inactive for very long periods. The soul-mind will arrange some event to get us to move and change our ways. You may wish at times to avoid life and escape through different practices such as meditating or drinking to excess, however, the change sense will not allow that to continue. When we reach a certain point of non-performance the change sense activates to redirect the energies of the person and those about them. This serves us by motivating and changing the stagnating life process.

Consider the fact that when the one person is activated by his or her change sense the energies influence others around the person. If any of those others were 'stuck' (so to speak) they conceivably set their own change sense into motion as a consequence of involvement in the energies surrounding them.

What if a whole nation of people were 'stuck' and were not exercising growth in harmony with the whole, in this case the whole being the planetary whole. Would this not set off a chain reaction that would reflect as a change in a nation and perhaps in the world? What would be the result of such a collective change? Would it not be chaotic for the collective group or nation?

We see mass changes taking place now all over the world. Nation after nation of people are reacting to their existing social conditions.

From the individual to masses of like-thinking people we see a personal and collective hyperactivity in action now. It is a response to the overall feeling on the part of individuals and multitudes, that nothing is being resolved and growth is being stymied or quashed through indecision and lack of purpose.

There are many souls who are fairly advanced in right brain conditioning that have come to the planet for this consciousness raising time. They make up a majority of the children and young people. This is a class of beings who easily see through the failures of society to solve problems. They are pushed to find challenges that will serve their soul lesson learning. They are easy to recognise because they seem to be ruthless and have little feeling for human failings. They appear to be insensitive, but they are extremely sensitive. Death does not have much impression on them and they can quickly find suicide as an answer to remove themselves from what appears to them as a 'no win' or 'no place' to be.

At a time when young people are caught up in a society that has nothing for them, educators are stretching out the time they must be in school. They are aware that much of what is being taught them has little value in the sense of growing from an inner perspective. The schooling is mostly left brain information which creates excessive mental stress. They are politically minded and see school as a machine designed to keep them locked into financial constraints. Their patience is strained in having to devote day after day in studies that have no purpose in relation to what is driving them. By virtue of their mental abilities they find life limiting and meager. They are a class which is 'stuck' in the sense of not being able to answer the need to change. They turn to violence easily and are curious enough about the unknown to take chances with their life that young people in the past have not normally considered. They need guidance on a grand scale that will orient their creative right brain into constructive ways of learning and just spending quality time.

FEAR SENSE

Early in the human experience the fear sense became a survival tool for the human animal. If we relate the fear sense to the change sense we can understand what might have happened to the human animal when the change sense began to force the human animal to move forward into a seeking mode, a response which was not natural to it. Being an animal who had no fear, it became exposed to more dangers when moving unnaturally because of the change sense influencing it. With its new sense it also had little capacity to understand if the danger it faced was real or illusion.

It was at this stage that the fear sense was developed. As a sense it is designed to emote as an energy which measures the surrounding environment. By measuring the quality of energy of that which came into the fear sense range, the human being could determine if it was threatened physically.

Unfortunately, the left brain as the dominant control part of the ego dynamics, has over-developed the fear sense. It has incorporated other uses of the fear sense in its controlling of the way of the person. The ego aspect of the brain deliberately creates conditions which activate fear in others and itself. By virtue of the law of attraction, creating fear for others compounds the fear level in the perpetrator of the fear. This distorted the fear levels among the human beings.

The fear sense developed as a means of measuring those things or energies which might harm the body. That was the original intent of its use. As a mechanism for that purpose alone it is still beneficial. If a person is standing in a place where the path of an oncoming automobile threatens it, the fear sense is designed to give notice to the cellular field to move the body out of the path of probable harm.

LANGUAGE

When I began my lessons on a daily basis with the masters from the 'other side', they attempted to teach me the original language of the human experience. I must admit that I was not able to fully grasp the use of the language, however, I did learn the fundamentals of it. What is significant to relate here is that words today are far removed from their original intent and thought particle power.

Most of the confusion and misunderstanding between people down through eons of time is reflected in the the misuse of words and sounds in our time. The primary influences on word distortion were the volleying of power and control over the human experience between the male and the female who use word sounds differently. Today we are in a cycle of control of the planet by the male energy, so we (male and female) have a patriarchal language to try to understand one another with. When the female controlled the planet, the female influenced the understanding of who God was and anything else that was talked about.

Here I wish to emphasize and give some understanding of the fact that we are now using sound and language from the male perspective. It is important for the reader to understand that I am presenting this material from both the female and male perspectives in the sense of vibration rather than from the idea of gender.

Females vibrate differently than males. Males vibrate on a much denser or courser level and there are important reasons for that. The primary need of all people is to harmonize and seek balance on the vibratory level. This of course requires proper thinking and behavior on the part of all to adjust to one another constantly.

Originally, sounds made by the human herd animal were limited as with all animals. Because of the soul-mind's need to create and to expand the human experience, it designed a simple language. This language had in its basic structure two kinds of expression. One expression were sounds (vibrations) which were primarily yin energy and carried the meaning of feeling. The other expressions were sounds (vibration) which were primarily yang energy and carried the meaning of will projection. Used together, these sounds, when projected with thought, carried the power to create or uncreate.

The world's alphabets retain a flavor of the original range of sounds. For most of them the first half of the alphabet contains sound (vibration) connected to yin expression and the last half of the alphabet to yang expression. There are some letters in one range which belong in the other, but that is to be expected considering the ways of the left brain hemisphere.

If we are to actually raise the consciousness we will be discovering more about the relationship between words (sounds) and the thoughts being projected with the sounds. We will also discover that conjunctive words often serve to destroy what we are trying to create. Consider what happens to the impact of our words when we sit in a creative writing class and then find ourselves limited by the left brain instruction that the rules of written English must be adhered to. I have been writing extensively for years, papers, short stories, poems, novels and channeled

130

works. My editors are always reminding me to change my style if I want to sell my writings, not because what I write is not saleable to the reader but because it is often not saleable to a prospective publisher. Many times I change my work to facilitate cooperation from that authority. I went through this same process in college being told again and again that papers are not to be written to create influence but to follow the manual designed to make all papers the same.

Language professors and people in control of grammar are important to the flow of communication throughout the world. These same people have the responsibility to see through the limitations of language paradigms. These same people are horrified when an ethnic group in some part of the world actively destroys an other ethnic groups in a frenzy of 'ethnic cleansing'. They fail to see the correlation between ethnic cleansing and grammar cleansing.

WORDS & INTENT AS FORCE

'Be careful what you pray for!' . . . 'What you see is what you get!' . . . 'We get the thing we fear the most!' We know in our hearts that these are old sayings that have meaning in the sense of, what we think about can happen. I have combined WORDS and INTENT in this chapter heading because what we think becomes a reality (a force) in direct relation to the emphasis we place on our words.

I am reminded of the time years ago when in great frustration and anger I blurted out to my secretary, 'I don't want to hear another goddamned thing.' I went to my home and took a nap and when I awoke I could not hear a thing. I had lost 100% of my hearing. A few hours later I was told by an ear specialist that I would never hear again. The doctor advised me that 'strangely' the blood vessels on my tuning forks had totally atrophied. It was strange to him, but I knew before he told me that I had destroyed my ability to "hear another goddamned thing." Fortunately I knew enough about healing to rectify the condition.

The point of my story is to illustrate that when something is said with great intent, and when the force of intent combines with thought, powerful creative forces are set in motion. Words, or combinations of words and their vibrations are the key to this energy or force. For the most part we have lost this understanding of words. Language does not have the power it used to have when it was simple and was more easily tied to intent from a generative perspective. Language today is distorted. Words are not used with their original meaning or intent. One can find words in which the meaning has been totally disguised and even reversed. Words when used in their original intent were designed to meld with thought projection. This knowledge is lost today, but again, as we rediscover the understanding of thinking and thought systems, words will eventually return to their purposeful uses and meanings.

The average person today speaks in generalities and only occasionally expresses a thought with intent. However, the choice of words used ultimately negates the power of the words. There is truth behind the observation that if a person talks long enough, they talk themselves out of what they originally intended. Thoughts have power and they can add, subtract or neutralize the energies connected with the word projected. Turned around, one can say that the spoken word, if chosen in relation to the intent of the thinking, can add, subtract or neutralize the energies involved.

Our use of language and sound today has been distorted by intellectual educators who have meant well in creating language structure. The left brain hemisphere has been the most instrumental in distorting language and sound usage. Its attempt to formalize language has resulted in a separation of sounds and meanings of the original method of communication which was designed to resonate with thinking projection.

When we discuss the power of the word, we most often think about Moses. With a word or two, Moses could activate natural forces that affected the air, water and material substances. It is an interesting fact that Moses rarely spoke. He was so cautious of speaking that he usually had his brother Aaron speak for him. He had good reason to do that, he was quick to anger and when his emotional temperature reached a dangerous level, the words he would blurt out had creative and destructive force.

Each one of us, on occasion, during our present lives, has had some example of speaking with power. If you examine your past you will find record of having used the power of the word in your life and almost instantly materialized the thing or condition you declared. The more powerful and spiritually balanced a person becomes the more s/

he has to watch word usage, because the more powerful will be the results thoughts and words.

EMOTION

To understand emotion I believe it is necessary to consider the analogy of working up steam to drive the old railroad engine. We can compare emotion to the steam. If we want more power to drive the engine we build up more steam. The greater the steam pressure, the greater the power. Steam engines have gauges to measure the level of pressure the steam is creating. The optimum steam pressure is just enough to create the power needed to drive the engine at whatever force one wants it to perform. Too much steam will create a pressure that exceeds the safe limit of power being generated. If the steam continues to build and the pressure exceeds the ability of the engine to contain the power, it will cause destruction.

Emotion is a power generated by combining thought particles. Thought particles contain negative and positive forces. As a specific combination of thought particles are processed through the thinking systems, combinations of positive and negative forces are being created. If there is a combination of thoughts which generate too much emotion (steam power) a chaotic reaction is created. Like the steam engine which has developed too much steam and is out of control, the human brain does the same when too much emotion is generated. If the human brain is caught up in an excess of emotion it becomes overloaded with thoughts attracted from mass thought fields. The result is a loss of self control.

As mentioned, the steam engine has a gauge to permit the operator to measure the amount of fuel needed to keep a balance of energy which is optimum. On the human being the gauge which measures the level of emotion is our sensing abilities working in harmony. The senses keep us aware of what our 'emotional temperature' is at all times. When we feel (sense) we are in a good place, our level of emotional temperature is where it needs to be to maintain our thinking balance. When we 'lose our senses', meaning we have lost touch with our ability to gauge our emotional temperature, we are in danger of saying or acting in an extreme or chaotic manner and are out of control.

Thought particles are the fuel of the emotion. Emotion is a field of energy we generate through thinking which has the result of increasing or lowering the actions of the mind chakras. These chakras are the centers which attract thought from the mass thought fields. The thoughts we attract contain energies on the particles that increase or decrease the emotion.

Emotion has a direct effect on our ability to create things in our lives. If we have no emotion concerning a thing we desire then it most likely will not manifest. If we have generated the optimum level of emotion needed, that which we desire will manifest.

WILL POWER

One cannot talk about emotion without mentioning the will. Will power is the ability to generate thought energies and focus them. At times, Hollywood creates a motion picture character who stares with intensity

at someone or something and the thing stared at is destroyed. This is an exaggerated idea of someone using their will power, however, it has left people with the idea that directed thoughts have power.

A person using will power influences the forces that are already existing. The correct statement would be that the forces joined to cause that which was already set in motion to happen. Will power can be used to influence matter, but only in connection with other forces such as desire and emotion.

No matter what we discuss in the way of forces and energies, scientifically we need to understand them in the sense of the laws of attraction. Voodoo practices are a perfect example of this. The voodoo curse cannot be willed into motion without the receiver of the curse being mentally prepared to receive it. This is often accomplished by the perpetrator of the curse seeing to it that the receiver gets a chicken part, or a pierced doll, or some other sign of what is being willed. The curse is dormant until the receiver discovers s/he is the target. When the target becomes emotional and enters an emotional temperature range called intense fear, the intense fear emotion activates the chakra of the target to attract to it what it fears. Whatever the perpetrator set in motion for the target is then received by the target, and the subconscious acts on the instruction which was unknowingly attracted by the target.

Levels of emotion such as desire, fear and passion, are nothing more than the levels of power (steam) being generated in the chakras (thought attractors). The emotional level of desire will open the second chakra to a certain degree. The emotional level of passion will open that chakra to a greater degree than desire. As the chakra generates, it increases the level of thoughts attracted through the person. The thoughts carry energy forces. As the amount of thoughts increases the level of energies (steam) increases. In the case of the target of the voodoo curse, as the level of emotion increases, the particular chakra expands and attracts the very thing that the target fears most.

Will is the ability to project thinking in a way that causes the thoughts to manifest by virtue of the laws of attraction. The key to the shifting of thoughts from one location (person) to another is to exercise the use of the eighth chakra which deals with communication between all human beings. Although there 'seems' to be a projecting of will force from one place (A) to another (B), that is not what actually takes place. Through the use of the eighth communication chakra (B) is influenced to attract to itself that which is assumed to be the curse.

6

Mass
Thought

MASS THOUGHT & THE PLANET FACTOR

Earlier, I described the planet and the fact that it is made of thought particles, and that it controls streams of thought particles which it sends to the different thinking systems of different species. I call it mass thought because it is just that, a mass of thought particles that is swirling and vortexing throughout the earth globe. It is mass thought which the individual attracts for use in thinking, an action similar to that between the television station (earth) sending out signals and the TV sets (human beings) receiving them. It is this process which explains the behavior of animals who act in a manner similar to other animals miles away without having any physical contact. Again, thought particles are attracted from the planetary sphere by the individual, to use in thinking.

David Bohm (1980) in *Wholeness And The Implicate Order* described mass thought without realizing what it is when he wrote,

> 'The new form of insight can best be called *Undivided Wholeness in Flowing Movement.* This view implies that flow is, in some sense, prior to that of 'things' that can be seen to form and dissolve in this flow. One can perhaps illustrate what is meant here by considering the 'stream of consciousness'. This flux of awareness is not precisely definable, and yet it is evidently prior to the definable forms of thoughts and ideas which can be seen to form and dissolve in the flux, like ripples, waves and vortices in a

flowing stream. As happens with such patterns of movement in a stream some thoughts recur and persist in a more or less stable way, while others are evanescent.

"The proposal for a new general form of insight is that all matter is of this nature: That is, there is a universal flux that cannot be defined explicitly but which can be known only implicitly . . ."

David Bohm had the idea but had not had the experience of seeing and measuring what thought is. He could only refer to consciousness to his idea of what thought might be. When he states that the 'stream of consciousness - this flux of awareness - is not precisely definable', he reveals that he is not aware that 'stream of consciousness' means 'stream of thought'.

In eastern philosophies we hear the term 'Akashic records' which describes a level reached by psychics and masters who access it for information about past and future events. It is sometimes called 'The Great Hall of Records' or 'The book of Life'. They are describing what I call mass thought which is the storage place and source of all our thoughts.

We can liken the content in mass thought to a 100 channel television network and all the channels were on at the same time. The information would be a likely representation of the planet's mass thought fields. One would be unable to comprehend all that was being observed as the conscious brain in the skull cannot manage such a transmission. There would be a cross section of entertainment, violence, education, childrens programs, social upheaval, history, business and so on, with an overwhelming emphasis on violence. All programs (thought streams) combined make up the consciousness (thinking) of this planet and are a reflection of the used thought in the mass thought fields. This conglomerate energy mix which I call the 'planet Factor' has an influence on all matter. It is in constant fluctuation as the planet's attempts to keep its material form in balance.

The planet factor can be likened to the term 'Zeitgeist', meaning the trend or way of things on a mass level. However, that would be a limiting representation. The planet factor is more; it is an intelligence. Elsewhere I have described the planet as being a living entity, and it is this, the intelligence of this living entity; which is the planet factor.

Imagine the situation of the planet before the human being began infiltrating its thought streams. Prior to any soul-mind having joined the human animal on the planet, no other creature could directly exercise influence on the planetary mass thought particles. Originally, the earth's mass thought particles retained a certain balance of energies that was not interrupted by other entities. Animals attracted the thought that they needed for their basic life processes without affecting mass thought.

Mass thought particles began to change when the soul-mind intercepted the particles coming to the human animal for its use. For the soul to be able to effect learning through a herd animal, it was necessary to change the created human animal's way of living like a herd animal. To accomplish this the soul-mind had to alter the standard mass thought particles before they passed through the human brain; this the mind began to do. Thus the planet factor and the human beings started influencing one another. As the planet factor reacted to human mass thinking which was causing mass disturbance of matter, the earth's intelligence was forced to expand.

For the first time in the planet's history, an entity other than the earth itself had control over its thought particles. By changing the content and quality of thought as it passed through the human animal, the soul-minds were creating fields of mass thought they could use to influence the human brain with. It was not long before most all mass thought particles in the planetary sphere had considerably different qualities and energies. What had been simple basic categories of thought particles became mass thought particles that contained energies which could create 'unnatural' illusions, desires and ideas in the brain of the human animal. After passing through the brain of the human animal and back into the planetary mass thought fields, these new thoughts mixed with other thought fields of like magnetic resonance, creating powerful thought forms.

As mass thought particles began to change energy and content to satisfy the new creature (human being) of the earth, the earth found itself in a situation where its very structure began to be changed and influenced. The basic formula of the mass thought particle always contains the law of like attracts like, that was not changed. What was changed was the earth's ability to manage all the particle streams as it had in the past. The earth suddenly had a creative partner, the human being.

As the human being changed and developed through the thinking process, it used thoughts and unknowingly changed their content and energy which in turn changed the earth's behavior. This cumulative effect on the thought particles created swarms of thought particles which we call thought forms. Human beings then began to attract thoughts from the planet in swarms, or thought forms, or beliefs (Jung's Collective Unconscious).

As human beings expanded their use of the mass thought streams, they began to abandon animal herd life. With the expansion of mass thought forms and beliefs, human beings drew together in groups in relation to the thought forms or beliefs they were attracting. This action of human beings collecting in smaller groups and attracting like kind thought, created group identities or what we now call races and nationalities. The animal herd instinct for the most part became suppressed and was substituted with intellectual reasoning.

MASS THOUGHT & THE SUBCONSCIOUS

The dictionary defines the subconscious as 'existing in the mind but not immediately available to the consciousness' and 'the mental activities just below the threshold of consciousness' (inferring it is not available through the conscious state). In this instance we have the dictionary referring to the mind as being something other than the brain.

The subconscious is that conglomeration of mass thoughts which are constantly being attracted into the soul-mind in connection to other thinking being processed and used. We attract into the mind in the range of several thousand unconscious thoughts to every thought registering consciously in the skull brain. The skull brain filters the thoughts, allowing only those which do not seriously threaten its belief structures.

Unconscious thoughts are those which are not triggering or activating into the awareness aspect of the thinking systems of the human being. Conscious thoughts are those thoughts which are triggering and activating through the awareness aspect of the thinking systems of the human being. Said another way, if you are aware of the thoughts passing through you then you are processing conscious thoughts. If you are not aware of the thoughts processing through your thinking systems (and there are volumes more of these thoughts than the ones you are aware of) you are processing unconscious thoughts.

Carl Jung experimented with the paranormal or subjective nature of the human being and discovered an aspect of planetary mass thought which he labeled the 'Collective Unconscious'. What he discovered were those streams of mass thought which carry the mythical, archetypal thought particles of all past thinking. Archetypal thought particles and forms, like any and all thoughts that were ever used by human beings, are stored in the planetary sphere and can be attracted for thinking.

Because Jung concentrated in his work on the archetypal idea, he attracted mostly only those kinds of thought particles. Consequently, he felt that that was all there was to the 'collective unconscious'. The law of 'like attracts like' ensured this to be the case. He did not understand the fact that he had in effect discovered a part of mass thought. This becomes obvious when we read his comment as to what he believed the collective unconscious to be. Giving a lecture at St. Bartholomew's Hospital in London, on October 19, 1936, he stated, "The contents of the collective unconscious have never been in consciousness, and therefore have never been individually acquired, but owe their existence exclusively to heredity." Jung, in making the statement that the contents of the collective unconscious 'have never been in consciousness', revealed that he had not reached the understanding that the collective unconscious (mass thought fields) consists of used thought, i.e., thought that has at one time been in human consciousness.

Rupert Sheldrake, with his 'Morphic Resonance' theory has come the closest to interpreting what mass thought is. He has contributed greatly with his research into the ideas that are similar to and illustrated in the book *The Hundredth Monkey* by Ken Keyes Jr. Sheldrake expanded on the idea that learning can take place for the whole species when an initial group has learned, whether or not there is visual or physical contact between those who do the act and those who automatically repeat the behavior.

At the 1992 Prague Conference, Sheldrake used the example of the human brain being similar to the TV set. With this example, he was saying that memory, somehow, is delivered to the brain. Sheldrake made reference to his belief that memories are not necessarily stored in the skull brain, and also to research by others which has failed to place memory in the skull brain. He speaks of memories being available through a process of morphic resonance, which acts as a natural habit. This leaves the impression that memory is something out there somewhere, and it acts on us through this morphic resonance attraction (mass thought).

Sheldrake has the right idea. Memory is out there, so to speak, and it is our need which attracts it to use. Actually, memory is everywhere if we interpret memory as used thought particles. Certain kinds are in the mind space, others are stored in the body. Memories of the past (thoughts) are scattered in the planetary sphere as mass thought and are used by the brains of all creatures.

To put Sheldrake's morphic resonance (which I can best interpret as vibrating body) into the perspective of this work, I take it as meaning the state of vibration a creature reaches that permits it to attract thought particles from mass thought. This interpretation of morphic resonance best fits the idea that as creatures of this planetary sphere, we are designed to resonate with things around us, and thereby become part of them. This is close to how thought and thinking works as a general idea, but it does not explain the processes involved. It leaves a question as to where is memory, what is memory, how do we use it, and how do we resonate?

MASS THOUGHT PARTICLES & THINKING SYSTEMS

I have mentioned that the earth has a thinking system which is connected to all creatures. Through this system the earth feeds thought particles with two results; it furnishes the creatures with energies and direction, and it feeds its own planetary illusion to sustain its material existence. As a result, the planet maintains its balance as a living entity. The thought particles it feeds all creatures enter their thinking systems on the basis of attraction founded in need.

The human being receives thought particles from the planet as do all other creatures. The difference between the human being's thinking systems and that of all other creatures is the ability of the human being to create unnatural mental thought forms for personal illusory needs. The human being can fabricate a false need and the planet will provide the particles of thought as though the need were fact. Because of the soul-mind system being connected to the animal thinking system, thought particles which have passed through the human being and returned to the planet contain energies unlike those thought particles which other creatures use.

The result of eons of time of thought particles passing through the human being is that the planetary mass thought is laden heavily with thought particles that are unnatural to the planet's existence or form. The planet has gained weight and has become less flexible because of the quality of thought particles it now processes. It is this condition of polluted thought particles permeating the planet which has caused the planet to react and violently destroy human populations through natural disasters, earthquakes, floods, famines and plagues. Such natural destructions cleanse mass thought particles of harmful levels of energy and returns mass thought to a more natural energy content. Because of the unbalanced thought human beings are spewing into the planetary sphere, we are time and again threatened with natural disasters by the planet.

Thought particles swarm together through magnetic attraction and are available to any person who is thinking with the same quality or level of emotional energy. One might say that an individual expressing a particular energy (resonance), automatically attracts thought forms of like force or energy, thereby compounding his/her train of thinking. If a person is in a heightened state of anger and is focused on a specific quality or level of thought, s/he will attract more like kind anger thoughts, thereby escalating the personal state of angry thinking and level of emotional temperature.

As to nonhuman animals and the quality of thought particles they are attracting by virtue of their expressions, they are receiving a different stream of thought particles than the human being. The dog, for example, has its own stream of thoughts fed to it by the planet. The difference between the dog's thinking system and its human master's is that the dog cannot choose its thinking and consequently cannot access the master's thinking systems. A master, using the human thinking system, has the power to access the dog's. I make this point about the difference between animals and the human being to emphasize the uniqueness of the human creation; it alone has choice and it alone pollutes the earth's sphere with energy laden thought particles.

MASS THOUGHT & PREDICTIONS

Recently there have been scientific projections presented by the media involving the likelihood of our planet having a major collision with a meteor in 2104. The projected damage, as publicized, would be disastrous to the world populations. I might add, this advertised threat feeds the consciousness of those who read predictions of world cataclysmic disasters and polar changes as foretold by psychics for the 1990s and early 21st century. This kind of psychological conditioning is furthered by scientific warnings of pending doom to the planet from ecological deterioration.

After the announcement of a probable pending meteor disaster, thought particles used in that kind of thinking circulate in mass thought to be attracted by anyone with similar thinking about natural disasters, planetary destruction, chaos and death. Such thinking can create an influence on the mass consciousness that can set in motion energies which would attract a meteor to strike the earth. If the meteor referred to is presently aligned to miss the earth, mass thought interference through the laws of attraction could cause the meteor to adjust its path to hit the earth. Human thinking, as a mass, has already reached such levels of mental influence on the planet.

There is a global need now for the masses to raise their level of consciousness to the extent that the whole becomes of more concern to the individual. The changes needed for the planet to heal socially and technologically, require a mass shifting of conscious thinking and a freeing of left brain belief patterns. It is the left brain, individually and collectively, which effects most of the control over human behavior. This amounts to humans shifting from literal thinking, to liberal thinking. Liberal thinking is right brain thought processing which promotes individual freedom. It is the soul-mind through the right brain which feeds art, romance and freedom into our thinking processes, and it is always trying to make inroads into human behavior. It does this

143

with some success, depending on how closed or open the belief system of the person, i.e., how conditioned the left brain is.

The left brain is losing its grip on the American consciousness. This in spite of the congress shifting to conservative control. The United States of America, from a thought projecting perspective, is now shifting consciousness into right brain influence on world mass thought.

How far world mass consciousness needs to swing in its right-brained movement towards freedom remains to be seen. At this time it appears that world changes may go to extremes, creating anarchy in individual's

and nation's collective thinking. It will take world leaders with good judgement in the management of yin and yang forces to prevent global chaos. This of course requires leaders who understand and have the vision to effect good left brain management of economics. These leaders would have to understand global needs in the sense of humanistic mass thought.

From the planetary perspective, there is the need for a balancing of the ratio of yin and yang energies. There is an over abundance of aggressive yang energy present on the planet whenever the left brain is in control of world affairs. When human wants are always seen as the primary need, ignoring the planet's needs, the planet's yin and yang energy fields become unbalanced. Mass thought through global communication is manipulated more quickly today, and it takes very little to tip the scale into the planet unleashing forces that are destructive.

MASS THOUGHT & RELATIONSHIPS

When I say 'relationship', I am referring to the inner need of the person to be in an experience with someone of the opposite energy. I did not say sex because part of the confusion of relating today is due to the misunderstanding of yin and yang energies and sex. Two people of the same sex can and do relate to one another because they attracted each other having an imbalance in their formula of yin and yang energies.

Most of the world automatically understands that female and male go together as a unit. Most of the world does not realize that it is because the energies compliment one another. When the two energies bond, there is the desire to attain balance - a primary need of the soul of each.

When two people of the same sex relate, one of them moves into the opposite energy. If they are males, then one of them generates and moves into yin (female) energy, acting out the female role, and the other stays in the yang energy, acting out the male role. If they are females, the opposite formula is true; one changes her primary energy force to bond with the other. There is no question that we can mentally subvert our natural energy and assimilate the opposite force. There is also no question that if the role reversal succeeds in any way, the one subverting his or her natural expression will begin sabotage and to alter the molecular structure of his/her physical body. This has consequences both mentally and physically.

MASS THOUGHT & BEHAVIOR

We like to believe that we are in command of ourselves, and only once in a while do we believe we are not in charge of our thinking and consequently our behavior. However, if we were to keep track of our behavior in relation to the chain of our thinking we would see that often we automatically stumble into another behavioral response which we had not initiated. When not paying attention to our thinking, we respond unwittingly, reaping the consequences of our thought.

To understand the power and use of thought and the resulting behavior, we need to examine behavior and its relationship to thinking. We hear the expressions, 'What you think is what you get,' or 'Be careful of what you think as you may get it!' From these kinds of comments it would appear that if we think something, we can expect it to become a reality in our life.

Often, when we are busy acting out some kind of behavior without thinking about it, a problem arises. When this occurs our thoughts focus on this new circumstance. We may desperately try to think our way out of the dilemma we are suddenly facing, but our thoughts change nothing. How did we get into the situation? The answer is: mass thought fed us the idea and we fell into it.

Without us realizing it, mass thought feeds us thinking that is related to what is really at the root of our being. It does this in relation to the level of magnetic attraction we create through our emotional temperature. We may be talking lightly with our mate about something which is not very important, and without realizing it something is said as a matter of habit which sets off a different train of thinking. The train of thinking builds emotion, and soon the thoughts coming from the planet accelerate. As the emotion builds the particles of thought pour through the system, carrying energy which finally builds to a level which forces the person to act aggressively or even violently.

Usually after such an experience the one who was flooded with mass negative mass thought is appalled at their own behavior and does not understand what 'possessed' them temporarily. There was no 'possession', it was simply the result of not managing the thought streams coming through from mass thought fields. What was needed was an understanding that increased levels of emotional temperature allow the mass thought fields to flood the thinking with world average thoughts and behavior related to such thinking.

Mass thought is always streaming through the person's thinking system. This is the way we get our thoughts, and it is constant. Thinking and speaking without giving attention to the fact that mass thought is ever ready to send floods of negative thought when the emotional temperature is raised, permits mass thought to take over and cause negative behavior.

MASS THOUGHT & THE WEALTH PRINCIPLE

I want to speak on this subject as an aspect of thinking, because having wealth has become an established need for human beings at this stage of life. The mass thought streams are loaded with thought particles which contain the energy of no wealth. When you understand how many brains believe that there is not enough wealth (money) to go around you realize how many thoughts are being put into the mass thought streams which reflect poverty thinking. When you examine how few brains believe that wealth is a natural gift of life, you realize how few prosperity thoughts are in the planetary mass thought streams. Understanding that all thinking works on a law of attraction, one can readily see that the few brains that believe in wealth are attracting all the money and that the brains which do not believe in wealth cannot attract it.

CHOICE OF THOUGHT

All along I have mentioned that choosing thought is extremely important. The planet is feeding a stream of thinking to you night and day. Think what that means! How often do you actually examine that stream of thought (particles with yin and yang energy) and choose what you want out of it? I believe you will say, 'rarely!' and you would be correct. In our early years no one is given the understanding that thinking itself requires specific management. We are taught some aspects of thinking such as letters, numbers, language, form and color, but not how to use the thoughts that come to us, or understanding how much magnetic force is behind the meaning of the thoughts and words.

If you do not choose your thoughts, that in itself is a choice. This is correct in a way, but how many know that if you don't actually choose what to think about, the planet chooses for you? When you do not pick thoughts deliberately the planet sends you mass thought related to the emotions you are experiencing and the essence which you are. Said another way: whatever your mood or attitude is, if you do not choose what you wish to think about, the thought you attract automatically is what the average person all over the planet thinks about when in the same mood you are in.

Most individuals believe their life is controlled by forces outside themselves, other people's wants and needs, society's demands, the doctor's orders, and even luck, good or bad. We also hear statements like, "It is God's will that it happened." All such sayings influence our thoughts and are nothing more than excuses for not making choices for ourselves. If we let everything and everybody choose for us, including God, then we can blame our life situation on everyone else but ourselves. Such thinking allows us to take the position that we are not to blame for the circumstances that seem to 'happen' to us.

On this planet the primitive animal does not have to think for itself. The planet will feed it thoughts and energy and it will live like animals have lived for eons, subject to the material laws of the planet. But as a human being you are a creature with a soul, and you have taken the responsibility of thinking for yourself and must make choices from what the planet sends you.

Thought is not permanent or stable, it is always influencing or being influenced by other thoughts near it, itself. Thought is in a constant flux. Its primary movement is subject to the basic magnetic laws of the planet, unless the human being takes control of it and manages its path. Human beings are responsible for the thoughts they attract and also for the thoughts they expel back to the planet.

If all the person does is merely respond to what is happening around him/her and does not take mental charge of the dynamics of thinking, that person will conduct his/her life without purpose. The planet will conduct that life experience. This is best seen in people who dedicate their life to taking care of the needs of others while ignoring their own needs. Their life is subject to the whims of others and there is no life of their own. This does not serve the soul's purpose, and it will arrange to make the life as uncomfortable as it can through the change sense and force the person to choose something for the self.

How does one know how to think? How can we choose from the thousands of thoughts streaming through our thinking systems? First of all, the very idea that you have to review all those incoming thoughts to be able to make a choice is of course unrealistic. This is a typical assumption the left brain mechanism would come up with. The skull brain says, "OK, if I am to choose between thoughts, then show them all to me so I can pick one." The tendency is to believe that you have to have an array of choices before you can choose anything. This idea is the result of over-conditioning of the left brain hemisphere and is misleading.

Learning how to think is simple. Staying in the mode of free thinking is the correct approach. Try this: stop reading right now and think of any one thing you want to think about. Continue to think about that one thing. As you think about that one thing, a thought about something else will suddenly enter the stream. Now is the time for choice. You can say to the self, "I want more about what I am thinking about now", and you will continue to attract more thought about your first choice. That is choosing thought!

Often when we are thinking about something, we get too involved in it. If you choose a thought and you find your successive thoughts becoming intense or emotional, it is time to examine whether or not to pursue the thinking. If continued thinking builds enough feeling to reach an emotional temperature which causes you to lose control of your thinking, there is an automatic takeover of your thought streams by the planet. Thinking should be done as though you are an observer who has the maturity to manage the emotions.

HOW WE ATTRACT THOUGHTS

Each human being wears an essence which is an accumulation of who we have been in the past. This includes genetic influence as well as incarnate influences. Whether you were a male, female, king or gardener in past lives has bearing on your essence. When we are first born this essence has primary influence on the law of attraction related to thinking. It is the ingredient which affects the quality of thought particles attracted from mass thought for thinking. As we age and add or subtract to or from our essence with the events of our present life, that initial essence changes, causing mass thought to send different thoughts to us.

Thought particles which are usually memories are a major factor in creating our essence. An unconscious memory, such as a memory of an injury, can have an influence on the essence of the human being. Forceful memories have the tendency to activate the mind chakras into being more dynamic magnetic attractors.

For every thought you consciously express, such as "there is a car I like," there are several thousands of other thoughts related to that car that stream into your soul-mind for editing. These are thoughts that are not surfacing consciously. They are about who made the car, where it was made, who owns it now, where has it been, where is it going, etc. The information comes streaming in and continues coming until your interest is focused elsewhere. Most of those 'secondary' thoughts never reach the conscious level, but they are there and available for use. The quantity, quality and details of the thoughts about the car are attracted in relation to the interest one has at that moment in time. The emotional temperature level is what sets the degree of attraction in motion. If your interest increases and your emotional temperature rises, mass thought will be sucked into the mind at an increasing rate, providing you with more related thoughts.

Some people have the ability to bring these subconscious thoughts into conscious awareness. We call this psychometry. The psychometrist holds an object (a shoe of a missing child, for example) in the hand and appears to be concentrating on some inner information. Through the balanced use of all her/his senses the psychometrist is able to give information that only the persons connected to the shoe would know about. The thoughts coming into the psychometrist are the several thousands or so thoughts mentioned in the mind. The information is coming from the mass thought fields as they are magnetically attracted by the psychometrist's thoughts of the shoe.

Two people arguing attract thoughts in relation to how intense their emotions have become. One may be saying nothing, trying to avoid the argument. This person attracts thoughts about the disagreement on that level. The other may have reached a degree of frustration where s/he is raising the voice; this person attracts another level of thoughts. When the argument has become almost violent, both are attracting thought that is high in destructive content. It is then that the mass thought coming into their thinking systems may become of a quality that is not typical for those involved.

Most of us have been in a conversation where we have lost control and in anger and frustration used words and made statements we have never used before. Afterwards we are shocked and embarrassed. We may have used language and acted in a way that is completely out of character. This is the result of having lost control of our thinking. When we do this the planetary streams of thought deliver an automatic dose of average negative thoughts.

If the emotional temperature is allowed to rise to extreme levels, the mass thought will include violent and deadly thinking of which there is much out there in the planet's mass thought. When a person is in an emotional state of blind rage, the destructive thoughts that come to them for their use can result in uncontrolled violent behavior. This is the case with the child who murders. It is also the case with the employee who suddenly kills whomever represents their source of

150

rage, including anyone who s/he thinks is in the way.

How often do you actually take the time to choose what you will think? Think about it! In a normal day, the average person might choose as few as three thoughts! Most people start the day out habitually and respond to all things without choosing the thoughts they use. The planet does most of the thinking for everyone. The reason for this is that we are at a primitive level of understanding of thought and thinking. On the ego level we believe we do our own thinking all the time. Careful examination of our behavior will reveal that we normally *not working* simply respond to what is there for us to react to.

When we consider the quality of human thinking on a planetary perspective, we realize that human beings are spewing forth used particles of thought of a very negative content. Much of it is greedy, selfish, angry, violent, bitter, controlling, and so on. This means the reservoir of thought from which we draw our thoughts is becoming increasingly negative and destructive. As a consequence, we attract for our use in daily interactions with others thoughts which are less respectful. When we use thoughts without care we fail to see that we are automatically lowering our own quality of thinking. Each negative thought we use has the impact of draining life force from our physical expression. The result of attracting negative thoughts is that the quality of our material life diminishes, our immune capability lessens and our susceptibility to disease increases.

Probably all of us, as children have been admonished by a parent to, "Think before we speak." But this is not meant when I talk about choosing your thoughts. Children are usually happy and exuberant and have a great desire to share their ideas and sometimes the thoughts come faster than the words. Whenever a person is happy and smiling, their thoughts and words are filled with life force and are energizing to everyone. This happy behavior is a right brain characteristic typical of children and most women. Being serious is a left brain concentrating reaction. Discouraging children from freely sharing the joyful creative expression of their soul-mind is forcing them into the left brain where *what about fathers didn't* there is criticism, boredom, anger, impatience and greed.

When we attract poor quality thought and do nothing to change it, we recycle used thought back to the planet with added negativity and distortion. This is the pollution I have referred to as being more damaging to the life of the planet than the chemical pollutions we worry about. The best defense against attracting negative mass thought is to find many joyful little diversions during one's day to day life, enjoying the moments and smiling often.

THOUGHT PARTICLE CONCEPT & MECHANISTIC THINKING

At first glance it would appear that the concept proposed here of all things being composed of thought particles, fosters hard science particle theory. This is not exactly the case. The thought particle concept fits with hard science particle concept up to the point in physics where quantum science enters the picture. There are matter thought particles and non-matter thought particles. Matter thought particles fit in with hard science theory. Non-matter thought particles are those which are not in the hard science paradigm, however, they do exist in quantum physics.

Annie Besant and C. W. Leadbetter (*Thought Forms,* 1901) were two who could psychically view and describe particles and thought forms. Following directions and with assistance from the masters I have learned to observe thought particles and thought forms as well as matter being created and decreated while in my astral form. What I see are energy forms merging and melding together. The smallest of these energy forms (thought particles) are in the shape of a vortex, something like a fat little screw. Depending on what is happening to the thought form being created or uncreated, these 'screws' are either rotating clockwise or counter clockwise. They also appear to be slowly melding with the energy mass or suddenly leaving or entering the mass. In relation to the size of an atom these 'little screws of yin or yang energy' would be like a pin head to a basketball; the basketball being the atom. These screws of energy merge and meld into forms that eventually become what science now refers to as the non-particle. Either as the individual 'screw' or as clumps of screws, their movement is either slow or speeded up far beyond the ability of the human brain to encompass the idea of greatest speed. Movement of the 'clump' of thought particles seems to be affected by the rotation of the individual 'screw' particles as they merge with the mass.

When we consider the world of non-matter thought particles, we enter quantum physics. At the quantum level the influence of the thinker has more impact on physical reality. In science it is the researcher projecting yin and yang energy on the thought particle which causes the quantum phenomena. I have pointed out before that the human brain is primitive in its ego identification. It remains this way because of its need to dominate thinking and stay within literal beliefs. Exposure to quantum thinking for a lengthy period causes the left brain to become very uncomfortable. Quantum thinking is three dimensional thinking.

The western left brain is grounded in the mechanistic principle and as a consequence is constantly demanding confirmation that 2 plus 2 equals 4. During the process of thinking, if the left brain can fit incoming thoughts into the mechanistic paradigm, it feels in control of the human experience and is not fearful. When the left brain discovers it is in the realm of quantum thinking, it loses its perspective and shuts down conscious use of thinking.

MEMORY

The dictionary definition for memory is: "That which one recalls of what has been learned and retained." On the surface this infers that some of what we learn is retained, and that which we retain we may recall. In reality there is a distinction between 'recalling memory' and what we call up from mass thought fields to think about. We might describe what we call up imagination instead of memory, but then we are bringing up the *idea* that we are mentally 'seeing' memory. This brings up the confusion about the concept of memory; science has yet to discover what it is. This confusion is compounded by the fact that many people insist they recall things they have never actually experienced. Why do people insist they remember something they could not possibly have experienced?

Science has had no success in finding specific locations in the brain where memory might be stored. There is the generally accepted idea that the brain holds within it all that has to do with thinking. Enough attention is paid to the brain to cause many to believe that somehow the skull brain holds everything. From the perspective of my research one has to think of the brain as a kind of chemo-electric pump which pumps thought and has a regulator of sorts that makes choices in thinking. The brain simply computes and pumps thought particles and thought forms.

Memory can best be described as used thought particles collected together in various forms. I have already stated that the planet and all that exists, material and nonmaterial, is made of thought particles; it is made of what we call memory. It would take volumes to classify and categorize the different kinds of thought particles with their energy essences, and so it would take volumes to classify memories. The point is that memory is the stuff of the universe and its forms, and the human being has the use of it all.

Some of the particles of memory you processed at the beginning of reading this book are now scattered throughout the earth. As you think, you expel the thoughts out into the planetary mass thought fields. Those thought particles make up part of your personal memories. When they are needed, as in memory recall, they are attracted back from the mass thought streams.

Anything and everything in this dimension is made of thought particles. If this is true, and I propose that it is, all things are made of memory. Your leg is made of thought particles. Your leg is made of memories which flow in and around it, reminding itself it is a leg.

If your leg was hit by a stick wielded by your father when you were ten, then the leg holds a clue or factor to the memory of the hit, the stick and who held the stick. It is memory recall ability in what I call the cell memory factor which causes the cut to heal. The memory recall ability is not the ability of the brain, it is the recall ability of the cell factor itself. If one used a method to stimulate memory recall to activate the process completely, one could grow back a lost leg.

Human beings at one time were able to totally renew the body, and I have little doubt that in the future we shall rediscover this process. The physical body has its own cellular fields of memory factors which can act on the physical parts of the body, independent of the nervous system.

Intellectual memories are keyed into a memory field process which surrounds and permeates the body. Intellectual memories are the beliefs, ideas, knowledge and training which we experience during this present life expression. This field of intellectual memory is directly connected to the left brain.

VEIL

There are fields of memory, such as ethnic fields, matter fields, non-matter fields, political and historic fields as well as many thought forms and other mass memory fields.

MEMORY AS CAUSE

The human experience appears to be in a constantly projecting, forward moving, seeking manner (see CHANGE SENSE). As individuals and as a whole, we are seemingly searching for our future. This urge to discover and find our direction has its roots in memory. It is the memory of where we came from, haunting us, we might say that causes us to move forward. We are constantly attempting to do something, complete something, in order to find where we came from. Our source, or beginning, is in our memory processes.

It would seem that if all we are trying to do is remember where we came from, then all we need do is sit and think, and we would find our answer. This would be the case but for the fact that our primary reason for being here is to learn to balance powers of the soul expression. To facilitate this, there is the 'veil' between the conscious thinking and the soul-mind which is that origin, that source of all knowing we seek to discover.

When the soul-mind first joined with the human animal, the human animal was not a mental seeker. The human animal, being a herd animal, was content to seek for food and to propagate. The soul-mind created a change sense mechanism in the animal brain to facilitate the needs of the soul. Within that original implant is the memory of what we were in the beginning and it is that memory which we pursue as seekers. The ingenious aspect of this implant is that to be successful in the search for our beginning, one must constantly balance the thinking. When thinking is balanced, the material life is projected in harmony and the total human being benefits.

155

When we hear the expression 'cellular memory field' we have this image of all the body cells joined together in some kind of field which connects memory in the cells. Although there is a connection between cells and memory, in reality all cells contain a reference factor to memory. These memory factor constructs act like triggers, activating a formula that attracts thought from the planetary streams through the mind chakras. The memory factor constructs of the cell are in the forms of two primary facets. One primary facet is the memory factor directly related to the human material form. The second primary facet of memory factor is the memory of the psychic essence of the cell.

The first primary aspect, the memory factor of the existing material life, deals with what has happened to it in its history (DNA). If the cell exists in a leg muscle and the leg muscle is injured during an altercation which involved the senses, the cell has recorded a reference to the event in its memory factor construct. This is the case whether the life is a past or present one.

How does an event get recorded in the material memory construct aspect of the human cell? To explain this I want to make the analogy of a piece of cheese cloth in a stream of water. The cheese cloth represents the human cells in a fetus and the water represents the thought streams around fetus and mother. Assume that the piece of cheese cloth becomes caught somewhere (in the womb) and the water is flowing through and around it. If someone were to throw a bucket of thick colored liquids (emotional thoughts) into the current, the colors would spread throughout the water. As the particles of colors flow through the cheese cloth some of the particles would get caught in the cloth. This is the idea of how the cells collect evidence of what is happening around and to them. When emotional waves of thought bathe the form of the mother and fetus, the cell factors in the fetus catch some of the information of what is happening around it. This is the memory source we reach as regression therapists going back to pre-natal trauma.

Emotion is a wave of energized thought particles which penetrate the molecular structure of the cell. Fetal tissue inside a mother's womb is being inundated with waves of energies (thought particles) when the mother experiences emotions. The thought particles reaching the cells contain the essence of the event connected to the mother.

The memory constructs in all the body's cells radiate and meld with one another, creating a composite field that constitutes an integrated field of communication. The memory factors in the knees are available to memory factors in the hands and visa versa. It is the total field of cellular constructs which conveys a message to parts of the body before the neural system can convey it.

I am reminded of a German tale about a pirate named Stortebecker who was captured and condemned to death with all his men. It was said that he made an agreement with his executioners that if he walked past his line of men after they had cut off his head, they must let his men go free. According to the story, he did just that, and the men were set free. From my point of view, the pirate captain was emotionally caught up in the need to have his men freed and (in effect) instructed his cells to retain the order to march along his line of men. This is the cellular memory construct in action.

The cellular memory constructs can operate to recall the memory of all events. It was the pirate captain's total cellular memory constructs field responding to the need to walk the body past the row of men that caused the body to perform exactly as suggested (post-hypnotic self suggestion).

Genetics is an aspect of the human physical evolving process. Cell memory constructs of passed-down life experiences of the person also transition through the cell process. What was in the cellular field of the parent or any ancestor for that matter, resides in the cell factors of the offspring down through the ages.

So far I have described the action of the first primary aspect of the cellular field of the human body from the perspective of the existing physical human experience. The second primary aspect of the cellular field is in its connection to the soul-mind. When the soul-mind bonds with the human body, usually at the time of the first breath of the infant, the memory references of past life bodies that are contained in the soul-mind melds with and becomes part of the cellular constructs field of the present physical body.

FALSE MEMORY

Although the term 'false memory' is usually used when referring
to hypnosis I put it in the memory category because it deals with
memory thoughts. Recent misuses of hypnosis by practitioners who do
not fully understand it have drawn attention to false memory recalls.
In a court, false memory means any confession taken through hypnosis
and is considered inadmissible as evidence. This is based on a
presumption that under certain conditions an individual can be made
to believe things happened which never did happen.

When we examine the idea of false memories we need to look at
the question of what is a false memory and what is a true memory. False
memory is the recall of what we believe as having transpired in an
event in our past and it did not. True memory is the recall of what we
believe as having transpired in an event in our past and it has. The
difference is that one event did happen and the other was a fabrication
of reality. As the recaller of the memory (true or false) we do not always
know which is which. As a matter of fact unless someone supplies us
with sufficient evidence to the contrary we have no way of seeing
through the false memory recall.

Countless numbers of times, especially in court cases, two
people seeing the same event have opposite memory recall of what
transpired. Being democratic in our western society, we accept the
majority opinion of which of the two has the true memory of an event.
What we ignore is the simple truth that for the witness of the event the
true recall is what the individual believes they have seen.

All of us have time and again listened to or been involved in the
changing of a true recall by an individual. If an individual is given
enough reasonable thought input about how an event happened that
person will adjust their belief about the event. Time and again
individuals have had their changed about what they witnessed by
another person's testimony (usually someone held in authority).
Considering how often others influence us, many of us experience
what we call false memory syndrome and we are not aware of it.

When we carefully analyze this principle of the thinking process we begin to grasp the influence hypnosis and past life therapy can have in altering past memories. In hypnotherapy we can do mind regression processes to adjust a past memory through giving the person understanding of past events that have been causing confusion in the present life.

This process of adjusting the understanding of past life memory alters the belief system. We could say that this process results in false memory. However, we can also say it is nothing more than the person having the advantage of reconsidering events of the past for the purpose of greater understanding and therefore more adjusted thinking and better behavior in the future.

The idea of false memory necessarily brings up the idea of changing the past. Having 'returned' the client to the past life and altering their belief of the the past circumstances, we have, not only created a different memory arrangement and adjusted the belief system, we have, in effect, changed the past life. We realise this is so if we visit a life time between the one that was altered and the present day or existing life, there is no longer a carry-over from those past beliefs (memories).

As an example, a woman was regressed to find the reason for some difficulty she was experiencing and could not understand. The regression took her back to be an event in 1700. Upon discovering the connection it was decided to go back even further to see if there was an earlier life that held a similar root cause. She found that in the 1300s she had a similar experience that resulted in the same kind of behavior as in the 1700s and in 1992. By altering the original events that had resulted in the traumatic condition in the 1300s, the client, using insight, averted that experience and was told to move forward into the 1700s lifetime. It was interesting to discover that in the 1700, life the old trauma did not occur. The client, applying insight to the situation that in the past had caused trauma, was able to avert trauma in the 1700s. Having resolved her part of the traumatic altercation was able to apply the insights gained from changing the two past-life experiences to her 1992 conditions and create a satisfactory change in her present day life.

Three questions arise: 1) Is this a process that can be repeated with equal results by others, and 2) Is this a false memory that takes away from the history of the individual or others connected, and 3)

What are the implications of tampering with history?

The answer to 1) is yes, this process can be repeated. There are many other cases in which the past was changed with equally positive results. 2) During the hypnotherapy process the past can be changed and subsequent experiences reflect this. The question about the false memory becomes irrelevant when the result is positive. 3) What of the principles of tampering with history? Humans are constantly reaching into the past and altering it using new understanding that contradicts or adjusts to what had happened earlier. What are the implications of changing or influencing personal history and are there other factors involved that should be considered?

I recall a case of a man who had reached a position in life when he could not hold onto a job. This was a person who for years had been a solid citizen, working as an engineer, and suddenly he became seemingly irresponsible. The trouble seemed related to the time when the client and his brother failed to return home in time for the father's funeral and burial. Through hypnotherapy he was taken back to a time just before his father's death for the purpose of having a talk with his father about his failure to be at the funeral. In the process his father discussed with him the pending death (that had already taken place) and the importance of the son realizing it would not be necessary to come home from another part of the world for the funeral. After the session the client went home feeling as though a burden had been lifted from him.

When he reached his home his wife told him that his brother, who lived in another state, wanted him to call as he had exciting news. He called to learn from the brother that (while he was undergoing the hypnotherapy session) the brother had taken a nap and in a dream the two brothers had a visit from the father just before he died telling them it was not necessary for them to come home for the funeral. He added that he now no longer felt guilt when he thought about their father. He added that the father had told both of them (in his dream) to go to a special place the three of them used to frequent years before. (The client had spoken about the same special place during the hypnotherapy process.) Was this a false memory? Was this a change of history? Was this an event that changed the sons? The client went back to a full working life, and the two brothers are closer than ever before.

For the individual, false memory can become the true memory

that has a lasting effect on the belief system. If the belief system integrates the false memory into the behavioral patterns in a way that frees the individual from trauma that has kept that person from functioning in a healthy way, then it should be accepted as a viable healing tool. False memory can be used for positive, lasting therapy, provided false memory is converted to true memory.

7

Male / Female
Game

ANDROGENY

The word 'androgeny' is a widely misunderstood term having to do with male/female relationships. It makes us think of the words 'equal' and 'same' and 'balanced'. I am one who believes the female is equal to the male, but I see through the misunderstanding of the idea of equality. Equal certainly does not mean sameness. Many who seek equality for the female are demanding sameness rather than equality. We have this confusion with the idea of androgeny. Many want it to mean that all human beings should be 50% male and 50% female in their energies, use of thought, and choice of emotional expression.

Like the word equality, in the feminist movement, androgeny is misunderstood when gender identity is discussed. Certain branches of psychology as well as many new age religious people are impressed by the idea of androgeny and the suggestion of non-sexual beings that are neither male nor female. At the same time we hear people referring to the androgynous person as being equally male and female, in other words a mix of the two.

In the dictionary androgeny is referenced to the word hermaphrodite, a condition of possessing both male and female reproductive organs.

Androgeny simply means having the characteristics of both, male and female. Many who seek the androgynous expression as the epitome of life are mislead by the idea. On the surface it seems desirable to be both, male and female, thereby removing the label of man or woman and reaching the goal of 'wholeness' or balance. This is an illusion, as the female must be female in order to fulfill her human expression, and the male must be male to fulfill his human expression. A primary ingredient of being a fulfilled human being in the optimum sense would be that the person, male or female, bond with their opposite power. This means that the male and female enmesh their energies. In our present period of evolution we are very much either male or female, and to fulfill the laws of energy, male must meld with female and visa versa.

At the time of birth the atomic structure of the male is constituted with atoms which are of a male (yang) energy essence. This essence is 'stamped' on the cells, so to speak, and is part of the formula of the material expression. This condition is also true for the female at birth; she is "stamped" on her cells with the essence of the female (yin) energy. This basic energy of the molecular framework of each, male or female, should be maintained for optimum health throughout the life of the individual.

The human being can influence the cells of the body with the power of thinking by insisting that the individual become more male (or female) than originally designed; the individual affects the energy and the growth of the cells with thought. Persistent, long term thinking of forcing the opposite sex structure on the self, will have an influence on the cells to change from their normal healthy structure to a mutant structure. 'Tampering' with one's own sexual makeup is much more serious than some may realize. To become androgynous - half male and half female - is not the goal in the human experience.

A great deal of the confusion about gender is caused by the failure to understand that we are a mixture of animal and mental being. Many reject their animal self. Others deny the animal influence in their lives. There is the tendency to believe we can reach beyond the animal self and attain a level of non-physical attachment (sans body). As souls we are not here to elevate ourselves beyond the physical being. When we arrive in this dimension we are specific in choosing the body we need to learn our soul lessons with, and we need the human body to accomplish this with. To accomplish the soul learning we must attain to becoming the perfect human being and this requires us to have a perfect body. The body after all is the reflection of our attainment of balance in the material world.

The gender of a fetus is often influenced by the energy needs of the planet. If there has been a major planetary loss of male energy, for example the deaths of many male soldiers, then the sex of the next generations of human bodies is influenced by the need of the planet to maintain a balance of yin and yang energies in the planetary form. The planet's need of yin or yang energy places a demand on the formation of the fetus as to gender.

On the surface it is not easy to accept that the planet influences the gender, however, one can look to history and note when a war has killed off a large segment of males (yang energy), soon thereafter a flood of male babies are born. When we ask the question of why this is so we have to consider more than the biological answers. Attraction or manifestation based on need is the primary cause in this universe of thought. If the planet needs more yang energy it will create the conditions that serve that end. The same is true for the human species as the human species and the earth are energy connected. Have you ever wondered why some families have only boys or girls and others have a balance of both? Humanly we try to find answers in biology, but the original cause for the balance or imbalance of yin and yang energy in the family unit has to do with the balance or imbalance of each family member and the lessons to be learned by each from one another. There are simply no accidents, we attract what we need and are to help us see that. This is so for our own choice of gender as soul minds, coming here is well planned and fits in with the dynamics of earth needs and individual lesson needs.

The soul-mind makes the choice of gender. Before the soul-mind connects to an infant it is aware that choice of gender means choice of yin or yang powers. It knows it wants to attach to a specific infant for its powers and abilities. The soul's choice of infant is prompted by lessons of balance it needs to learn. It takes into consideration that the planet functions on the two basic powers of negative and positive, which are normally reflected in the human expression as yin in the female and as yang in the male.

Some human beings are confused about their gender and

unwittingly work to change it. There are many influences that can cloud the purpose for the original gender choice. Primarily, the soul-mind desires that the individual stay with its original gender choice. I might add here that I make no personal judgement of sexual choice. I am fully aware that those who do choose to alter their sex, or behave as the opposite sex have a right to such choice. I am also aware that if someone chooses to act as the opposite sex, or chooses to be sexual only with someone of the same sex, s/he must eventually deal with having made such a decision from a soul lesson perspective.

Those who make such choices fail to realize that there were soul lesson reasons for the gender choice made by the soul. The soul-mind will insist on the lessons being learned, no matter how many lifetimes it takes.

When we consider that the human animal is just that, an animal, then as the light being and a soul, we are responsible for what happens to the body. Every choice we make has its consequences. This includes forcing an opposite gender energy on the human manifestation which alters its molecular structure. When we are not satisfied with our original gender and we change the body we confuse its memory patterns.

WORKINGS OF THE FEMALE EXPRESSION

To understand the female human being, we must examine her from two points of view, the female as animal and the female as mind of the soul. The female animal has the instinctive need to be protected, the need to propagate and give life, and the need to nurture and manage life. These are fundamental urges of her animal nature. If the soul's needs for learning are better served in the human experience as a female, then the soul-mind attaches to a newborn female infant. This choice is made because the projected female essence and powers are expected to serve the particular soul's intended progression better than male powers and energies might.

The female is the giver of life, she serves as the channel for the human body to manifest on the human level. The female is also the nurturer of life, feeding life force and wisdom to the male. On the material level she prepares and gives substance to the life. As the intuitive expression, she provides life with a connection to that which is greater than the human. She serves as soul-mind communicator, the natural link between the male's brain as it expresses yang thoughts and the mind. The female's natural expression of power is through the use of yin energy.

WORKINGS OF THE MALE EXPRESSION

The male animal expression is easy to see acted out in herd animals. In examining male herd animals we see some basic behavior patterns that are natural and instinctive. There is the need to dominate a group of females for the purpose of propagating. There is a need to dominate lesser males to maintain strength of the species. There is the need to select areas of feed to sustain the group. There is the need to avoid or combat predators to survive. These behaviors are primitive and basic, however, they are part of the essence of all human males. Animal traits may be prominent in the human male or not, depending on the strength of the animal essence in the individual.

The soul-mind who desires to become one with a male form examines the probable human needs of that male before it attaches to it. If those needs reflect that it is more desirable for learning to be in a male body than in a female body then the soul-mind melds with the male at its birth.

The male is the keeper of life; he is responsible for keeping life in its progression. Being the driving force, the male must take action to continue the life he manifests. Ideally, because he has the strength of the protector, the female he attracts into his experience can feel free and secure. He is the manifestor of matter and the projector of will. His natural power of expression is through the use of yang energy.

SEXUALITY & LIFE FORCE

Males and females have very different ideas about the human sexual experience. There is good reason for this as the two are vastly

ALL

different in their thinking processes. As a rule, the female uses the upper three chakras to attract thoughts. These three chakras deal with non-matter kind of thoughts, meaning that the thoughts a woman naturally attracts for use are not physically oriented. She may have thoughts about meeting a man and having an intimate sexual experience, but it is thought about by her in the essence of a loving, romantic experience. This may include holding hands, or dancing, or intimate talking and petting. The focus for the female is on doing things together romantically.

The male is normally using the lower three chakras to attract thoughts. These three chakras attract thoughts related to physical matter. When he thinks about an intimate experience with a female, his thoughts include physical sexual activities. His focus is not romantic togetherness as the female thinks about it, his focus is on what each is going to do to the other sexually/physically.

Looking at these roles from the perspective of yin and yang energies, we see these forces in action during the sexual experience. The yang (male) energy is matter oriented and aggressive, expressing in a projecting manner. The yin (female) energy is nurturing and receptive, adding a bonding essence to the yang energy.

In the western world there is a trend for women becoming more aggressive sexually, using yang power, and men becoming more submissive, using yin power. We see it also in the growing gay movement. However, the greater world population still acts out in the typical yin/yang roles.

It is important to understand how thinking is influenced biologically and also from the mental perspective. In the human male there is the animal need to mount the female for propagation; this is a drive that is in the genes. In the human female there is the animal need to hold still while the male injects his sperm to assure impregnation, this is in her genes.

As mental beings we at times resent the implications of the sexual act being an animal experience. At some point during the sex act desire and emotion on the primitive level causes behavior that leans toward animal responses. Again, as mental beings we usually want to approach the idea of sexual intercourse from the position of the experience being mostly emotional and mentally acceptable.

There are many other factors that are not physical which come into play because today we want to believe we are more mental and less animal in our experiences. Because of this we bring into the sexual intercourse experience many influencing factors such as moral good or bad, marriage rights, social pressures and much more. These are mental conditions placed on the sexual act and have a considerable influence on the outcome of the experience, both psychologically and physically. These influences make the experience satisfactory or not, meaningful or not, healthy physically or not, guilt ridden or not and so on.

One of the most powerful factors of male/female relating is the need to feed one another life force. There is a natural need on the part of the female to feed life force to the male. This exchange of life force energies happens on a deep inner bonding or mental melding level and requires the female to be 'connected' to the male psychically. Even though this connection occurs at the psychic level, it becomes reflected as a form of possession on the awareness level. This bonding and 'energy feeding' is not restricted to married couples or adult male/female relationships.

We can witness a one year old daughter in the arms of the father, and this bonding becomes obvious. The mother may attempt to join the two by moving as though to hug the father and daughter. When the mother does this, the girl child will often ruthlessly claw at the mother's face or in some way push her away. The child is feeding the father life force energy and does not want anyone to interfere, especially another female.

The coy actions of the daughter snuggling with the father and teasing him in play as the child ages, is the process of daughter feeding father life force energy in yin form. She is doing the natural thing for the female, feeding the male yin energy he needs to make his yang efforts successful in the material world. Sometimes this leads to a confrontation between daughter and mother when the child is 'felt' by the mother to be a female threat to her bonding with the father.

The exchange of affection and life force between adults and children, particularly between girl child and male adult, is generally not viewed for what is truly being experienced on a deeper level. On the surface, many times the exchange of energies is viewed as sexual innuendo on the part of one of the parties or both. Most certainly, from the perspective of a third party, such as the mother, sexual innuendo seems to be what is happening. The unfortunate cases of abuse happen when the male misleads himself into converting the surges of life force he is experiencing with the female child into sexual feelings.

In not understanding what is taking place, the male often will fall into the trap of experimenting sexually. The result of course is that the child is emotionally damaged. The emotional damage is increased by the psychic reaction of the mother responding as though the child were usurping the role of the mother and therefore is no longer trustworthy. The child becomes alienated psychologically and attempts to bury the event in repressed memory.

All human beings are in need of life force which we get from loving, happy thoughts, joyful interactions with others and play. Expressed sensuality is one of the main sources of life force energy for the male and he actually depends on it. The female, being generally right brained, gets her life force from the many happy light hearted events of her day. Yang energy being much denser than yin energy, makes it more difficult for males to get life force in a light hearted way. The only time the male ever feels energized and free from the demands of life is during and immediately after the orgasmic ecstasy of intercourse. The male is dependant on his life force supply almost totally from a happy female and will become extremely uncomfortable and irritable mentally and physically if his supply of life force, which he equates with sexual intercourse, is not forthcoming.

In many religions, including the Christian, women and sexuality were connected to sin. For centuries there has been the mass thought idea that the female misleads the male with her sexual powers and traps him into a kind of sexual slavery. Even today, some religious teachers caution males that too much sexual activity will strip them of their life force. This goes along with adults in the past telling teenagers to not masturbate or they will harm themselves and possibly go blind.

These ideas about males wasting their power is a false belief and does not serve the human relationship. For teenage males, masturbation relieves the pressures of acting out sexual fantasies on defenseless females. For adult males masturbation can be the very medicine the body needs to offset a prostate problem.

Sexual activity does not deplete life force; it replenishes it. The idea that it strips males of their power is absurd. The orgasm gives the male complete release from the material world; he feels totally free of all demands on him physically and mentally.

If a male is so involved sexually with a female to the point that his work suffers and he shirks responsibilities in his life, it is because he is driven to avoid life. The sex act makes it easy and convenient for him to not face the world.

Their are some women who are addicted to sex, however, they are a small percentage. The average woman could care less whether or not she becomes involved in the sex act. For the most part she enjoys sex because it makes her male happy, and this is why she seems quite ready to become involved in sex. When we examine sex from this perspective we can easily see that the female is more or less trapped as far as sex is concerned. The reason being that she knows that sex is the prime interest the male has in the female, and she wants to be the one who is there for the male she chooses in life, thereby keeping his interest in her. This situation is not too rewarding for female, because no matter how available she is to her mate for sex, as a rule, he still views other women as potential partners for the sex act.

Educators fail to provide a real understanding of the roles and differences of males and females. They are transfixed in the need to educate based only on equality of persons and fail to include the importance of the differences. Sexuality as a power and an energy exchange is ignored altogether.

MALE & FEMALE BONDING

I use the term 'sub-atomic bonding' to make the point that the male and female bond is something that takes place on a chemo-electric level that is pre-matter. It is a bond that is mindful and has an essence that is beyond the common understanding of the human idea of material or physical relationship.

Individuals consider themselves separate from others even though there is an eternal 'knowing' that on some level there is a joining of one to the other, especially with the one chosen in love. But there is still the idea that there are separate entities involved. On the material level this is true. On the mental level this is not always the case. When the female completely accepts the male there occurs a bonding on the sub-atomic level that transcends the physical separation. No matter how far apart in distance the two are, the mental bond creates a union or unit.

In a true bonding, the soul-mind of each has access to the essence of yin or yang powers of the mate. Wherever you may be, if you are bonded with someone of the opposite sex, your soul-mind field stays connected to the energy of your mate. You may draw on that energy to assist you when you are in need of your mate's support. Mental transfer of yin or yang energy between a bonded pair is instantaneous and has the same effect as if the partner were standing right by your side, supporting you with their physical presence.

The male and female have gifts they bring to the relationship by virtue of their essences, both genetic and transpersonal. One of those gifts is the giving of life force to one another. This life force is carried on the thought particles which make up the yin and yang energy forces. This is a gift to one another that gives power to the couple to manifest together those things they desire in their union. Additionally, the female gives other gifts that are basic to the female, such as the nurturing; and the male gives other gifts that are basic to the male such as protection.

A true bonded relationship between a 'natural' female and a 'natural' male has its roots in the thought systems of each. Their behavior toward one another is the result of either deliberate thinking, choice, or non-deliberate thinking of mass thought. Both, males and females, are driven by their instincts, essences and powers and by their memories, their beliefs, traits and habits ingrained in their thought systems. Both parties are animals at one level and are acting out their animal needs. At the same time, each of them have a soul-mind attached to their bodies and are constantly urged to act out the needs of the soul. This animal and soul-mind balancing act is basic and is what drives much of the behavior in the relationship.

When melded on the mind level, there is a giving over to one another at the level of essence. The minds are joined and therefore inter-connected at many levels. This giving over has its roots in trust and commitment. Each is totally open to the other on a psychic energy level. It is this deep bond of commitment on the mind/body level that is the basis of intense reaction for physical communion and conflict.

Being open to the other in the relationship, one is highly vulnerable. Being open to the other and vulnerable, if that trust is violated, there is intense inner shock to the essence of the person. This inner violation is often the cause behind extreme violent behavior of one toward the other. It is also the reason that the one violated is constantly in fear of the other in future relations. This is a mass condition today and makes forgiving almost impossible.

One might say, it appears that times have changed and men do not need nurturing, or that women do not need protecting. This is not so, these two things are basic to the animal essences of human beings and are not something that can be intellectually considered as no longer relevant. They are inherent to the natures of the human expression and do not just go away. What appears as a change in social behavior in bonded relationships is nothing more than the individuals confusing their roles while trying to relate.

Basically, the female wants a permanent relationship, and basically, the male knows he needs to relate one on one. It is the mass of humanity which is engrossed in intellectual pursuits that is confused about relating. The idea of expanded freedom and independence has distorted into confusion and lack of identity. Western education has unwittingly fostered the confusion of gender differences. The idea that males and females should learn the same things in the same manner so they can compete in the field of business is at odds with the true natures of males and females.

Most people give little or no consideration to the two powers involved in the male and the female, the yin and yang forces. The bonding of the male with the female is more than an animalistic ancient rite. Each of the sexes represent a certain kind of power that escalates the individual ability when it bonds on the inner levels. The male brings certain abilities and powers to the union, the female brings certain other abilities and powers to the union.

These human powers and abilities could be nurtured by an education system that recognizes these differences. Rather than force each of the sexes to learn and function as the other, the true abilities of each should be nurtured. The female brings the mind power to the experience as she is functioning mainly from a right brain oriented thinking system. The male is usually functioning with a left brain influence and brings literal orientation to the human experience.

172

Together they constitute a balance that enables them to move far beyond the present individual level of thinking.

The consciousness of human beings could be raised more rapidly if the leaders of education would take into consideration the differences between the male and the female, not just the sexual difference, but the mental differences, specifically. Not long ago it was noted that medical science had ignored research on women in business when it came to heart attacks. There was a presumption that there was a difference, but the difference was accepted as 'job' oriented and it did not matter because women were not having the same rate of heart problems. When women moved into the fields of intellectual business competition they began to reflect increased heart problems. Why this would amaze researchers is hard to understand.

Unfortunately, the mind/intuitive aspect of the human thinking is still under valued and this is a predominant reason why women have moved into using yang energy and left brain/intellectual careers since that is what our present society values. It is time that we fully integrate and appreciate the female gift to the world and teach our daughters the value of their yin energy when used correctly.

When women act like men, using left brain orientation, they will be into the same causative effects that men have been into; worse, they will experience job related harm as men do and maybe more. The female has a finer vibration and yang energy tends to distort it. Research can show that women who use yang thoughts distort their physical structure. What is interesting is that in many jobs women are better equipped to do the work men do, provided they stay in their own yin energies. If they did so they would not experience the same level of heart problems the male does in the same work. In the future, when there is an understanding of the use of bonded powers by the individuals, there will be less heart trouble in the body of male and female.

WOMAN'S CHOICE OR MAN'S CHOICE

When we examine the relationship between western man and woman today, we find there is a stalemate existing. On the one hand the female has a desire to create her own security and be independent, and on the other hand the male has reacted by separating himself from the need to protect or provide for the female. Each defend their position of isolation. Reasons for this separation can be traced back to the time of the 2nd World War when females were moving out of the home environment and into the industrial war effort. This move created a world of personal experiences outside the home life for the female. This was new to many women and gave them a feeling of independence.

After the war there was a decisive shift in the cost of living and the family was slowly forced to have both adults bringing in income to keep up with the changes in economics. In the work place the scramble for position and higher wages involved everyone. This condition contributed to a psychological push on the part of the female to be treated equally in the work market. The need for equal rights began to create aggressive behavior on the part of the female and defensive behavior on the part of the male.

The couples who should have banded together to politically demand that one person's income should take care of the needs of the family, failed to see they were becoming victims of economics. Today there is a blaming of one another for the failure of the family unit to survive. The male is suspicious of the female and the female resents the male. Women, in their hearts, need to be bonded to a male yet cannot find the respect or the acceptance by the male. The man who needs to bond in his heart with the woman avoids commitment like it is a plague. The gap is getting wider, and the family unit has reached disaster conditions.

Many women are trying to raise a family on a single income which has lost its earning power. They often fail; they fail emotionally, and the children suffer the pains of existing in a bondless environment which is unnatural for the child. I listen to the common ego talk of men and women who blurt out their right to be free from one another. However, when talking personally with the woman who is failing financially and emotionally, I feel the pain in her heart over her failure to find a male willing to bond. When talking personally to the man, I hear him moaning over the failure to find a woman who wants him simply for who he is. Both fail to see the real cause of conflict between them which is the lack of a true bonding between them, nor do they see how one can give in to the other to create a true bonding.

Beside the obvious differences between the male and female, the physical, the intellectual and the emotional, there are the subtle differences which are not so obvious but are more influential than the obvious ones. There are the yin and yang powers, there are the different uses of language, there are the different uses of the thinking mechanisms, there are the different uses of sexual powers, there are the different needs materially and psychologically, and there are the intuitive differences. Are males and females evolved enough to grasp the understanding of their differences, and is each capable of actually shifting consciousness to put together a bonded relationship that serves them individually and as a unit? Today it seems not.

MARRIAGE

Of all the ventures we experience in life, none is more meaningful than the marriage experience. Many couples who live together and have not socially registered their union, believe that they are in a marriage. When they do get legally married life in the relationship changes and involves a lot more thought and thinking than they had previously experienced together. We fail to realize that marriage is not just living together physically, it is a psychic experience as well.

As a psychic experience marriage has far deeper meanings than the agreement to live together. Psychic means there are realms or levels of connection in the marriage which are unknown and mystical. At a level below that of the atomic particles of each there is a bonding of energies which takes place when two people give themselves to one another. This giving to one another is specific and psychic and becomes ritualized in the marriage ceremony.

REASONS FOR MARRIAGE

Although many people give love as the reason to be married, most are not clear on what was the basic purpose for their marriage. This failure to be clear on the reasons for marriage usually is caused by the levels of emotional temperature experienced by those about to marry. When we act out of emotion, the real reasons for our relating become clouded.

There seem to be several reasons for marriage such as love, sex, money, influence, tradition and so forth. However, if we examine all of them, we would find out that there are really only three basic reasons for being in a marriage. The three reasons are family, security, and spiritual growth.

A young man driven to relate sexually to a specific female may not be able to articulate why he 'must' marry her, but the simple truth is he is 'driven' to create a family. A woman caught up in the passion of a new romance may simply be seeking security. And finally, the person who seeks to marry for the purpose of companionship and sharing life, is usually looking for a spiritual partner.

Physical desire is a powerful part of the courtship and of great influence in the bonding. With so much intellectual conditioning, desire is the potion that allows the intellectual one to abandon cold reason and experience engulfing emotion. Oftentimes physical desire serves to help two people to find it within themselves to commit to a marriage. After the marriage has run its course for a period we find that desire was only a part of the courting.

So, we have three real reasons for marriage: 1) to create a family and perpetuate the race; 2) to create security and ensuring control of the life experience, 3) to grow spiritually by sharing and learning from one another. The first two reasons for marriage are dictated by the planet feeding mass thought to the animal aspects of us just as it feeds any other animal brain. Propagation and security are basic for the survival of any specie. Some form of what we call love can be an aspect in the reasons for getting married or may not exist at all for one or both of the participants in a courtship and marriage. A person may be married for family reasons alone. Another may be married for security reasons or spiritual reasons alone. Another person may marry for all three reasons; family, security, and spirituality.

Of the three reasons, perhaps the reason of spiritual growth needs more clarification and understanding than the other two. Spiritual growth is often thought to mean religious training, but that is not exactly correct; one can be religious to the point of fanaticism, and that could hardly be called spiritual behavior or growth. Religion can be part of the spiritual growth process, but it is not a requirement for spiritual growth. Spiritual growth is a stage of mental growth that places personal harmony with all of life as more important than things that are material.

Because it requires interaction with other human beings to manifest a spiritual life, marriage is the ideal condition for advancing spiritual growth. It is in marriage that we find ourselves constantly confronted with those things that create emotional conflict. It is in managing, moderating, and releasing conflicting emotions that one grows spiritually. In a marriage whose reason for the bonding is spiritual growth, both parties are in the experience to reflect the needs of the other and to share with the other the wisdom of the learnings. When we grow spiritually we are fulfilling the soul's purpose for being in this dimension, manifesting balance through a human being.

TRUE MARRIAGE (TOTAL COMMITMENT)

There is the opinion by some that a marriage can succeed without traditional commitment in the form of social acceptance. Some say the legalizing of a marriage is not necessary or important. We often hear the comment, "Why destroy a beautiful relationship by making it legal." If the relationship is a real marriage how could legalizing destroy it?

Actually, what is at question when discussing the merits of legal marriage versus 'live in' relationships is the depth of bonding between the two people involved. Two people can be legally married and not have a marriage involving total commitment; the marriage is legal but there is no true meaning of marriage as marriage is meant to be.

For a true marriage to function with any degree of success there must be total commitment. A marriage without commitment is nothing more than a temporary agreement to relate. It is through commitment that the marriage can be true and successful no matter the reason or reasons for the joining. If the reason is family, then each must give entirely to the building of the family for it to achieve success as a family. If the reason is security, then both must be committed to creating the security that ensures success of the marriage. If the reason is spiritual growth, each has to give totally to the spiritual growth of one

177

another and this means total commitment. It is commitment that sets the framework for the evolution of the joint experience. If only one is totally committed and the other is not, then whatever the reason behind the marriage, it suffers accomplishment in the total sense. If there is total commitment by both to the joint purpose, success is much more likely for that marriage.

The question of whether there is a true marriage or a mock marriage is settled by the depth of the commitment on the part of each to the common purpose of the union. True marriage has a depth that goes beyond all other kinds of relationships. Besides being a social bonding and a physical joining, true marriage contains the aura of a psychic bonding that takes place in the essence of the pair. Pair-bonding of the essence of two people has meaning that transcends the normal physical experiences of relating such as occurs in friendships or family relationships.

THE FEMALE CHOOSES

The actual choosing of the mate is finalized by the female. Until the female commits totally and accepts the male on the level of their essences, there is no true pair-bonding or true marriage. I like to refer to this as the pre-atomic bonding level. I call it that because the union causes a merging of the vibratory psychic energies of the two people involved. The female is the receiver, the nurturer, the holder, the healer, of the union, and it is for this reason that true bonding cannot take place unless the female totally commits and accepts the bonding experience.

The male ego likes to believe that it is his choice as to which female he accepts in marriage. This fiction is easy to understand when one views the behavior of the male and female in courtship. It appears that the male pursues the female until he convinces her that she is his. What actually occurs is that the female prepares herself for 'hunting'. She chooses the courting conditions, and she 'lets' the male have his way. Old sayings are rife with truisms: "She let him chase her until she caught him." When the female chooses she usually makes a total commitment.

This aspect of the female making the choice can have far reaching consequences in a separation or divorce. Unless the female releases the male on the psychic or pre-atomic vibratory level, he will not be free of the relationship. It may appear that a male leaves and relates to a new female, but that is appearance only; in ways that are deeply subjective, the first wife still holds some part of the will of the male who has gone.

COMMITMENT

Total commitment is the giving of the self, in the marriage, to the other person on a level that is unconscious and pre-atomic. This means that the female gives over her will (her yang energy) to the male, and the male gives over his mind (yin energy) to the female. From then on they each have the power of both together, In the unit each has the role they agree to but out in the world separately they have the dual power. When the essence of one person is committed to another person, there is an exchange and melding of energies on a level the human brain does not understand. Anyone who has made such a commitment can tell you that there is a deep shift in the psyche of the person that is not explainable intellectually, but it leaves the person with a knowing of total commitment.

Commitment is exactly what Webster says in the dictionary: 'The state of being obligated or emotionally impelled.' Such commitment is needed to relate on a deeper level than the surface reasons for marriage. It is the mind of the female which is far more than an intellectual brain functioning, that makes the choice and commitment. When the female does this she releases her will to the male she commits to, for his use. In doing this she automatically has both her and his will.

When the female has committed to the bonding process she expects the male to do the same. If the male commits on the intellectual level only and does not do so at the mind level, then he does not release his mind to his mate. When this occurs the mind of the female knows there is lack of total commitment and an unconscious uneasiness permeates the union.

Many couples marry who are not committed at the pre-atomic

level and their minds have not bonded. Most often the female has committed, but the male has not reached a point of giving up himself totally to the union. Until both have committed at the level of their higher selves, bonding is not complete.

ROLES IN MARRIAGE

In order to discuss roles in marriage it is necessary to talk about the energies of the two beings involved. Eastern philosophies recognize and consider the yang powers and the yin powers of human beings. In the west we refer to the masculine and feminine natures in a general context. I use the eastern references of yang and yin energies in discussing roles.

Yang power is normally attributed to the male person; yin power is normally attributed to the female person. To understand how a male can have yin powers and a female have yang powers, we need to examine what these powers are. Yang is a positive magnetic electric power that has the essence of projected force. Yin power is a negative magnetic electric force that has the essence of cohesion. Yang force builds or destroys; yin force binds and welds.

A female person can have yang power along with her yin base essences. A male can have yin power along with his yang base essences. The female can project male thinking; when she does this she uses yang power. The opposite is true for the male when he uses female thinking. Yin and yang energies are projected by thought, and either sex can learn to use one or the other.

A female can create, build and destroy using yang power or male thinking. A male can manage, bind, and heal using yin power or female thinking. When we witness a major role reversal, we say, "that female is masculine," or, "that male is feminine."

If the marriage is not balanced in yin and yang energies, there is confusion and disharmony. If both partners in a union use yang force, there will be an inevitable clash of power, usually resulting in the weaker yang person (female) being controlled or abused by the stronger yang male.

There are very important reasons for males and females to remain true to their biological gender and use their respective mental power for the benefit of the unit. When faced with a problem, the couple should first determine whether yin or yang energy is required to solve it. Although both should have equal input on what to do, the unit is best served if one makes the decision. If yang energy is required to solve the problem, then the yang oriented person should make the decision and act on it. If yin energy is the solution, then the yin oriented person should make the decision and act on it. If the thing to be done requires force, that is the role of the yang person. If the thing to be done requires managing, that is the role of the yin person.

All

Whatever the basic reason for marriage, the power of the total bonding lies in the melding of the yin and yang forces; if they are balanced and managed and their use is understood, the unit can have great successes.

When the two partners have reached a level of harmony and the forces and energies are in complete balance then each has the use of the other's powers without having to act out the opposite energy or role. The power of one's mate becomes tangibly available mentally by simply 'tuning'

into him or her. This mutual use is the ultimate desire of the experience and results in attaining the material things of the marriage readily.

THE MALE/FEMALE GAME

When we understand the true differences between the male and the female we can begin to appreciate the "game" they are involved in. It takes little reasoning to realize that the male speaks differently than the female. It takes little reasoning to realize the female acts differently than the male. It takes little reasoning to note the physical differences between the male and the female. One can make a long list of things the male does differently than the female. In examining their spiritual energies and essences we find that they are opposites; the female 'takes in', holding to herself; the male 'gives out', pushing from himself.

This difference between male and female was exemplified in an article in the San Diego Union newspaper of August 5, 1993. The author berated male behavior, calling it 'Stupid Men Tricks'. The article made fun of male behavior, such as his use of the dishwasher to wash clothes, use of the microwave to dry clothes, and fluffing his hair with fabric softener. Instead of making men look foolish and immature the article could have given understanding of the difference between males and females. Male behavior has its roots in the yang energy laden thoughts that the male uses. He attracts thoughts for use which have an essence of investigation and query which influences him subliminally. What was criticized pointed out as 'stupid men tricks' was really the evidence that men have a driving need to investigate, to test things, to create things.

Women are also pointing out this behavior of the male adult when they state, "he acts like a little boy," What do we notice about little boys? They take things apart. They convert things whenever they can. They make up new things using anything they can find. They would gladly wash their trucks, tanks and other stuff in the dishwasher if they could get away with it. In fact the only thing that saves the dishwasher from many boys is that the door is not glass or see through. If they could see what is happening inside anything that is mechanical they would soon 'invade' it and take it apart. This is the creative male and this is the function of the male yang force. Males are driven to inquire and invent. It is this creative male drive that has given us all the modern household appliances making our lives easier.

Women are creative also, but in a different sense. Yin energy adds warmth and beauty to life. Woman, in her traditional role, make the home warm and beautiful, men supply the utility. On the level of thought, yang power supplies the building blocks of material manifestation, yin power is the glue that holds them together.

We have plenty of evidence that men and women have a need for each other, not just a casual need, but a driving need. There is a mental seeking for the self through a process involving the opposite sex. It is the eternal 'memory' of once having been bonded or melded together that insists we seek out one another for the serving of the need. What is the need? This is a question which plagues many who try to understand the human relationship.

From the animal perspective the need, like with all animals, is to propagate and to survive. This is a powerful force between the male and the female. However, the need to propagate is often superceded by needs which we can describe as rooted in the mental being. The mental makeup of the male and female, as individuals and as a mass, drives them to bond and meld on the mental level. This is an expression of the soul's need to evolve.

The driving need to be together is for the male and female to balance and perfect themselves in an ongoing mental process and is part of the human search to discover and understand the self. The human female and male accomplish this when each has the other to interact and 'vibrate' with and discover what is needed to balance the vibration into harmony, both mentally and physically.

How can these two energies and belief systems come together and find harmony when they are so completely different? I call this the human game because that is what it is supposed to be, a game. It has all the components of the most sophisticated games. If it is played out in ignorance of one another, the game becomes painful. When played successfully it is a happy game.

THE PSEUDO MALE/ FEMALE GAME

One cannot talk about the human game without including the male who wants to be female, and the female who wants to be male. This combination seems to fly in the face of what the majority desires as the optimum relationship. The person who acts out a behavior pattern which is not acceptable to the majority is in violation of prescribed social rules. It is not a matter of good or bad. Good or bad is in the eye of the beholder, and if the majority believe certain behaviors are unacceptable then they rule what is good or bad. This is the case, no matter what the choice of behavior is.

Whenever the 'gay' person 'threatens' the exclusiveness of the majority, the majority will feel a violation has taken place and react accordingly. The style of life is dictated by the majority as far as acceptability to the whole of the society they live in. Examining the human game from the perspective of soul growth and balance of power, we must look beyond good or bad in the human sense. In truth all people should be free to be who and what they are so long as they do not violate another person's right to a peaceful life. Being 'gay' is a way of life chosen by a person and that is their right. The question raised here is what is behind the choice?

The larger percentage of 'gay' persons do not understand the dynamics of their choices as to gender orientation. Those who are not gay are just as confused, believing that sexual behavior is the underlying cause of the confusion of identity. There are different reasons underlying the drive to be gay. In many cases where the belief of the person is that they are of the opposite gender of their body, they are a soul who did not leave this dimension when their last body died. They chose to immediately reincarnate. This meant there was no time spent on the 'other side' to release certain essences such as the gender essence. The result is that in the new body, which is opposite gender of their last body, there is the underlying essence of belief that they are still the other gender.

Strictly speaking, only those who identify with and act out the opposite gender role are truly 'gay'. They are the ones confused about their gender. It does not take much common sense to recognize that if a male is acting a male role in a gay relationship he is not insisting that he is female. He is insisting on the right to a gay life style and is playing the game of being gay simply because of a control issue or fear of the female. This is so also for the female who is acting out the role of a female in a gay relationship. Her underlying issue may also be control, or fear of the male.

Many individuals are exercising defiant behavior, acting out the gay life style for the sole purpose of preying on others who are confused about their gender. There are many in this kind of role for the sole purpose of sexual exploitation and the garnering of life force energy through the sexual experience and are not aware of the energy dynamics that propel them.

DIVORCE, CONFLICT & CHANGE

On the surface, no rational being really wants conflict; we see it as causing misery and pain. The dictionary defines conflict as a clash of forces. Earlier I spoke of yin and yang as opposites, and on our planet opposites create clashes and upheavals; it would seem then that conflict is inevitable between the male and female. It also seems that conflict is something bad, and we tend to think that way. Actually conflict constitutes the beginning of change. Whether the change is explosive or gradual, it has its root in conflict.

Change is the natural progression of all things on the planet; nothing stays static. It is the process of evolvement and progression that all things are subject to here, and it cannot be avoided. If we do not change when it is required of us, we are left behind; we die. Argument in a relationship is a sign of the need to change and adjust; when argument begins it is wise to see it as the need for adjustment. Adjustment in a relationship requires change on the part of all in the relationship. If one changes as a result of conflict and the other does not, the conflict will become greater.

A relationship should be projected to flow through the events it will encounter. The people in the relationship should prosper and grow. If the relationship is a male and female union, the bonding will be challenged by many forces trying to change it into a stronger or weaker union. All external happenings to a bonding are mirrors of the inner attitudes between the yin and yang relationships. External happenings can be allowed to reflect a failure of the bonding or they can be used to strengthen the bonding. Conflict/change should be grasped as an opportunity to adjust and balance a relationship by both the yin person and the yang person involved.

Change is probably the most frightening thing that humans have to face. A person can be living in a relationship that many would consider unpleasant and degrading, yet the thing that keeps the person from making a change for the better is the fear of change. Fear is not natural to the human being, it is a learned response that is deeply rooted in the belief system of the person.

Fear in the parent is conveyed to the infant and as the child grows, each parent is constantly warning the child about the unknown that 'might' happen at any moment if he or she is not careful. We grow up with fear as a staple in our lives and this fear causes us to not want to face change. Show me a successful person in life, and I will show you a person who has no fear of change.

The feeling which propels us to move forward, searching for that which we are not sure of and causing us to change, is the memory of where we have come from before being born, the place we refer to as the 'oneness'. We are forever seeking that 'oneness' we know exists.

Change is inevitable, one can attempt with all their being to prevent change, and it will still occur. Failure to adjust to changes as they unfold around us, results in the inability to do anything about them, whether they be material changes or relationship changes. In relationships it is healthy to keep one another aware of all signs of change so that whatever is occurring can be managed in a balanced, harmonious manner.

Conflict, as mentioned above, is the stage the relationship has reached when the ability to look at things with understanding has failed. Conflict means confronting, and confronting is what we do when we do not have the wisdom to mitigate what it is that disturbs us. When we examine the thinking being done by those in the relationship who are in conflict, we find they are locked into streams of mass thought. They have allowed themselves to reach an emotional temperature level where they no longer are able to choose their own thoughts. The law of attraction is automatically bringing to them the average negative thoughts that are standard responses to that which they reacted to. When conflict reaches a certain point in a marriage, divorce automatically surfaces as a solution to the conflict.

When I am asked by a couple if they should divorce, since they are at a complete stalemate in communication, I always give the same response. I ask, "Are you wise enough to dissolve the partnership so you both will be successful after this?" Usually the answer is no.

As frustration between two people mounts, it becomes more and more difficult for them to be objective. By the time they reach the divorce stage, whenever they see one another, mass thought floods their thinking.

The most important thing to consider when the question arises about divorce is whether or not the separation can be truly amicable. If there is anger and hate, any divorce will be an incomplete dissolution. The fact that a legal document exists that says two people are no longer bound together does not mean they are not still bonded on a far more subtle level. Reason for divorce is to sever the bond and set free the parties.

186

Because of a deeper bond than the couple is normally aware of, I often refer to the 'Divorce Engagement Period' when commenting on newly divorced behaviors. This deep bond goes beyond or deeper then the legal separation, and because of it there is usually a jockeying of control of one another's lives after the divorce. The male attempts to keep some physical control over his ex-partner. The female attempts to impose psychological control on the past. Neither the male or female is thinking these things deliberately in the sense that they are aware of the 'inner' control efforts. Her control is usually exercised on a psychic level and she controls the bond. Unless the bond is released by her there can be no complete bonding by either one with new partners.

In psychology we know that people who divorce are usually still emotional about one another. This means that something is holding the couple together is attributed to the emotions involved. Couples are usually advised to avoid seeing one another as a solution to the emotional entanglement. This advise is short sighted and does nothing to solve the real problem which lies in the deeper psychic bond that brought them together in the first place. Without understanding there is never any resolution or completion. Understanding of the meaning behind the deeper bond will allow divorcing couples to free themselves from one another.

I can recall years ago, in a class on relationships, one woman emphasizing that she 'certainly' was free of her ex-husband she had been divorced from for nine years. She insisted that she had forgotten him completely and he had no meaning in her life. I could tell from her defensive tone of voice and comment about the 'bitch' he had married when she left that this woman was still very much involved with her ex-husband. She insisted that when she left the town in the east where they had lived together she had 'washed her hands of him.'

I commented that her way of talking about him meant that she still was bonded to him. She denied even thinking about him. To help her see through her involvement I asked her if she would be willing to call him on the telephone. She was quick to say "yes". I handed her a telephone. The class expected her to call the town for information to get his phone number, instead, nine years later, without hesitation she dialed his number. This revealed she had thought about that phone number many times.

The class listened as she spoke to someone who had answered her call and we observed her as she turned white and nearly fainted. She had reached the woman who had replaced her to discover that her ex-husband had died of a heart attack five years before. Later this woman admitted that she had periodically considered calling to tell him how much she hated him. She eventually commented that she knew 'deep inside' that she had never stopped loving him nor did she ever 'give him up' to the other woman.

Like this woman, whatever is driving the individual to hold on to the other person has to do with not making correct choices in their thinking. Unfortunately most people who divorce have no concept of the soul involvement with one another in the relationship and that there is far more to separating than one realizes. This of course makes the right choices of thought about separating difficult to understand. Most of us get emotional and then we function using the average mass thought streams of the planetary thinking system about divorces causing us all to behave similarly in not letting the other go.

 ## WHERE IS FEMALE THINKING TODAY

Where is the western woman psychologically? What does she think unconsciously about relating to males? Why does she look upon the male as a 'little boy'? What is the root of her mistrust of him? What must she do to be able to nurture the male and be accepted by him on an equal basis so she can accept him at the bonding level? These are questions that are basic for all yin oriented females.

For the most part there are three general categories western woman fall into (with exceptions); there is woman A who accepts that she needs a male in her life; there is woman B who has taken the position that a male is not a necessity in her life; and then there is the young woman C, just out of school, who is torn between her belief that there is little or no difference between the female and male, and in her confusion she does not know what to believe about males.

Woman A, who knows she needs a male in her life is looking for that male who will commit to a permanent bonding. She is willing to become a bonded mate in a lasting relationship. She is struggling with the need to survive economically and works many hours. She is single, unmarried or divorced with a child on her hands. Like B and C, she is burdened with the subtle essence need to bond with the male. Unlike B and C, she is vitally aware of the need to bond and suffers the urgency that propels her to relate to that one male, causing her to be vulnerable to the predatory male who will use her. She harbors an anger toward the male which is rooted in the frustration of not having her gifts received by the male in a commitment framework. She suppresses the anger, turning it on herself. She has not understood the nature of her yin powers and lacks the knowledge of how to use it to attain the bonding she needs.

Woman B, the one who feels she can get along without the male, has become competitive with the male. Her need to bond with him is latent and buried; it smoulders in repression, giving more power to her competitiveness. Her anger at the male is on the surface and does not require much raising of emotional temperature for it to flair openly. She attempts to relate to males in a pseudo equality context, using left brain (yang) reasoning to prove her status and level of equality. This leads to her becoming involved in the male aspect of her own nature regularly. The constant demand on her yang energy and male nature keeps her in conflict with herself and others. She ignores the need to bond with a male on the sub-atomic level.

Woman C, the young woman just out of college, is confused about gender roles. She has moved out of childhood into an education system which is designed to force her into linear intellectual conditioning. Competition with males and females is standard processing. Her natural connection to her intuitive abilities has been interfered with. She comes into the adult world as either A or B in nature, but is indoctrinated by her education in the competitive equality standards that demand she move into the world and establish herself alone. It not being the nature of the female to survive alone, she creates pseudo togetherness situations with roommates, male and female, while setting parameters of isolation. This is a very confused female who has an over-developed intellect which is more encompassing than A's or B's and which causes her to flounder in all relationships.

Today the western woman is caught up in a confused debate about what her powers are, who she is and how she should relate to males. Unconsciously, the planet is feeding her mass thought that contains the average global thinking about males in relation to the emotion she is experiencing at the moment. This mass thought has a high content of negative thoughts about the male and trust. The root of the mistrust goes back into ancient behaviors of the male toward the female. Besides physical and mental abuse it lies in the many lifetimes of the male leaving the female to go off to some adventure, usually war. As a consequence of him going off the woman was left alone to survive whatever way she could. Since the females biggest unconscious fear has been to be left alone without love, protection and direction, today she is unconsciously torn about having to provide for herself and still be there for the male when he needs her. This is compounded by his history of not complying with his obligation to provide security.

The male now faces a confusion of adjustments about his attitude toward the female and an improved relationship with her. It is primarily his responsibility to nurture relationships toward a more equal balance. This is especially difficult at this stage of human experience since globally, from a mass perspective, the male is still the controller of the human experience. Since mass thought feeds all brains the average mass thinking for behavior, males are still attracting the old thinking toward the female. It requires specific choice of thinking for the individual male to not be caught up in the mass stereotypical thoughts. His choice of thinking should be done in a calm emotional state.

The 'little boy' thinking about the male by the female can be put to meaningful use today to facilitate equality thinking on the part of the male. By thinking thoughts such as, "He is a struggling male seeking equality for a happy relationship." the female can help the male make his changes. Such a statement should be accompanied with a nurturing smile on the part of the female.

WHERE IS MALE THINKING TODAY

Where is the human male psychologically? What does he think consciously? What does he think unconsciously? Why can't he accept the gifts of the woman? Why is he not able to trust when relating? What must he do to accept the gifts of the female and bond with her on that subatomic level of oneness?

Like the females, the males can be considered to fall into three types today. Type N is the older male who accepts his inner urging to bond to the female. He is the traditional male who is looking for a permanent relationship and has feelings of incompleteness without a female in his life experience. His reaction to the move by the female to act independently of the male has been to take an attitude of, "Go ahead, see how you like being independent and doing it all yourself." He acts out this attitude, but he has a frustration bordering on anger rooted in his objection to being rejected in the ego sense.

Type O is the male who is the opposite of the competing female (C). He feels intimidated by the aggressive, independent female who is expressing yang energy. As a result he has a tendency to withdraw into his yin energy. This makes him seek less threatening relationships and often leads him into a pseudo bonding with another male. After two or three years in this way of living, he becomes sensitive and effeminate in character; if not effeminate then very passive.

Type P is the young male who is out of school and is in competition with everything. The co-educational/equality life he was taught has given him a false impression of what a female is about. He tries to relate with her as a buddy while struggling with his natural tendencies to dominate her. He, like the C female, is confused about what is expected of him as a male in a relationship. He is quick to anger, and most of the time the planet is conducting his behavior with mass thought.

Western man is caught today in a struggle which is world wide. There is a monetary desperation building which has survival overtones and this energy affects the nature of all males, causing them to want to act out aggressively. At the same time there is a psychological mass demand put upon him by the female to be more gentle, communicative and more like she is. These two forces which are fed into the consciousness of all males are at opposite purposes.

Caught between these two influences, the male is losing more and more of his identity, and he is brooding. We have reached a point where the brooding is causing males to be more explosive and susceptible to mass thought influences. We see this today in violent individual and collective male energy outbursts. There are senseless killings happening everywhere. In this mass thought mode male behavior is devoid of humanistic feelings.

This destructive condition is not confined to males today because many females have slipped into an abusive use of yang (male) energy, abusive in the sense that their use of male energy is excessive and misunderstood. As those females go further along the male path, they are increasing the levels of confusion between males and females, thereby adding to the distorted mass thought energy levels now in existence. At the same time as a reaction to this phenomenon, males are avoiding relating and consequently are feeding the mass problem.

Added to the misuse of yang energies by both sexes is the minimal nurturing of the male by the female. This compounds the male's need for life force energy, which equates in his thinking to libido starvation. Confusing the need of energy from the female as the need for sexual contact, the male's tolerance of the female diminishes. This feeling in the male has the effect of stirring physical survival needs which will cause males to be more brutal and demanding of physical sexual contact, often resulting in domestic violence and abuse

These combined forces on the male; fear of monetary survival, loss of stature and identity and loss of life force which is seen as lack of physical sexual contact, causes the male to feel unworthy and without goals. He is without purpose, and a creator without purpose is a brooding angry person who does not desire to be in this life experience. By nature, if the male finds himself forced to leave this life, he wants to take as many with him as he can. We are seeing more and more of this kind of thinking throughout the world.

On a deep spiritual level, the male needs the female as much as she needs him. This drives him to bond with the female because she is his connection to the inner or spiritual world. He has a sense of the inner gift the female holds for him. The female with her intuitive nature provides the link to the inner expression for the male she accepts in bonding. It is the female who brings him to his spiritual truth.

Any male can test this if he is bonded to a female. All he need do is be aware of some problem he may have in his work which frustrates him. Then, at a time when he is in privacy with his female and she is happy, all he need do is mention the problem without emotion. She may not even know what the problem is about intellectually, however, out of her mouth will come the answer to the problem. She will automatically access the inner aspect of their natures and deliver forth the answer he should use on the problem.

The male must recognize that most failures in relating are the result of him not modifying his levels of emotional temperature. If he can understand that he needs to release aggressive yang thoughts about life before he communicates with the female, he can build a healthy, equal relationship. He should leave aggressive, work related thinking outside the door of his home before he enters. This is done by 'shaking off' energies he has attracted to his physical body before he enters the front door of his home. A vigorous 'wiping down' of the body with the mental intent of 'grounding' such energies into the planet beneath his feet will do the trick. This frees him of negative energy that has been attracted during the work confrontations of the day. When he enters the home he should refrain from discussing work with his mate until he has adjusted to the home environment.

MID-LIFE CRISIS

Mid-life crisis is the time when we realize that life has different meaning than it had when youth was the prime driver of energies. The first half of life we are preoccupied with the material aspect of the existence. All our upbringing and early education focuses on competition for recognition and money. But eventually we reach a point where we step off the conveyor belt and watch our life going by. At that time we ask the classic question, "Is this all there is?"

When the realization comes upon us that we have been on a treadmill, we often go into our midlife crisis stage. For some that becomes a long drawn out period, sometimes plagued with depression and a deep feeling of being without purpose. This is a period of adjustment in major aspects of our belief systems.

There are those who do not adjust very well during this period, and the result is continued confusion and a final acceptance of life being a drudgery. Others manage to eventually see through where they are, and their beliefs become adjusted to a new outlook on life. This second group begins life anew, finding new purpose and enjoyment. The mental adjustment and the acceptance of the change in beliefs results in an understanding that we are and have been mental beings all our lives. Learning lessons of the soul was not the dominant idea in that first half of life. Getting ahead materially has been the objective.

We usually spend the first half of our lives involved in the physical things of life, establishing economic security and building a family. It might be looked at this way: the human animal needs to be raised, its brain has to acquire a belief system with which to function on earth and to be readied for the purposes of the soul's interests in coming here. This period varies in time depending on several factors, all having to do with personal growth in matters of life experience.

Males and females approach midlife crisis in different ways and different years. The basic mental differences are always there between the sexes but at mid-life crisis males shift closer to the female usage of thinking. Females usually adjust to mid-life crisis more readily than males. This comes upon her almost automatically if she has children. The children leave home and she is faced with 'the empty nest syndrome'. For women without children there are other triggers. In either case the feeling is one of no longer being needed in a major way.

As a right brain oriented thinker the female is intuitive and already has connection to the mind. The male does not have this connection as he is oriented in left brain thinking. This means the female is more readily adaptable to the mental searching stages of life. We see this in churches and in spiritual groups where the females far outnumber the males.

When we wake up to the fact that we are really not going anywhere, we get the chance to work on the meaningful aspect of the human experience in this dimension, the mental lessons of the soul. We often come to the realization we can choose to work on anything that makes our hearts happy. We understand that it is not the goal that is all important, it is the way we go about getting to the goal that is important. Once this is understood we phase out of the mid-life crisis stage and become 'butterflies', we metamorphoses into who we really are. In a sense meaningful life really begins with mid-life crisis.

MID-LIFE CRISIS & THE MONASTIC STAGE

There are times in the male's life when he avoids intimacy with the female. This is a phase that is devoid of sexual interest. If he is in a close relationship in which sexual participation was the norm he will

194

act disinterested in the sex act. I call this the 'Monastic Stage' because it fits the concept of the life of the monk which is celibacy. The Monastic Stage can occur at any time after puberty, however, it is often an aspect of the mid-life crisis. I have included it here as a section of its own because of the impact it has on the male's sexual relationships.

A sudden seeming withdrawal of interest by the male in the female will oftentimes cause stress and fear in the female. His withdrawal from intimacy appears to her as though he has no desire for her and she has lost him. In her fear of rejection she will badger him and insist that he tell her what is wrong. He will not be aware of any rejection of her and will not understand her sudden change in behavior. This situation can lead to a breakdown of the relationship.

The female's reaction to the Monastic Stage he has entered is that she suspects he is being intimate with another female. All his verbal assurance that he is not seeing another female will not reassure her. Because he is in the Monastic Stage he looks at her reaction to his non-sexuality as childish and oftentimes pathetic. He has sympathy for her frustration, but his mental state does not allow him to take the situation as serious or threatening to the relationship. He says to himself, "She will get over it."

The truth is, he will get over it. The Monastic Stage will pass, however, it can last for a few months or as much as a year. It is a time when the male withdraws from material life and adjusts to the more mental period of living. When it wears off he will usually become aggressive sexually.

To save the relationship the couple may consider a sexual liaison which has spiritual tones such as the 'old' tantric ritual of *maithuna*. At least the part of the ritual where bits of food and drink are taken in a pleasant manner before the act is entered into contributes to good relating and what might be called spiritual sexual joining.

It is also helpful to the relationship for the partners discuss the Monastic Stage and incorporate it into their lives as a wholesome growth process. For the western man the Monastic Stage holds the danger that he will slide into a non-productive period which threatens the security of his family. This does not have to be a problem, however, it requires that managing the material life is kept in focus and acted upon to maintain unit security.

FIVE KEY MECHANISMS INFLUENCING BEHAVIOR

As human beings we have five primary mechanisms which motivate our behavior. They are: (1) the heart, (2) the soul-mind, (3) the brain, (4) male power, (5) female power. These are the forces through which we express the human experience. It is important to *understand* the roles of each of these influences in order to *understand* how matter is manifested and changed by thinking.

In reappraising these five influences, if there were an order of first importance, it would be the 'heart'. The heart is the keeper of record of all that is, was and will be in the life of the individual. Because the heart holds the lessons, that which is secret within us and which we must do, we might say the heart is first in importance. Yet, the soul and its mind, seeking balance, is equally influencing behavior. The soul-mind can be seen as the bridge between what is in the heart and what the brain uses.

The brain manifests the human experience. Nothing transpires for us unless the brain processes the thoughts each human aspect is wanting to express. The brain has the final say about what becomes material reality; it has the last word.

We cannot express anything without involvement of the yin and yang, or female and male powers. The male expression is the keeper of life, driving force, strength of the protector, manifestor of deeds and the will. The female expression is the giver of life, the channel for the body, the nurturer, the substance giver, the intuitive force and the bridge between mind and brain.

As I said, no one part has first place in importance as far as human behavior is concerned. At any given instant each of the influences is involved in the whole expression. All five, heart, soul-mind, brain, yin and yang energies are the motivating forces of the human experience. Thus they are constantly interweaving and expressing as we live and think. Thinking can be conscious or unconscious, however, these five influences must go on expressing continuously.

As to the use of and character of yin and yang energies, you may recall that the basic thought particles themselves carry different yin and yang energy contents. I liken the consistency of yang thoughts to being the building blocks, yin thoughts to cement or glue. When melded, yin and yang thoughts have a strength they do not have separately.

We can readily look about at humanity and see the male putting together things and the female giving them continuity and adhesion. If the female is removed from the male who is 'empire building', the empire crumbles. Without the yin 'glue', the 'building blocks' of yang thought lack adhesion and will not hold material form. I am using these examples to reflect the properties of the yin and yang energies. It is vital in the harmonious workings of all five key motivators of behavior that the yin and yang - female and male - energies serve to balance the other parts. Whatever the deed of the heart, the soul-mind gives soul direction, the brain manifests the experience, and the energy creating it is a blend of female yin and male yang.

If a male is projecting the manifestation, and he uses his own yin energy with his yang energy for willing the creation, that creation will be weak of form. If a male is projecting the manifestation, and he uses a woman's yin with his yang energy in the willing process, that creation will be strong and lasting. Couples who are bonded and accept the gender energy role of one another, automatically use one another's yin or yang energies. Consequently, whatever they create together has durability and power.

If you have no close mate, it is only necessary to include in the thinking process the knowing that someone of the opposite sex, whom you believe in and who believes in you, agrees with your way and would share their yin or yang energy with you. If someone of the opposite sex is willing to agree with what you think, then you have the use of their yin or yang power and are able to accomplish the same as a bonded couple does.

8

Consciousness
& Altered States

CONSCIOUSNESS

We are living in the age of the search for the meaning of consciousness. Everyone has something to say about it, how to raise it and how to improve it, but no one has yet clearly defined it. The word 'consciousness' is like the word 'miracle'. A miracle is something we cannot easily explain, but we know it has to do with something unexpected happening. Consciousness is not easily explained, but we know it has something to do with awareness and some kind of thinking. The countless books written about consciousness treat it like there are levels we are supposed to move through. Others describe it as if it were a spectrum of some kind.

There has been particular effort on the part of several consciousness researchers in the immediate past who have helped to focus attention on this subject. A few of these would be Willis Harman, Charles Tart, Julian Jaynes, James Hillman, Stephan Priest, Daniel C. Dennett, Larry Dossey, Ken Keyes Jr., and Ken Wilbur. There are many more and this concentration on consciousness points out that it is time in our universe for consciousness to be understood.

The dictionary defines consciousness as 'being aware' and 'being wary or watchful.' This is not a clear idea of what consciousness might be either. This lack of clarity about consciousness is further compounded by western beliefs and eastern beliefs, which reflect different interpretations. It is especially interesting and more confusing when someone who has studied eastern and western philosophies attempts to equate the two ideas of consciousness.

Science is determined to find the source of consciousness and is busy researching the material aspects of the human brain to discover what they refer to as the 'seat' of consciousness. Science will not find it in the brain because there is no 'seat' of consciousness in the brain.

When we examine what consciousness is, we look upon it as something to do with our thinking, as the dictionary implies. If we ask the question, "does the new-born baby have consciousness?" we can answer in the affirmative. So we presume that some 'place' in the newborn turned on, and that started the consciousness. It is this 'place' that turned on, that science has searched for cutting up and testing the skull brain in multitudes of ways, looking for that 'seat' of consciousness.

As I stated above, there is no 'seat' of consciousness. What we call consciousness is what the universe is composed of; that composition is made up of fields of individual and conglomerate thought particles in material and nonmaterial groupings. The universe is made of thought particles. Those thought particles and conglomerates of thought particles are there for any thinking system (brain) to access and this is what is consciousness.

When the infant takes in its first breath and activates its chemo-electro-magnetic being, its thinking systems automatically receive thought streams which pour through the human being all the time. Consciousness begins with the flow of thought particles through the infant thinking systems after its body is excited into functioning on its own. What is called consciousness is the act of the personal thinking systems receiving and expelling thoughts consciously and unconsciously. When the human brain is turned on through the excitation process at birth and the joining with the soul-mind, it opens automatically to the mass thought streams of the planetary sphere. It thereby participates in the existing consciousness with all other thinking systems of the planet and its creatures.

The human being, having two primary thinking systems, processes the incoming mass thought particles through: (1) the non-material thinking system called the mind which processes unconscious thinking, and (2) the material or skull brain thinking system which has to do with conscious thinking. For example: We all have experienced having an unexpected thought or idea and asked ourselves, where did that thought come from? That thought or those thoughts came to the conscious thinking system of the skull brain from the unconscious thinking system of the mind. Consciousness equals awareness, equals thinking.

As to the so-called spectrum, levels or hierarchy of consciousness, these need to be viewed as ways that thought particles are attracted and processed by the mind mechanisms, the skull brain's mechanisms, and the combination of both systems, when the two are in harmony.

Presently, what is behind the west and east insisting on their way of thinking, is the habits of thought usage each has locked into. As a mass of human thinkers we can and must move beyond this limited idea of the use of thought. We are supposed to be fully into the third dimension with the aggregate of our thinking, east and west, however, we are not there yet. Fear of the unpredictable (the miracle) has kept the west from expanding into the mind, and fear of dependency on the material has kept the east from expanding into the left brain. Both need to expand thinking into the framework of the third dimension or quantum energies.

There is an optimum quality of thinking to function with in this third dimension. I might best describe this by making the comparison of second dimensional thought and fourth dimensional thought. In two dimensional thinking we use two surfaces as our immediate reference for thinking. Things appear flat and without depth. In four dimensional thought there is thinking which we are unable to comprehend or describe as it is vast in concept. In between the second and fourth dimension is the third dimension; things are not supposed to be flat, neither are they beyond our ability to comprehend. Objects, ideas and concepts in the third dimension are supposed to be viewed and comprehended beyond a flatness, with depth and imagination and with calculable reason.

When we examine the present state of thinking of the average person on this planet we must admit that it often is flat and unimaginative. People get up in the morning, and as the day progresses they go in a typical non-thinking kind of way. They are not creative, nor do they consider the thoughts that are coming to them. How often do you hear someone refer to the fact that they had thoughts which they had to give consideration to? Hardly ever. Most people think as a habit. They simply act out what the planet is sending them based on what their essences and emotional temperature level dictates and attracts.

In describing consciousness, all there is to say is that it is the thinking being expressed at the time. This is true for the individual consciousness, and it is true for the collective consciousness. People often say, "There is consciousness in everything: plants, animals, rocks, cells and more." They are technically correct in the sense that all things are of thought particles. But human consciousness is different in that there is choice involved.

Consciousness does not end because there is a death of the body with its brain. The brain only stops processing the consciousness that exists. After death the consciousness continues on and although the brain is dead and can no longer use the consciousness, the person continues to use the mass consciousness during the death transition to other states of being.

Consciousness can only end when this dimension no longer is functioning. Thoughts are the food of this dimension that thinking systems must have to exist here. Thoughts as particles, non-particles and energy factors constitute consciousness.

CONSCIOUSNESS RAISING

The very words 'consciousness raising' seem to denote that we are getting smarter, that we are accelerating our intellect with inventions or computers that think as humans, as well as expanding human rights. This is all misleading and is nothing more than an expanded version of the existing mechanistic thinking paradigm. Some people think we are moving into a time of androgeny, and the many who are 'coming out of the closet', demanding equality for gays are all part of consciousness raising. All that may have its roots in the need for consciousness to raise, peace movements, the 'Berlin wall' breaking down and other examples of unrest, but the reaction to what appears as freedom is not in keeping with consciousness raising.

We have this general idea that consciousness raising must mean that thinking somehow grows or expands so that life becomes better than it has been. This could be the result of consciousness raising, but it does not give us a clear understanding of what it is and how exactly it is done. Let us go back to the dictionary definition which says 'consciousness is the state of being aware'. Aware is 'having knowledge of something'. Raising consciousness according to the dictionary definition is becoming more aware and more knowledgeable about something you already are aware of. This is a good starting point. If consciousness means thinking, then raising consciousness means simply increasing and making more quality choices of thoughts.

What greater way of raising consciousness could there be than becoming more knowledgeable about that which we are! At present, our schools are teaching that we are an advanced type of primate who has learned to use tools and imagination and has 'somehow' become self aware. Let me propose that what we seem to be (primates) has been a reflection of our limiting education and belief in an evolutionary, mechanistic paradigm.

As long as we stay within that belief structure, we are destined to limit our ability to raise our consciousness. As long as we see ourselves as primates, limited by a mechanistic evolutionary principle, we can do nothing about our consciousness but wait until we have evolved over eons into something acceptable to the paradigm that is greater than the educated primate.

If we step away from that limiting concept of what we are, we might raise our consciousness. One way we might do this is to make an assumption based on scientific principle. Quantum physics reveals that the researcher affects the answer to the question. Said another way, no matter the formula, there can be no answer without the researcher. Said still another way, it is because of the researcher that there is an answer. No researcher, no answer. This makes the researcher first cause.

Researchers are human beings who think, without thought there is no researcher. Now thought becomes first cause; before there is a human being there is thought. It takes little imagination and understanding to realize that the difference between the human and the ape is the thinking.

Science has tried vainly to prove that the consciousness of the ape can be raised. The ape will never raise its consciousness, because the ape cannot make a choice of thoughts. The ape simply feeds on the thought delivered to it by the planet. Whatever behaviors apes have displayed that are out of character for an ape, they did because human thought interfered with the thought streams fed the ape by the planet.

I have talked about different ways of defining consciousness raising. I have said that it involves becoming more aware and knowledgeable and that it also involves making choices and expressing thoughts of greater quality. I will now condense it into a definition that fits with the human thinking systems as they were described earlier in this book.

I suggest we accept the following idea of consciousness and its raising: consciousness is the act of processing thoughts as they are received from the planetary sphere. The end result of consciousness at any given moment is what we call understanding. Examining consciousness from this perspective, we come to the conclusion that consciousness raising is simply that act of deliberately raising the quality content of the thought being attracted and processed through choice. In summary: consciousness raising is the raising of the quality of thinking. Consciousness itself is the state of thinking, either individually or collectively.

When we examine thought particles and thought fields and streams of thought that are used by the human species, we find they have a mass meaning, or Zeitgeist. The thought particles which make up the mass meaning have attained destructive and constructive energies which collectively act on the human skull brain. For centuries planetary mass thought particles have accumulated destructive energy, more so than harmonious energy. Human beings, in their thinking processes, have slowly polluted the thought particles with negative forces. For example, at this stage of relating between the male and the female, the thoughts people have about relating are polluted with negativity. Relating between the sexes has become a negative experience for many. Thinking about relating as being a bad idea creates a negative layer of energy that feeds human brains. This has an influence on the individual no matter how much one wants a relationship to be a positive experience.

In as much as thought comes from the planetary mass thought streams, to raise the quality of consciousness about relating or anything else, we must raise the content at its source. When individuals expand their beliefs to include understanding the thinking processes for the betterment of the whole of humanity, we are raising the quality of consciousness. The more people comprehend the fundamentals about the power of thoughts, the more understanding of what thoughts are will reach others throughout the planet. Understanding how thinking works causes us to be more selective of thought, and as a consequence of selective thinking the planet will feed mass thought accordingly to the many millions who are ready to attract such thinking.

CONSCIOUSNESS RAISING & DIVINING

While researching for my doctoral dissertation on the source and meaning of hearing of voices and psychic channeling, information surfaced that seemed to point to an evolving religious paradigm that correlated with the raising of consciousness of human life on the planet. The records revealed that those who had major roles in affecting the consciousness of people were often doing it through psychic channeling. They were setting a path for others to follow which would lead to world consciousness raising. Being specific, there was Abraham, Moses, Muhammad, and more recently Joseph Smith and the 'new thought' leaders such as H. P. Blavatski and many others in the 1800s and 1900s. Added to these are the more recent forerunners of consciousness such as Paramahansa Yogananda who served to bridge east and west.

There were many others not listed here who have and are contributing to the raising of consciousness. What appeared to me as a religious paradigm turned out to be a combination religious and consciousness raising paradigm. Simply stated, the 'voices' heard by those leaders gave guidance down through the ages that followed a specific pattern for evolving human consciousness.

Early 'voices' of biblical characters helped establish the belief of masses in a 'one god' principle. In the beginning the 'one god' was a god of wrath, one who punished those who varied from the 'one god' principle. We find this in the teachings of the prophets and kings as well as in the Moses experience. Muhammad reinforced this 'one god' principle, following commands from a 'voice'.

The era of Jesus was accompanied by a change in the god principle from a god of fear to one of love. This became another raising shift in the mass consciousness of people. During the 'Age of Reason' we began another shift or raising of consciousness which seemed to spawn confusion and distortion in religious themes and this went on until the 1800s. Joseph Smith's (the Mormon prophet) hearing of voices resulted in a last surge of reestablishing the 'one god' principle at a time when spiritism was breeding countless of religious and metaphysical churches which appeared to confuse the god idea.

A new shift in the late 1800s eventually adjusted the one 'god' theme to a partnership with God by the individual person. Spiritism or what we call spirituality became entrenched in mass consciousness. The consciousness of human beings was turned inward in a pseudo partnership with the 'one god'. Channels who have been hearing voices over the last two hundred or so years give messages that reflect a partnership based on the 'one god' having given choice to human beings. This meant God was no longer solely responsible for what happened to that person. This raising of consciousness meant the individual could see him or her self as the god of their life, taking personal responsibility for personal acts.

One need only listen to the channels of today to hear the voices tell us that God is there for us, but we alone create our circumstances through making choices. This I construe to mean that consciousness went from a human living in fear of a zealous god who owned the life, to freedom of self expression and self responsibility.

The connection of these voices and the trend of religious change and consciousness raising is undeniable and extensive. They reflect that divining channels have been at the center of mass consciousness changes down through the ages.

HEARING VOICES & CHANNELING

Hearing voices covers a wide range of the human experience. It includes those who think they hear 'voices' but are not sure, those who hear 'voices' and think they come from outside the head, those who think some thing (non-human) spoke to them, those who think they hear someone from their past speak, those who believe someone who died spoke, those who are labeled as crazy because 'voices' made them do something irrational, those who are called prophets and holy men, those who are in institutions because they hear voices, and those who are labeled schizophrenics.

Hearing 'voices' (usually in or near the head) is not as uncommon as some might believe. By simply researching history one can discover that hearing voices has been a special ability of many people down through thousands of years. At the time of the Greeks when gods were many, entire communities and countries lived their lives asking the 'voices' for direction. Divining was an accepted practice and leaders sought the advice of the 'voices' through those who heard them. It has been noted in today's times that United States President Ronald Reagan sought the advice of one who heard 'voices'. Major religions of this world exist today because someone heard 'voices' or the 'voice' of God. Christianity is one. Islam is another.

Abraham, Moses, King David, Jesus, Muhammad and others heard 'voices', a practice which today is considered schizophrenic or psychotic. When we examine history's 'voices' we can trace the beneficial influence of such phenomena on the societies of the world. There are some other 'voices' who echo warnings of the end of the world, but then those have always existed. This is to be expected in a humanity which has an element that often wishes it already were dead because for them life seems impossible to do.

There is another level of 'voices' which one can find all down through history which seeks to confuse and cause harm to the listener. This is a lesser type of 'voice' which can drive the listener to lose reason. There is evidence that the lesser, trouble making 'voice' can be managed by involving the higher 'voice' which also seems to be with the listener of the lower voice.

Through my own research and experience with voices and in my doctoral dissertation I sought to find the source and meaning of 'voices'. I determined that we as individuals are subject to at least two 'voices'. One 'voice' is that which can cause us to lose touch with our better nature. Then there is the higher 'voice' we can call on to guide us into a better way of life. Those who are interested in discovering more about the higher and lower voices may read Van Dusen's book, (1985) *Hallucinations And The World Of Spirits* and the article titled, *The Meeting Ground Between Inner and Outer Reality* in J. White's *Frontiers of Consciousness*.

Many hypnotherapists, and especially those involved in regression processes, report having clients who have communicated with an inner messenger. The inner messenger is often referred to as an angel, a guide, a master, inner teacher and other. These messengers, from the perspective of my own research, are usually with us to facilitate our personal consciousness expansion. Time and again, I have found that voices from the inner are available through a hypnosis process. To me this says that there is a level of trance state, which all persons can access, which is the level of inner communication with 'the messenger'.

'Voices' can come from many different levels of consciousness, however, all of them access our awareness through the right brain hemisphere. Different forms of mental communication can come from the immediate energies around us or they can come through our thinking systems. If the communication is mental, in the form of telepathy or mental transference, it comes to our awareness through the right brain hemisphere.

MEDITATION & PRAYER

Years ago, as a Catholic boy, I would sit in church after confession and do penance which amounted to repeating so many 'Hail Mary' prayers. Years after that I found myself sitting in an eastern meditation, repeating my mantra over and over again. The difference, for me, between the prayer and the mantra is that in the prayer I was asking for something, in the meditation I was not asking for anything. Today I realize both of them were serving the same purpose; they kept my brain busy in a certain place so that the rabble or chatter of thoughts would eventually subside and I could be in a state of no conscious thinking.

There are many other methods of reaching meditative states. Repetitive physical acts that develop a hypnotic effect can place a person in a mental neutral state. This can also be accomplished by doing a repetitious movement of the fingers such as habitually passing prayer beads through the fingers. Every religion has developed its own special way of getting in touch with the inner.

Now that I have had years of training on the thinking systems and the soul-mind thinking, I have the understanding that what serves eastern philosophy is for eastern thinking, and what serves western philosophy is for western thinking. Easterners train for years to quiet the thinking and stay in a 'no place'. This 'no place', from the perspective of their beliefs is where they must go. Westerners believe thinking is something you do to get you somewhere and 'no thinking' gets you nowhere. For the westerner who measures his life in terms of accomplishment, hours of meditating daily can be a waste of time.

For westerners who are seekers of spirituality and who have not found it in western practices, it is natural to venture into meditation. What westerners have found through meditation is a quieting of the conscious thinking which serves to remove excessive outside pressures to perform. This is a great assist to relieving work related stress. There is no mystery to why meditation relieves pressures and stress. In meditation one deliberately slows down conscious thinking. Prayer, practiced as regularly and intently as meditation, will relieve the body of stress just as meditation does. I find that there are a few excellent meditation teachers, however, the average westerner learns about meditation from those who are barely trained or have little knowledge about the different meditations. They are given simple mantras and receive instruction to sit quietly and either block out thoughts or refuse thoughts until there is nothing.

I want to say a few things here about stopping the thinking. If we actually stopped our human thinking processes for an extended length of time we would die. I have commented on the continuous streams of thoughts bringing life force to the human body and that this is a part of the life sustaining process on this planet. We do conscious thinking and unconscious thinking. With conscious thoughts we either imbue the self with life force or we drain life force as we project our thoughts.

When doing meditation it serves us better if we do not approach the excercise with the idea of stopping the thinking. What is desirable is to create a neutral condition which permits conscious thought to pass on through the system without activating the need to mentally respond. Think of it in the sense of placing your automobile in a neutral gear, the engine is running and all is available to you, however, nothing can operate unless you choose to - process, organize and elaborate the random thoughts coming to you.

As a westerner, subject to the mass thoughts of the western world, I take the position that I am best served by being part of the western process of thinking. It is vital to the well-being of our body to be in harmony with those forces surrounding us. As the westerner, when doing either prayer or meditation, you must ask for that which you are seeking, as that is our way.

A word of caution about meditating. Going into a deep, prolonged meditation immediately after eating one invites physical problems. I recall several instances during my psychology training where students were instructed to begin class with a half hour meditation. This was usually at six and seven in the evening, at a time when the students had been rushing to get to class and more often than not eating hurriedly before class. At the first break, many students were complaining of violent headaches and nausea. These ailments were brought on by the defusion or separation of physical and astral bodies while the body was trying to digest the food they had eaten. If one has just eaten before meditation there is a struggle between the primal brain and the meditation process. The hindbrain has the responsibility for the care and well-being of the physical body and that includes the processing of food. The hindbrain needs to remain active as the body processes the food. Meditators often give a mental instruction to the brain to 'stop' thinking. When this conflict between self instruction and the need for the body to process food is going on the subtle bodies at the sub-atomic level get mixed messages. The result is that the cells in the body begin to mutate. It is similar to a person jumping into a cold pool of water after having just eaten a heavy meal. The physical energies were busy at work digesting food and are suddenly drawn away to take care of an emergency, leaving the body struggling for balance. Psychics often die prematurely from the mutation of cells because of the failure to understand that the bodies defuse and becomes misaligned during an altered state. When the meditation is over there is a major shift in the electric processes as the cells of the body work to regenerate themselves.

There are grounding meditations and non-grounding meditations. Grounding meditations are those which involve the planet in some way. For example, meditating on a mountain stream, 'seeing' it, 'feeling' it, 'hearing' it, are methods of grounding the body while meditating. Non-grounding meditations have nothing to do with the ground or anything material. Meditating on the illusion of something or on 'nothing' is non-grounding and causes the body to disrupt its planetary connection.

What is the purpose for prayer and meditation, and what can be the expected result from it? One should understand why one meditates, for what purpose, and then choose the meditation which serves what is intended by the process. Are we asking for healing, or are we trying to learn to be more at peace, or are we seeking to get in touch with the inner, the All-in-All; or maybe we desire to learn to channel, talk with our guides. Whatever the reason for meditating or praying, we must be clear, otherwise we will accomplish nothing except getting restless and wonder why nothing extraordinary ever happens to us in meditation.

So rule one for meditating is: know what you want. Rule two is: you must ask to receive. The asking does not have to be to a god; it must rather be an inner acceptance of that which you desire.

We do not need to sit in meditation for hours to accomplish what we desire. When your intent and acceptance is pure you can attain instant results. Meditation or prayer is not a matter of proving to God that you can sit perfectly still even though you would rather be doing something else. Many have the idea that it is spiritual to meditate. Meditation in itself is no more spiritual than doing the dishes. Being spiritual has to do with balancing your inner and outer life. Sometimes it is more spiritual to do the dishes than to be spending hours in a non-grounded meditation.

There are those who have been told and believe they will suddenly become enlightened in meditation. Perhaps they are not certain of what enlightenment is. Maybe what they are seeking are psychic phenomena experiences like hearing voices or seeing apparitions, which have little to do with enlightenment. We hear words like fully enlightened, self realization, transcended, astral, sensitive, mystic, and somehow they all seem to be connected to meditation. These words do have different meanings even though they seem related. They are all states of being that are accessed through the right brain.

Enlightenment involves more than right brain processing. The idea of enlightenment through meditation is founded in the eastern belief that life is an illusion. This is partly true. Enlightenment encompasses all that is, illusion and material life. Meditation helps to give us westerners a perspective on enlightenment that usually escapes us. The more we understand our soul lessons and ourselves, the more enlightened we become.

Meditation alone does not lead us to enlightenment or what is sometimes called illumination. When we consider the enlightened master we are speaking of someone having transcended to a high state of being. There are many masters who have returned to the human experience, and even with years of meditation fail to find themselves in the mastership level they attained in the past life.

Masters have incarnated many times only to find themselves mentally blocked in some karmic aspect of the human experience. Everyone coming to this dimension for the human experience seeks enlightenment at some point in their life if the karmic traps they encounter do not destroy them. This is so whether one is born into eastern traditions or western freedom. The enlightened state is attained through learning to balance ones powers in a manner which reflects ones ability to be truly spiritual. Truly spiritual means to understand the self to the degree that one can pursue the soul lessons and resolve them while maintaining a flow and harmony with everything and everyone. To accomplish this means one is able to understand all of the human experience.

Today we have multitudes of westerners seeking enlightenment through meditation and by following eastern teachings and philosophies. I think it is a worthwhile pursuit if not carried to an extreme. We are experiencing a major resurgence of spiritual seeking. Many people are having visions and hearing voices without having meditated. This is a normal occurrence when we move into right brain usage. This in itself is not necessarily spiritual. Spirituality is the balance of the right and left brain in harmony, in other words, applying the wisdom from within to the outer human experience.

It is through the right brain that we become those states which are altered states of thinking. Some of these, such as channeling, may require hours of sitting in meditation with a specific purpose or 'asking' in our thinking. Other processes, such as stress release, do not require long practice sessions.

The following is a meditation I refer to as 'Quiet Time' which works well for stress relief. 'Quiet Time' is a mental and physical state one can practice once a day for about ten minutes. This can be done anywhere, in your home, office or on the commuter train. Sit straight with the spine erect and the head well balanced by tucking the chin slightly inward. Take three normal breaths using the pit of the stomach, not the chest. Release the body from your thinking after the third breath has exhaled. Deliberately tell yourself to limit the rest to ten minutes. Then, whatever thought comes into your thinking, patiently tell it to pass on by. Continue to tell each thought that comes to you that you are not interested in it. Soon you will find that thoughts will come and go, and you can simply ignore them. In about ten minutes you will find yourself peaceful, aware and refreshed.

In the following section I give an example of a body regenerating meditation called 'Ener-Pulse Meditation' that does not require much time. It has as purpose the aligning of the rhythm of the body with the basic planetary beat, which allows the cells of the body to adjust away from mutating states and into a regenerating state.

As I have written above, meditation requires use of the right brain which in turn has access to the soul-mind. It is in the soul-mind that we can reach creative dynamic information. I teach students to access the mind for such information when it is needed. This is especially important in times of immediate need, when confronted with a difficult situation. An example would be the introvert who suddenly finds s/he has to address a room full of people. Usually this person would suddenly be at a loss for what to say or how to say it. This would be an occasion for what I call an emergency meditation, a meditation that can be done in seconds. I call this the 'Mind be my life' meditation.

The 'Mind be my life' meditation is a quick self instruction, a thought altering mini trance. It is a successful right brain accessing statement one can do in seconds. It works very simply. By examining the statement 'Mind be my life' one can read into it the fact that the person is asking the mind to take over. When the mind takes over it draws on its creative power and unlimited sources of information to do what is needed, such as giving a speech that was not planned for. The process is very simple. When in need of the mind it is only necessary to distract the left brain from control of the thinking. When the left brain is distracted, or confused, the right brain takes control, and then there is access to the mind.

To induce the meditation of 'Mind be my life' readily, it helps to be familiar with meditation. In the beginning it would be good practice to do the 'Quiet Time' meditation before using the 'Mind be my life' meditation. This is not necessary, however, one will respond more readily at first having relaxed a bit in meditative trance. In any case, practiced in meditations or not, anyone can do the 'Mind be my life' meditation. If in a situation where you feel you need help, simply do something to confuse the left brain. You could roll your eyes upward and backward to destabilize the left brain, this will do it. Next say the words, 'Mind be my life' with the intention of something greater than you being in your presence. then begin your speech, or do whatever you are having to do. You will be amazed at how well you handle whatever it was you were confronted with.

ENER-PULSE MEDITATION

A recent news article entitled, *'3000 Spontaneous Remissions'* was telling us that medical science is finally looking at healing that is not typical of the results of standard medical treatment, but is miraculous. Thousands of holistic type healings are occurring that can not be explained scientifically. Holistic healers and researchers have spent many years developing methods of relaxation, meditation, and visualization. Their successes are attained through applying and refining and practicing their methods. This kind of research is not the scientific traditional type, but is subjective.

Understanding the body means more than knowing about material parts, it also means understanding the effects of thoughts on those parts. Balance and health are influenced greatly by mental attitude.

When we observe the skin through a powerful microscope we can watch decaying cells flaking off as new skin pushes to the surface. If we scratched the skin, we could watch new cells fill the scratches. If the skin were cut, we could watch cells fill the cut in an orderly growth process. This process of new cells replacing old or lost cells is automatic on the outside surface of the body, and also on the inside of the body. We do not have to think about the process to make it happen or even be aware of it; the process of healing is natural and spontaneous.

We know instinctively that we can affect things by thinking about them. But when we do think about repairing the body, we are usually interfering with the healing process. This is because we do not fully understand how the body heals itself. Even so, we still try to heal ourselves, or others, and sometimes we stumble on the way and have success; usually we fail. What is important to realize is, the body has a way to heal itself.

If the body heals itself then one should stay out of the way of it doing the healing. There is only one way to get out of the way of the body healing itself, and that is to remove interfering thoughts.

Have you watched a small child sit and rock back and forth? Some children bump their head again and again against their crib or a wall in a rocking, back-and-forth motion. When we see this it disturbs us because we belive they are hurting themselves. Examinations usually reveal nothing wrong with the child. In most of these situations the child suffers from a cellular disturbance and is simply trying to get its body in tune with the natural beat of the planet and is working to adjust the body into a healing pulse rate.

All creatures and creations of this planet have a natural pulse rate which is supposed to blend with the planet's pulse rate. Even the lowly auto has a rhythm of its own, and the sensitive auto owner can 'feel' the vibrational beat of his/her own auto. Most owners ignore this vibration. However, if they kept a record of the kinds of problems their auto has, they would soon see a similarity between disturbances in their car's performance and their own attitudes and emotional and physical states of wellness or disease.

The Ener-Pulse meditation is a healing exercise I discovered while researching the effect of words, sounds, and syncopation related to meditation. Ener-Pulse is a simple and effective process for providing relief from body pain, as well as assisting healing processes. The Ener-Pulse meditation stops thoughts from influencing the body, thereby permitting the body to heal itself. From the moment you begin to sound the words of the Ener-Pulse exercise it takes approximately three minutes to attain a natural state of separation of the body from the thinking processes. A few moments in the natural state of Ener-Pulsation is sufficient for the body to be free of interfering thoughts, balance subtle energies and regenerate cell life. When the body is disconnected from the thinking processes the body cannot feel pain.

I have named the exercise Ener-Pulse because it facilitates the blending and harmonizing of energies in the body to the earth's natural pulsating rhythm. The Ener-Pulse healing meditation is designed to mobilize energies that maintain the optimum pulsing of human cells.

214

The planet has a basic energy pulse which the healthy human body harmonizes with. If we can prevent the constant stream of thought particles which process through the human system day and night from interfering with the primal brain, the body will harmonize with the earth beat and naturally balance and regenerate. The Ener-Pulse meditation assists this process.

Inner city business activity and traffic conditions distort the natural earth beat and confuse the human being's pulse beat. We call this condition stress. If one permits the body to rest quietly in a natural environment without mental interference the body cells will energize and renew themselves. A few minutes of Ener-Pulse meditation each day helps the body get back to harmony.

As with any meditation: it is important not to eat for at least sixty minutes prior to doing the ener-pulse excercise. During the meditation the energy is withdrawn from the physiological processes, such as digestion, and cellular interferences will result. The freer the body is from processing food and creating enzymes, the better it is for the cell alignment and regeneration processes of the body.

Also, before doing the Ener-Pulse meditation, or before any meditation, be aware of your mental attitude; do not do meditations unless you can be free emotionally. You can test your freedom from an increased emotional temperature by simply smiling; if the smile is forced, you are not ready to meditate.

Begin this meditation by sitting in a chair so you can align and keep the spine erect and in balance. If the spine is straight there is a better flow of messages and energies. The head should be facing straight ahead with the chin slightly tucked back; there should be a slight feeling of the back of the neck being stretched.

Take a deep breath and exhale. Breath normally, using the stomach.

With eyes closed, think of the tick-tock of a grandfather clock. Imagine the pendulum of the clock swinging back and forth, tick - tock- tick- tock- tick- tock.

Keeping in time with the imaginary ticking of a grandfather clock, begin speaking softly to create sound and vibration, saying:

"I - AM - THE - MOVE - MENT - OF - THE - BODY."

Say again:

"1 - AM - THE - MOVE - MENT - OF - THE - BODY."

Say again:

"I - AM - THE - MOVE - MENT - OF - THE - BODY."

Repeat the words over and over, keeping time with your idea of the tick - tock of a grandfather clock.

As you repeat the words, allow the body to rock in tune with the tick - tock of the words. Some will swing the body from side to side in a pendulum motion, and others will swing forward and backward. Let your body choose the way it wants to rock.

Repeat the words and rocking until the body comes to a stop of its own accord. Depending on your condition, you may rock back and forth a few minutes or fifteen or more.

When the body has stopped, the exercise is over; it has adjusted as much as it can manage in the one sitting. When it stops, tell your body it is all right to move and stretch. It is a good idea to talk to the body occasionally and tell it you know it is wise enough to tell you what it needs.

ENTITIES & POSSESSION

The subject entities is vast as there are many different levels and dimensions which sometimes interact with our dimension. I will comment on what kind of entities the average person might encounter.

What is an entity? When we are looking at entities as being thought forms, we begin to understand them. The human being is an entity, a thought form which is materialized in this dimension. The dictionary says that an entity is a 'self contained existence'. That is what you and I are, and is also what entities are. Entities exist on dimensions next to ours, they are like us only they have no material form.

Non-physical entities cannot exercise any influence on physical matter unless they get the energy from a material being. In other words, they have no power except that which they can get from a human being. They can access human power in two ways: one is for you to give power directly to them, and the other way is for you to give them power unwittingly. In the first instance of giving power to a disembodied entity, one does this most often through ritual. This is practiced in some cults (and in some religions) who encourage entities to become part of their worship. The ritual deliberately arranges a vibratory series of events for this. Beating drums, or chanting, or praying raises the vibrations until the energy reaches a pitch which opens the psychic door to our reality. The entity then 'wears' the energy being projected by the worshipers and enters the material world. Once an entity gains this position most are wont to give up material influence and do what they can to sustain the energy level of material manifestation.

The indirect way one gives energy over to an entity is through being fearful or in some vulnerable state in which the entity can assimilate the vibratory emanation. This brings to my thinking a client who came to me because she was experiencing the presence of an entity in her bed at night. The entity was beginning to get enough material power that my client began to feel its physical touching of her even though she was unable to see it. Her terror of this thing began to reach a level of near panic.

One might ask how could an entity get the energy for materializing in the first place; she was not even aware of any such thing? There are many ways this can happen, but I will give this one way to show how simple it can become reality. Let us assume she had been at a bar or social event where dense vibrations and suggestive sexual energies are common place. Many entities seeking to experience base human vibrations will often congregate in places with these kinds of energies. At such a place it would be highly probable that if she became emotional and densified her vibratory energies, one or more entities might stay in her somatic field. After following her vibration to her home they would sustain their connection to her by trying to intensify the dense energies she was involved in. If she were to go to bed with thoughts of anger or frustration and also entertain thoughts of sexual fantasy and or masturbation, the entities would use the heightened energies she emits to densify their own existence. If they attained enough energy from her they would attempt to use the energy to feel her body. If she suddenly became aware of a strange presence, her fear sense would be activated and as a result the entity would have even more dense energy with which to become more dense and solid in the material sense.

Many professionals do not believe in ghosts or disembodied spirits or entities of any kind. They maintain that 'somehow' the person having the experience with such phenomena is creating the illusion through their own mental processes or are having hallucinations. Rather than take issue with this kind of thinking one must allow everyone to think as they like. The reality is that if someone believes they have an experience with an entity of any kind, then from their perspective they have had the experience without question. If it is believed, it is real and should be looked upon as having occurred.

There are people who have an experience with an entity and doubt their experience. They find intellectual, 'logical' reasons why the event could not possibly take place. If this is done, the experience becomes buried in the mind, and like the caged animal which digs its way out, the buried suppressed event may at some time resurface. It is best to honor ones subjective experiences and beliefs and attain understanding of why one would have an experience with an entity (real or not). In accepting the responsibility for the experience (real or imagined) there is the opportunity to find out why it is there. Facing our fears in whatever shape or form, will eventually dissolve them. This is true for solid material fears, the monster in our dreams, or a disembodied entity. All these lose their power over us when we decide to stop running, hiding or denying and fearing them.

ANGELS

Angels are another form of entity. According to countless reports and stories there are many angel appearances taking place at this time. Michael Landon, the movie star of the television series Bonanza who has died in the recent past has been reported in many places, appearing to do the work we usually think of as angel work. The work of saving lives or transforming personalities in a miraculous way. We hear of Mary, the mother of Jesus, appearing in angelic form to give solace and reassurance to people all over the world. There are countless reports of personal angels appearing in the lives of many these days. Are they

218

real? Is this just some kind of mass hysteria? How can we explain so many people, over so many years, reporting experience with angels in their lives?

I like to relate this to my own angel experiences. I have mentioned that old masters came to play with me and teach me beginning in the 1920s when I was four and five year of age. To me, they were and are what is called angels. They have come to me over the last 65 years. Not just those original playmates, but many others, for different teaching purposes.

Angels to me are those beings who have chosen a life of guidance for those who are manifested here and are in need of guidance. I do not consider that those who receive visits from angels as being special or something more than someone else. All of us have one or more angels watching over us for the purpose of giving guidance if we are open to it.

Angels come in many forms and have the ability to transform themselves into what we are able to accept as special to us. Angels come in the form of kind old men, of wise motherly visions, of playmates in animal form, of pixies or tiny fairies, and some of them have wings and others do not.

In my experiences I have communicated with many angels who have come to me for many purposes. Often they come to me because I believe in them. In their not being able to get the attention of those they are trying to guide, they ask me to intervene for them. Sometimes I do pass on a message, and sometimes I feel I would be encroaching and I choose not to do it.

An important thing to realize about these angel beings is that there is a kind of hierarchy. We think in terms of someone being more important then someone else when we use the term hierarchy, but that is not the case among angels. All angels are equal; it is simply that some have certain things to do in the human scheme of things and others do not. Their dimension is like ours. There are specialists in knowledge about many things, medicine, science and so on. Their assignments as guides are usually taken in relation to their particular expertise.

There are occasions when we communicate with what we assume to be an angel, however, the seeming helper, guide or benefactor is ourself. It would be more proper to say, one of our selves. In the section

MULTIPLE PERSONALITIES & POSSESSION I discuss our many selves, or egos, of other lives. These egos or selves, at times will visit us for various reasons. One of those reasons might very well be to help us through a difficult situation. Or it may be that the other self has expertise in that which we are facing in this life and is there to aide us. This occurs more often than most people are aware of. It also points out that at times, in an unconscious state, we too can move to another time to assist another self who needs help of some kind.

There are angels who oversee the whole world process and work to help the human experience transition through what we call evolution. Those would be the angels who helped guide the Abrahams, the Moses, the King Sauls of the bible as well as the Buddhas and the forerunners of the 'Age Of Reason', etc.

Human beings have free choice and can choose their own social paths, however, human beings are always going to extremes and are causing chaos for themselves and others with their zealousness. If it were not for the intermittent guidance of angels, guiding us on the personal level and the collective levels, human beings would not live very long. A destructive aspect of our creative nature is continuously us to bring chaos on ourselves, individually and collectively. Angels are always around saving us from ourselves.

I have mentioned that our education system is going completely out of balance, concentrated primarily on left brain development. If this trend continues the left brain will completely dominate thinking, and humankind will find itself confined into dogmatic, authoritarian societies. This kind of conditioning results in 'mindless' control of human existence. Life would be rationed and meted out for the benefit of the machine at the top of the left brained schemes of thinking. This would ultimately be a global condition that all of us would have to live under.

At this time, angels who have chosen to assist and guide the overall way of humankind, attempt to influence thinking on the planet through certain individuals to steer us away from the left brain path we are on. They do this several ways. They work globally, trying to give guidance to receptive individuals to choose free ways of living. They also guide certain leaders of various fields toward the revelation that right brain thinking needs to be nourished. They may choose to come back to an earth life as a human being to become a specialist in a field which could influence many to move toward a more right brain thinking society. All of this is done to guide us toward a more balanced way of living the human experience. Angels are very limited in how much they can influence their charges. Humans have free choice, and angels must work in ways that honor the rights of the individual to make free choice.

Direct communication between angels and human beings is not difficult to establish, but it is not a popular idea. Societies are wary of those 'voices' which give advice to those who would listen. This is rightly so (to a point), for there are negative entities which would love to take control of some human being's free choice, and they often do so, creating havoc in the life of that person. For this reason people are uncomfortable if they hear a 'voice'. Society at large considers the hearing of 'voices' as pathological and unstable. Individuals are afraid to tell others they heard a voice for fear they will be labeled schizophrenic or 'crazy'.

I myself for years hid my angel communication. I hid it from my original family and my first wife and children. It was not until I was in my fifties that I felt I could tell certain people aspects of it. Today angels are noticed everywhere, and it is safe to reveal an angel experience for the most part. However, if one is a member of certain groups in our society, particularly religious groups, it is wise to keep your angel to yourself.

As to whether or not the voices one hears are from angels or some negative source, this is a personal matter. There are voices that are from ones angel. There are also voices from some source which is negative and possibly harmful. The idea of lumping all voices into a negative, unwanted category is not reasonable. Wilson Van Dusen, (1985) *Hallucinations As The World Of Spirits*, found that many hear voices whose messages are consciousness raising and beneficial to the life experience.

SPACE ENTITIES

I am reminded of a woman who came to me, asking if I could help her stop space aliens (entities) from impregnating her. Like many who have had a similar strange, life-like experience, it all began with her thinking something or someone was in bed with her when she was alone. The state she was in reminded her of being sedated. She felt she had awakened and someone was on top of her, and there were others near her bed. She struggled, but her seemingly drugged state won, and she sunk into a helpless stupor. The next day she felt as though she had somehow been molested, but decided it was all a dream.

She then went through a morning sickness stage with her friends telling her that she acted as though she were pregnant. She had forgotten the sleep connected incident and discounted the pregnancy idea as she had not been in a relationship for a year. After three months she began to feel pregnant and blamed it on an intensified desire to eat. She was eating more than usual. She gained considerable weight and her abdomen bloated. She had a ten year old daughter so she was familiar with pregnancy symptoms. She half felt that she was pregnant but could not accept the idea enough to get a medical examination; she blamed her eating.

Five months after her molestation dream she received visitors in the middle of the night. They appeared to be space aliens, and she felt confused and as though she was dreaming but more real. Again she was feeling dense and drugged. One of the alien beings told her they had come for their baby. They circled the bed and then she noticed they had instruments. She began to feel that her dream was suffocating her and panic began to mount. Suddenly a warm calm come over her as though she had been sedated. As she settled in her body, one of the aliens held up a fetus and the others exclaimed about it. She remembered frowning as the one who seemed in charge leaned over her face and thanked her, saying, "We will be back for another."

She awoke the next morning feeling refreshed and better than she had in months. When she sat up she saw that her stomach had subsided and she no longer looked fat. It was as if she had given birth and was empty. It was then the dream experience of the night before came to her. She struggled with the whole idea and then she clearly remembered what happened with the aliens. She bathed and dressed and slowly convinced herself it was all some kind of mental experience and she had never been pregnant. She was happy to feel freer than ever. It wasn't until the end of the day that the words, 'We will be back for another', came to her.

The aliens did return, according to her, and after several such experiences of becoming pregnant and having the pregnancy terminated she came to see me. Hypnotherapy regressions verified that she had been visited by aliens beginning when she was seven years old. Several sessions confirmed her impregnating experiences and the removal of the fetuses. After discussing what was happening I gave her suggestions on how to deny the aliens from controlling her.

She was certain they would return, and we rehearsed a set of possible questions and answers to confront them with. They had always talked her into acceptance of what was taking place, and I felt if she had a way of meeting their requests and to deny approval, they would not be able to go further. This plan was successful. When they returned she used the rehearsed answers and they did not force the issue.

How to handle alien beings is standard of how to manage any experience with an entity of any kind. I had explained to my client that if she exercised her power of choice and saw through the fear, no entity had any power over her. The power they have is hers to begin with, and if she denied them that power through understanding rather than fear, they cannot access the power she has.

MULTIPLE PERSONALITIES & POSSESSION

There is a difference between possession by a non-human thought form, whatever kind (alien, discarnate entity, etc.) and possession by a personality related to the self. It is important to make a distinction between full possession and temporary possession. The more we investigate this subject, the more we discover how complex it is. As we examine the many different states of consciousness - sleep, day dreaming, hypnotic trances, meditations, possession - from the perspective that all of our experiences are manifestations of our thinking, we realize we are just now beginning to understand life and the many 'strange' and unexplained occurrences. As we gain understanding of the thinking systems of earth, animals and soul-mind, we will come to accept that every state of consciousness is real, not just the waking state, that indeed waking, sleeping, dreaming, imagining, are all the same. This will help expand our knowledge of multiple egos.

There is considerable attention today focused on the multiple personality condition. The idea of multiple personalities has been around for some time. However, psychology has only recently, since the 1980s, included it in the category of pathology. This raises questions in regard to treating the condition. What does one do with all the personalities? Which of the personalities is the prime one? Is there a prime personality and should the others be integrated? There are many more questions that are unanswered. Where do all these personalities live? Who are they? How can one aspect of a person know how to do some special work and another not know anything about it? Why, when a personality changes, do physical problems, such as defective vision change also? How is the biology tied into the change of personality? Is there a 'place' where these lives hide?

There is one state of consciousness which offers us insight into multiple personality influences and that is hypnosis and regression therapy. When we examine the person's life from the position of multiple incarnations, we find that people have been many different personalities in what we call past lives. It is not unlikely that those who have multiple personality interferences are temporarily allowing a past life ego or personality to take control of their conscious state. These other selves were the primary egos in past life experiences.

When we consider how many lives a person may have lived, we find a vast source of ego personalities available to access or connect to the present day thinking self. After all, by using hypnosis we can bring forth these different personalities. Unlike our present life ego, our other ego personalities are bodiless and remain in different realms or strata of thinking inside our soul-mind, the sphere of thought surrounding and permeating our physical body. But the egos of past incarnations are vibratorily available to the present day ego and may surface under certain circumstances when there is need. All these incarnate past life ego memories may be brought forth deliberately by tapping into the soul-mind information. This is how hypnotherapists attain past life information, by accessing the soul-mind to access the egos. Keeping in thought that there is no time or space as far as the soul-mind is concerned, we need to consider that all incarnations are in progress together, at any given earth moment. When we shift consciousness into the soul-mind we are able to access any life experience in any period, at any instant.

Inside the mind no one life is past life, all life is simultaneous life. All the lives are going on at once. This explains how with regression work we are able to discover and examine our other lives. At any time, by taking the client into the mind, using hypnosis, we can 'open' the vision to any past, present or future life.

There are times in our present lifetime when these other egos, or selves, from other lifetimes manifest simply to support us on some mental level. This is sometimes done without our conscious knowledge. In other instances the other ego from another time may actually manifest or in some way use energy to help us; I mention this kind of communicating in the section ANGELS. We can actually call on these selves if we have the training or understanding of how this works.

In the situation where the present life ego of the person is not able to manage life, a past life ego may be substituted. There could be any number of reasons for the exchange. One common reason is that mental or physical abuse may have been traumatic enough for the natural ego to want to escape responsibility for the life. This is most likely to occur when the person is young and the aware state is intolerable. On the other hand, it may be a simple case of the soul-mind taking advantage of lapses of control over the thinking by the ego, using the opportunity for soul-mind learning purposes. Or it may be that the soul-mind has substituted a past life ego to prevent an alien thought form from entering and taking control of the body when the natural ego has temporarily lost control.

When a multiple personality or alter ego interferes with the present natural self it does so because of a need in the life of the person. The ego is normally reluctant to vacate the position of control to any other ego, no matter if it is a 'good' or 'bad' personality. If the person can easily switch personalities it may mean that the soul-mind is in control and is using the altered state condition to learn lessons.

I recall a situation where I helped a woman integrate an alter ego personality for the purpose of freeing the primary personality from obesity. Jane (fictitious name) was depressed because no matter what she did, she could not lose weight. During a hypnotherapy process she revealed that whenever she reached for food she had a strong empty feeling in her hands. Focusing on the feeling in her hands resulted in her experiencing herself as another female named Nancy (fictitious) in another life during the early 1940s.

Nancy was a teenager who was in full term pregnancy and about to give birth. She (Nancy) began crying because she had to give up the baby after the birthing, and she voiced her anguish over the coming loss. Taking the position that I was observing two people, Nancy of the 1940s, who was pregnant, and Jane of the 1990s who was sad and over-weight, I suggested they help one another.

I explained to the two of them the problem as I understood it. There was pregnant Nancy who had to give up her baby against her wishes and would suffer from the experience in the future, and then there was Jane who was suffering fatness because she was holding onto a false pregnancy condition.

I suggested that they talk back and forth what each could do to help the other. After some discussion we arrived at a solution. Based on the fact that the baby had been adopted after it was born, I had Jane (over-weight person) explain to Nancy that the soul of her baby had used her body to find its way to the people it wanted as parents.

Jane, after understanding that her fat layers symbolized her holding onto the pseudo pregnancy, made an agreement with Nancy: if Nancy could be happy with the gift she gave to the baby and its adoptive parents, she, Jane, could become slim and beautiful and maybe some day have a baby for both of them. Nancy agreed to this and they both were satisfied. Both personalities hugged a large pillow and each in turn spoke to it as though they were hugging one another. Toward the end of the event Jane promised Nancy, "When the baby comes I will name her Nancy in your honor." Though there was no real possession of Jane by Nancy for any extended length of time, the Nancy personality was influencing the body of Jane.

This is an example of using two egos to make an adjustment in the life of the primary ego. From the soul-mind's perspective, when we resolve a lesson in one life experience, we can resolve the soul lessons in every life experience at the same time (no time or space). The changing of personalities is a continuous process in those who are learning soul lessons. Changing personalities is common for most people in the dream state. In dreams, when there is a shifting from one ego to another, the soul-mind may be conveying a message to the natural ego, using alternate past-life egos to assist the person to adjust the life.

REINCARNATION & PAST-LIFE THERAPY

Although a major part of the peoples of the world believe in reincarnation western societies have not embraced the idea. From the point of view of the theory of relativity and the perspective of 'no time or space', there is no reincarnation, no past lives, as there is no linear perspective. From the perspective of 'no time no space', reincarnation does not exist because all things are occurring simultaneously. The many lives one has are all taking place in the now. At our present level of awareness (second/third dimensional), we can only understand reincarnation if we apply the rules of time and space. So, in this phase of our thinking, in the dynamics of our present western thinking systems, reincarnation as a reality is a time and space phenomenon.

Recently there has been a wave of interest expressed by leading national talk shows in past-life therapy and reincarnation experiences. Psychiatrist Dr. Brian Weiss by coming forth with his early experiences in regression therapy and giving national attention to it has done a great deal to further this field of healing. In his book, *Many Lives, Many Masters* he reported past-life experiences that came out of his hypnotherapy treatments of a patient. These past-life experiences proved to be the source of healing for his patient.

Marge Rieder, Ph. D., a hypnotherapist in Lake Elsinore, California, in her book *Mission to Millboro* documents the present lives of several citizens of her community in Lake Elsinore, California and their past lives together in Millboro, Virginia during the civil war. There is some pretty convincing evidence to substantiate reincarnations.

Ian Stevenson, in *20 Cases Suggestive of Reincarnation* (1988), presented case histories supporting the idea of past lives and reincarnation. There have been countless other writings about past-life experiences and reincarnation over the years offering proof of its existence. I recommend the above books as well as those by Jess Stearn who wrote about the late Edgar Cayce, a Virginia psychic and his reincarnation reports.

I have revisited many of my own past lives with the guidance from my own 'inner' guides or angels from which I experienced emotional and physical healings. Assistance from my guides was not limited to myself, but also included my wife and children. I want to share an experience of past life therapy with my family and our guides. This involved my son David when he was nine years old.

There were nights when David would come screaming downstairs to scramble into bed between me and my wife Joni. David would be in a state of panic and shivering from fright. After a few times of this we decided to ask our guides if there was something that could be done to resolve David's nightmare problem.

Our guides suggested we ask David to talk to them about it, and if it was his decision they would assist him. Even though we knew David was aware of our communication with guides, Joni and I were a little surprised at how readily he was willing to accept their help. That evening we sat in meditation together, and soon the guides addressed him, using his name and speaking to him as though they had been doing so all along. David responded as though the experience was a natural process. They first of all brought up his attitude toward old women.

One of the things that dismayed my wife and I about David's behavior was his attitude toward old women. He was a normal boy, but the thing I would get after him about were his sometimes berating comments about some old lady he had seen. For example, we might be driving along a street and there would be an elderly woman in a cross walk, and he would blurt out a comment like, "Hit the old bag." This shocked us and he would reap a stern reprimand. This was the first thing the guides brought up for him to consider. They followed that with the remark that his nightmares were related to his attitude about old women.

At first, upon hearing the direction the communication was taking, I thought to myself that the guidance was making an error if it thought it was going to impress David with a talk about his attitude toward old ladies. I watched David's face for signs that he was bored, but his expression showed eagerness to hear more.

Then the guides shifted the talk to a surprising connection between David's 'old lady' act and David's last wife in his immediate past life. The way the talk had shifted to David's past life surprised me, and I was even more surprised that David was nodding affirmatively as they continued telling him about his past life.

David was nine years old when this occurred. His guide proceeded to plainly advise him that nine years earlier he had been married to a woman who was angry with him because of how he had treated her, and who hated him with a passion. They had two sons in their thirties who lived with them and who were just as bad natured toward the mother as he had been. He had suddenly died of a heart attack, and this had further enraged his wife. At the funeral, in a passion of angry frustration for leaving her abruptly with two abusive sons, she vowed that when she died she would find him and kill him.

Over the next eight years she repeatedly renewed her vow of hate and threat to find and punish him when she died. The guides then told David that the year before his wife had died, and as she had vowed, began to look for him. Now that she had found him, she was trying to get at him through his dreams.

The guides told David to think about that for a day or two, and they would try to keep her busy and out of his dreams until they could talk to him some more. He accepted what they said and went off to school as though the experience were an every day occurrence, which surprised Joni and myself. We cautioned him to keep the experience to himself and avoid telling his friends at school.

Later the guides told us that for the process to have results, David would have to have proof established in his belief system of the information given to him. When I asked them what kind of proof, they said they would give him what he needed, and we were to cooperate by doing what they and David together asked of us. Having experienced a long record of communication and consistent evidence of the truth of what had been given to us by these guides in the past, we agreed to accept their way of handling the rest of the process with David. That night David slept without interference.

Before school the next day, David asked if that was the end of the problem, now that 'those guys' (his reference to the guides) had kept her out of his sleep. I told him that that was temporary, and his guides wanted to tell him more after school that day. When he came home from school he sat with us, and we listened to the guides and his comments which went like this:

Guide - "David, we are glad you slept well."

David - "Yea"

Guide - "David, we are aware you understood those things about your wife, but we also know that you are not sure if it really happened, is that so?

David - "Well, a-huh."

Guide - "Would it help you to understand more if your Dad talked to your sons on the telephone and you could listen?"

David - (looking at me) "Ah- I think so."

Guide - (speaking to me) "Ask of David those things he would like to know of his past life with his wife, Ruth Jones (fictitious name)."

Me - "David what would you want to know if I talked to them?"

At this point I was unsure what was going to take place. I had no phone number and I was at a loss as to what I would ask if I were David.

David - "Gee, I don't know, Dad. Maybe their names?"

Guide - "Their names are John and Stewart Jones (fictitious names). It is good if you ask more."

Me - "What else, David?"

David looks at me and hunches his shoulders with a questioning face.

Me - "What about asking about their mother, about Ruth?"

David - "Yea. What about where they live?"

Guide - "They reside in Lever, Kansas at 158 Winton Street (fictitious address). It is good if you ask."

I mentioned a few more things to ask and ended it with David asking how we would know what number to call. At this point I had an idea which I thought would be simple and be easier for David to understand, so I asked the guide what color their house was and if there was a trim color.

Guide - "The house is white with green around windows and corner trim. Call them now at 123-456-7890 (fictitious number)."

Using a telephone on which Joni and I could listen also, I had David dial the telephone number given to us.

1st Voice - "Ya-what-da-ya-want?" The voice was coarse and defensive/aggressive.

Me - (noticing David react as he watched me answer) "Is this the Jones residence?"

1st Voice - "Who wants ta know?" The question was curt and demanding.

Me - (at a loss as to what I would say, I said the first thing that came to me) "This is Roger Smith with the Chicago Fidelity Insurance Company."

1st Voice - "We don't want any insurance!"

Me - (speaking quickly) "I'm not selling insurance its about - eh - a Mrs Ruth Jones."

1st Voice - (after a pause) "She's dead."

Me - "Yes, we know. I am verifying the policy now that she is deceased." I winked at David who seemed transfixed at the moment.

1st Voice - "Insurance huh! This mean we got money comin?"

Me - (not admitting one way or the other) "Well I do need to verify some things about Mrs Jones. Her husband is David Jones?"

1st Voice - "He don't get nothing. He's been dead ages. I'm her son."

Me - "I see. How long has David Jones been deceased?"

1st Voice - "Nine - ten years. What difference does it make how long?"

Me - "I'm just filling out this form, Sir. Now are you Stewart? You are the legal son?"

1st Voice - "Ya - I mean no - I'm the son, but my name is John."

At this point I could hear someone else in the background curse and ask who was asking about him. That was followed by, "Give me that goddamn phone!"

1st Voice - "Wait a minute. This is a Chicago insurance company. Something about Ma's insurance. Maybe its money."

I could hear the other brother say, "Huh, we were goddamn lucky we got the house. You can bet that nag never left us any money."

1st Voice - "Let me see! - - Mr. - how much money is there?"

Me - "Well, you know I must verify - Let me speak directly to Mr. Stewart Jones."

1st Voice - "He wants to speak to you, Stu."

2nd Voice - "This is Stu. What's going on here?"

Me - "I represen -"

2nd Voice - "Ya, I know. What da ya want?"

Me - (feeling awkward and the need to end the call) "I'm simply verifying the information - and - is your house white with green trim?" I knew I had said something wrong at that instant.

2nd Voice - (after a silence) "Who the hell is this? You some kind of nut? If you're in Chicago, how the hell come you know we painted our house this week! I find out who you are, I'm going to kick your -!"

It was at that point that I decided to end the conversation and quickly hang up the phone. I looked at David and his eyes were round with astonishment.

Guide - "David, now that you have listened to your sons, we ask that you discuss this with your parents, and we will again talk to you before you go to bed. It is time to deal with your Ruth Jones."

David, Joni and I discussed the phone call. I was impressed with the level of questions and comments that David brought up about the phone call. During dinner we discussed it some more, and later when it came time for bed we went back to another session with the guides.

It was explained to David by his guide that it was important to realize that all things which were thought and spoken never were lost. They told him that in listening to how his sons spoke, and having his past wife in his dreams, he had experienced the depth to which hate and anger can carry a person from one life experience to the next. They gave simple explanations of the dynamics by which his former wife Ruth, using David's own anger, got the power to enter his dreams. Once in his dreams, she would then attempt to access his own angry or confused vibrations to cause himself some kind of physical harm.

The guides advised David that Ruth was aware that all of us were

The guides advised David that Ruth was aware that all of us were conspiring to prevent her from bringing him harm, and this would make her try harder to punish him. At that point David asked what he should do. They suggested that he go to bed and think about nothing else but meeting her and telling her he was sorry for his past behavior - if he really was sorry.

David assured them that he really was sorry about how he had treated her and felt bad that his sons were so mean. He promised that when he met her in the dream that night he would stay calm and try to make her feel better, no matter what she tried to do to him.

After the session he went to bed, and for a bit we sat on his bed to assure him that we believed he could settle things with this Ruth person. It was then he asked what he should do if he wanted to be friends and she did not want to be friends. I told him that his obligation was to stay firm in being humble toward her, and if she could not accept it, it would be her problem, and she would leave carrying that into her own future life. That satisfied him, and we all went to bed.

In the morning, when the rest of the family was up and ready for breakfast, David was still upstairs. I yelled up to him until finally he came down. I met him as he reached the bathroom, and I was shocked to see his face had caked, dried blood on it. I asked him if he was hurt, and he said that he was not. He was not aware of his face being bloodied. I took him into the bathroom before his mother could see him and washed the blood from his face. There were three scratches running down the side of his face and across one eye. They were deep enough to have bled quite a bit. Strangely, David thought it was humorous; he also said he felt nothing.

I asked him about Ruth and if he had dreamt about her. He said that she had come to him and he kept insisting to her that he was sorry, and that was all that he remembered. He added that he felt she left, still being angry. That was the last of his nightmares and of Ruth.

Later the guides told David that she had managed to get energy into his hand and force him to scratch at his own face. He was told that he handled the experience with wisdom, and she was no longer able to come into his dreams. He was free of her.

I have been witness to other examples of reincarnation, but this one is my favorite. The result was a greater son with much more compassion and wisdom. For a short time following this incident, there was more communication between David and his guides, but not long after that he advised us that he would not ask anything more of them until he grew up, as he did not want to get too serious about things. These were words of wisdom from a nine year old.

Scientists and researchers in many disciplines argue about the mental reality of the human experience. There are all kinds of positions on what is going on between mind and matter. Some think that this human experience is not a reality, that it is a dream and that the planet and our part of it is an illusion. I take the position that if you do something and you get results which affect your life then you have experienced something real and given the self a gift. It matters not whether or not someone else believes what you saw, felt or did; your life is your reality. If you see a UFO, and the end result is that you have marks on your body, your life experience changed. You have lived reality. It matters not if others do not believe in UFOs, it is your reality, not the other person's.

I have seen many people change their emotional and physical well being for the better after having experienced past life regression events. This has been the case regardless whether the regression only went back to childhood or infancy in this life time, or to a past life in 1400 BC, for instance.

Rather than argue about the validity of past-life regression, I take the position that it really does not matter if we actually lived in 1400 BC or not. If we went through the memory and relived 1400 BC, and the result was an emotional or physical cure, that is good sufficient reason for doing the process. Where one gets the memory to go back with is irrelevant. What is relevant and important for the individual who has past-life therapy is that the present life is improved.

As I mentioned earlier, I have experienced many past-life regressions. Becoming involved in reincarnation began with one of my guides coming to me in the middle of the day, in astral form, and informing me that I had an opportunity to work on one of my lessons if I would go into the past with him. I agreed to go with him after he informed me that in a past life I had been shot because of my arrogance, and I could now change this.

We returned to a lifetime in the 1800s where I was about to be killed by two men with guns. Watching myself in the scene, I noticed how belligerent and arrogant my attitude was and how this brought out the anger in the two men who were facing me with guns at the ready. My guide then told me to slip into my past life body and calm down my own emotional temperature as well as those confronting me. This I did - with some difficulty, I might add. By entering my past-life body and dealing with my arrogance at the time and humbly reasoning with my captors I escaped being shot. The very next day, in this life time, I was in a confrontational situation which nearly caused me to excercise my arrogance, when I recalled the past life I had experienced with the guide the day before and changed my behavior accordingly. The result was that the situation reversed itself to my personal benefit.

Past-life therapy can be accomplished without the guidance of a hypnotherapist. The two examples I just shared were guided by inner guides who are always there for you, David's through channeling of the guidance, my own regressions through a combination of self induced trance and astral traveling with my guide.

There are various other ways of processing past-life experiences and reaping the psychological benefits. Dreams are one of the greatest tools for soul growth, and we can learn to go to past lives using our dreams. Although much practice is required becoming proficient in dream work and interpretation, it is a great rewarding process. As the dreamer we can learn to manage/change our dreams. This is called lucid dreaming, a method one can develop to do ones own past-life therapy.

Self hypnosis is another tool for doing self guided past-life regression. After becoming knowledgeable in self hypnosis one can use ones ability as a lucid dreamer to guide ones past-life process while in a self induced trance. To attain this ability requires considerable step by step training in self hypnosis. Patience in processing is a great factor in these methods of developing self regression.

I need to mention here the importance of finding a wise, experienced hypnotherapist. One can be easily mislead and harmed by an inexperienced hypnotist with meager training. I am reminded of a prime time TV exposure of psychologists using hypnosis to expose devil worship that was nothing more than leading the client into imagination and fantasy. The harm to the lives of the patients/clients was considerable.

If you wish to experience an effective and safe past-life regression be certain it is with a competent hypnotherapist who has had considerable training in clinical and past-life therapy. Simply being a trained psychologist or psychiatrist is not enough to qualify the therapist to do past-life therapy.

One client told me that a psychologist had regressed her to a horrifying past-life experience where she had been attacked by wild dogs and eaten alive. The terror and pain had traumatized her, and she would shudder at the recollection of the dogs tearing the flesh from the inside of her thighs. The therapist had told her she needed to go through and re-experience the horror exactly as it had happened to become free of the memory. She became so terrified during the process that she ran screaming from that therapist's office.

A well trained professional hypnotherapist knows how to guide the client through such events without him/her having to feel the flesh ripped from their bones. Trust in the therapist is a vital prerequisite for a successful regression. If that link is abused, or never established, there can be no healthful completion of any process. The ability to be regressed into a past-life is often influenced by the belief in the therapist. There has to be a bonding of minds between client and therapist during a past life regression session. If either the therapist or client has fear or disbelief, the bonding might not occur.

Some clients have an intense fear of regression, and that in itself may prevent the past life process. This fear can be subconscious. Clients may vocalize their readiness to venture into past lives, but that unconscious aspect of them which knows otherwise will prevent the process from succeeding. The higher self knows the order of adjustment which is acceptable to the belief system. Often the higher self will reroute the attempt to enter a past life into a present life trauma or experience. It's as if it is saying, "Do this first, and then maybe we will move on into past lives."

There is an inner knowing that by processing a trauma in the present life the person can get prepared for the deeper past-life trauma or visit. For these reasons, I never get disturbed by the failure of the client to jump into a past-life experience, nor does it concern me that the client seems disappointed. I take the position that regression does eventually come; when it does, there is a greater readiness and acceptance of the experience after seeming failings.

I stated before that when asking the question if past lives are real or not, we can take the position that it matters not. If someone experiences a past or future life and can benefit emotionally and have an improved life, then it works. However this does not mean that any fantasy or idea one experiences in regression is therapeutic. The regression must fit the psychological needs of the client. Leading a client into fantasy can subvert the intent of healing.

The danger here is that if a therapist gets a client into a fantasy event about demonic rituals or child abuse, that therapist can unwittingly expand the fantasy to a level where it becomes an aspect of the client's belief. Once that fantasy belief is set in the belief systems, the individual will suffer the belief as though it were a reality.

A false belief, once entrenched in the thinking systems, will be acted on by the whole human thinking mechanism as though it were fact. The false conditioning can be extracted, but it is a lengthy process. The soul-mind can and will use fabricated belief data to unravel other aspects of the personality which may be in need of adjustment.

I have previously pointed out the position the soul-mind takes when editing thoughts coming from planetary thought streams for the person's use: the mind does not concern itself with whether the untrained therapist has made a mistake. For indeed, there are never any mistakes from the soul's perspective. If a person has a strong emotional reaction to any circumstance, s/he a lesson to learn in connection with the circumstance. The mind does not care if there are family troubles because of a false accusation of child abuse. It will use the fabricated circumstances to influence the person into more soul growth. Other minds connected to family members will also use the fabricated accusations to advantage to cause soul growth in their own life experiences. Morality is not an issue for the mind; it matters not to the mind if the deed was good or bad, reality or imagination.

As far as the overall thinking mechanisms are concerned, a false accusation is food for self growth. Examination will often reveal that the falsely accused person has set up a magnetic field of attraction of guilt, doubt and other self punishing thoughts which resulted in the false accusation. In other words, their own inner need brought the experience of false accusations to them. It is advisable when falsely accused to act as quickly as possible to offset the accusations. The sooner we release all emotions which give fuel to the magnetization of the 'set up', the sooner we will be free of it. The law of attraction will be broken, and the matter will dissolve as the illusion it was in the first place. Holding on to and dwelling on any emotions connected to the accusations feeds the process by attracting more mass thoughts to all those involved.

I have heard some individuals say that belief in reincarnation gives some the idea that life has less meaning. This is said in the context of, "Since I am coming back in another life anyway, what does it matter if I do not take things more seriously?" Actually, when one understands that we are here to learn soul lessons, and that ignoring the lessons results in a progressively more severe testing (or karma), then there is good reason to be the best human being one can be in this lifetime. After all, it is in learning to be that best human being we can be, that makes it possible to move on to greater spiritual learning.

Regression and past-life therapy is rapidly becoming an important area of study, research and education. Although clinical psychology, at the present time, looks at past-life therapy with some disfavor, and universities, as a consequence, have not provided any extensive education for past-life therapy, the public interest is forcing a need for more professional work in this area.

At present there are individuals like Dr. Raymond Moody and others who are personally sharing knowledge. There are also organized efforts to bring knowledge about past-life therapy into the mainstream. The organization that leads this effort to bring past life information to society and the academic/professional world is the Association for Past-Life Research and Therapies Inc., headquartered in Riverside, CA. This group has members in seventeen countries and is dedicated to furthering the knowledge about past lives and healing through regression.

PROJECTED FUTURE LIVES THERAPY

We can predict the future based on what is occurring in the present, provided that all factors involved remain constant. If there is a variable, a change through choice, then the future will not be what was predicted a moment before. This is similar to our weather reports;

based on all present conditions and on past experience, we can predict the future weather conditions with a fairly high accuracy for the next day, even the next few days, but beyond that it becomes less and less accurate.

At any present moment, mass world factors are moving all things in the world towards events that are certain to occur. If one accesses all the world information and sees it being projected (which some psychics do) then they see the natural course of events unfolding based on that moment. However, if one thing alters the predestined course, that then affects all other aspects of the future. When we think in global terms, it is easy to see that for the world to change its predestined course requires some major changes to occur. This is hardly true for the individual life which can be changed in its entirety by one seemingly small decision.

I have had clients who have a very consistent life program, and one can see that their life will change very little over a year. Then there are those who are not so set in their path, and predicting what they will be doing in one week is risky. It is these factors which make a fortune teller a good or a poor predictor.

Earthquake predicting is very risky because anything happening in China can effect the San Andreas fault in California; there is a global influence involved. On the other hand, what a predictable, stable person might be doing in one year does have a chance of being accurate. For this reason, if I do any future-life progression with anyone, and this is rare for obvious reasons (chances are there are too many variables), I use birthdays when projecting ahead. For example, if the client is with me in June, and their birthday is in December, I may suggest we visit their future life on their December birthday. This method can and does work.

Future projection is not unlike predicting the future except that the purpose for this process is not to predict the future. Just mentioning predicting the future in connection with any psychological process causes one to discount the process. However, when we recognize that predicting the future is a common practice in our society, we need to reconsider our first opinions. One is predicting the future when one says, "I will meet you tomorrow at this corner."

When we examine the idea of predicting, we realize that the

lowliest statement about meeting someone on a date tomorrow, or the most scientifically involved computation of when a space vehicle will pass Mars, are examples of prediction.

Scientists are now engaged in predicting earthquakes. To people with left brain orientation, predicting is more acceptable if it is done by prestigious groups of scientists. If a psychic uses common sense (left brain thinking) and makes a prediction that comes to pass, it is looked at as being amazing. I find a psychic's predictions no more amazing than the journey of a launched space vehicle reaching its predicted mark. The scientist, with the aid of a computer, is usually predicting the behavior of a machine related to time and space. In these predictions success can be given a percentage factor. The psychic uses his intuition (all of his senses in balance) to calculate the behavior of other human beings. This is much the same as the scientific process, however, it is subjective science and is outside the mainstream of accepted reality.

EDUCATION

There are many great educators belying the condition of education and the fact that students are ever more at odds with what is taught. From my perspective, the inability of education to keep up with consciousness changes lies in the fact that left brain intellectual conditioning is layered excessively onto the belief system of the student. The drive of educators to create left brain genius is slowly collapsing.

One can easily see that the student's needs have changed drastically in the past few years. Memorizing historic dates such as the day, month and year of a military event as being vital to be remembered is meaningless. The focus of history is planetary today. Not so much which country did what when, but what the economic or military strength is and how that affects the planet as a whole is much more important now. It is vital that students gain understanding of world influences and forces and how those affect the future of the planet.

There needs to be a new approach to learning and teaching that covers the total spectrum of education from nursery school to college.

The answer is in a balanced right and left brain system of teaching. Linear learning should be balanced with subjective learning, thereby expanding the individual's ability to think with a broader belief base. Focus should be on the individual's relationship to the forces affecting the world and individual life experience.

The world is presently caught up in a system of mechanistic principles that dictates the modes or methods of teaching. Essentially that framework is confined to ideas that spring from principles anchored in evolutionary and biological paradigms. These are good foundations for education, but they are limiting. They are limiting because they limit subjective ideas which are fountains of creativity. Teaching that is founded in the present day principles fits primarily with left brain functioning. Examination of left brain activity reveals a mechanism which creates structure that is limiting, whether in the material sense or the behavioral sense.

The rapid move into computers has been the result of the inability of the human brain to keep pace with ideas due to its confined to left brain dogma thinking. When we look at the idea of the computer we realize it is designed to give the left brain more ability and speed. What the computer has done is propel the mass thinking into a realization that there are greater ways to think than we have been used to as a race of human beings. It also has pushed us into some understanding of this time of enlightenment or consciousness raising. The so-called 'Information Highway' is forcing us to face our mass changes toward fully experiencing the third dimension and all the wondrous aspects it holds for the human race.

In the fall of 1993, I was teaching a class on 'Thinking and the Soul' in the San Diego area. During the break a woman came up to me to ask a question. From her halting use of words I could tell English was not her native language, Spanish from Mexico was. She seemed very shy and was speaking low enough to be sure no one else was listening as there were others nearby. To some her words might have seemed strange, but having had contact with people from many places and experiences I was not surprised. Our conversation went like this:

She - "Dr Costa, my name is Maria (fictitious) and I am from Mexico city. I was sent here to ask you if I could have an appointment with you this week."

Me - "Yes Maria, who sent you?"

Maria - "My guide sent me."

Me - "I see. Is your guide a human being or what?"

Maria - "He comes to me. He speaks through me."

Me - "You are a channel then?"

Maria - "Yes"

We made an appointment. In the interview Maria told me she had been channeling an ancient guide who gave messages to those who came to her for guidance. I asked her if her guide was similar to the entity known as Lazarus, and she advised me that he was more like Jane Roberts' Seth. After further questioning her, I realized she did not know why she was meeting with me; her guide had sent her and he wanted to talk to me. I agreed to it, and she went into a trance state, relaxing into the chair.

After a few moments her body straightened somewhat and a husky male voice greeted me, saying "Greetings brother seeker." I returned the greeting and asked him who he was. He told me his name was Atma. I asked why he was coming through Maria and what was his purpose in coming to me.

Atma - "We are aware of your work on this planet, Brother. I am the being responsible for the seedlings we have sent to earth. It is also my responsibility to see that they accomplish the work they have come to do. I am here with you to share information and ask that you assist this one as much as you can."

Me - "How can I do that?"

Atma - "Simply by doing the work of bringing the teachings to those who come to you."

Me - "I am doing that now, but I do not understand why it is important, from your perspective, for her to come to this school. Is there some particular teaching you wish her to have?"

Atma - "Perhaps I should explain it from our point of view?"

Me - "Please do."

Atma - "As you are aware, humanity is struggling to move into its higher vibration. We have committed a group of beings to assist in this consciousness raising, as you call it here. We are aware of the likelihood that the ones we send to manifest here will be lost through the system of education. For this reason we have seeded many of our beings among those who live in what you call third world countries and primitive areas. This will assure that some will not be lost in the intellectual teachings here and they will be able to retain their connection to what you term as the mind of the soul. Like this one here, (Maria) several have now reached an age ready for involvement in the world activities, however, as you know, without education or human recognition, their ability to speak truth and be listened to is limited. You have come to our attention through those who teach you that you are giving not only the principals, but are also guiding students to attain human recognition and status in society."

At this point Atma remarked that the position the body (of Maria) was in was uncomfortable, and he asked if I would mind if he stood and walked about as we talked. I assured him it was alright with me. Using her body, he stood and stretched, and then, holding the mini skirt out to the sides with both hands, he asked if what she was wearing was appropriate and respectable. I told him it was considered appropriate attire here. He then continued to talk about the importance of the 'seedlings' getting an education after they had gained the mind communication. After I reassured him that I would do what I could to guide Maria in the direction of a degree, he decided to leave.

Atma - "Dr. Costa would like to make the acquaintance of Maria's guide, Juno?"

Me - "I thank you for your visit and your curtesy and would by glad to meet Juno."

Atma had been walking around my office (using Maria's body) with eyes closed the whole time while talking to me. Now he stood before my desk, and after he wished me well I watched as Maria's body seemed to stoop as if she had suddenly aged, a gentle male voice greeted me.

Juno - "Doctor Costa, this is a pleasure."

Me - "Welcome to my office. Can you share a little of what you teach through Maria?"

I listened as he compared what he was sharing with my own work. For ten minutes or so he spoke on as though speaking from one professor to another. I finally had to interrupt him to say I had another appointment waiting for me.

Juno - (both hands held up apologetically) "Forgive me Doctor Costa, of course you have someone waiting on you. I thank you for the sharing of this time. My own work has been rewarded. I will be leaving now."

Before I could say anything he sat in the chair and Maria's body collapsed. Immediately thereafter she regained her awareness and asked me if I had met her guide. I told her I had and why they had come.

What is most important here is to consider the idea that too much education too soon is a detriment to mental growth. I personally am distressed when I hear about a pregnant woman already teaching her fetus about math or some other kind of left brain education. It is unfortunate that babies and small children are force fed left brain teachings. I find it odd that mothers, especially, cannot see that they are turning their offspring into human computers, limiting their ability to be free thinkers and creative.

DREAMS

Most dreams are messages from our soul-mind guides. They usually relate to the most dominant or urgent issue of the previous day or days and they try to tell us how to look at an issue for the purpose of our overall growth and learning. We can ask for a dream to help us solve a problem. Many times the message of a dream is, "Take a look, this is what you are doing", or "If you keep going the way you are going, this will happen." When we have the same or similar recurring dream it means the mind is trying over and over to make us change our behavior, and we are not listening.

When making reference to brain and mind and the thought processes, it is important to include dreams. We have mind dreams, and we can have brain dreams. The mind uses the dream to give us the truth of what is happening in our human experience. The brain uses dreams to gain or maintain human ego control over the thinking processes.

There are reasons for dreaming that have to do with things not directly connected to the physical human experience. People experience altered states that appear to be dreams. Often visions are taken to be dreams, but they are not. Astral projections often appear to be dreams, but they are not. It takes considerable practice to differentiate between dreams, visions, past lives, predictions, nightmares, psychic connections, etc. Here I write about dreams that are directly connected to the soul and its human experience. Every time we reach a sleep state which is beyond the interference of left brain control (often referred to as REM or Rapid Eye Movement stage), a mind dream is given to us.

Mind dreams are given to reveal the truth of what is occurring in the life of the dreamer. These dreams have to do with the chosen or unchosen path of life. They serve the purpose of keeping us on the path of lesson learning.

Dream work is a most important tool for spiritual growth and is the basic method of channeling gifted to us. Every child should be encouraged to share his/her dreams and every parent should learn the meaning of dreams. Sharing and interpreting dreams is a fun and meaningful way for a family to be in touch with what is happening in their unit. It gives the parents an appreciation for the child's growth and unfolding and it gives the child a sense of equality and accomplishment. I have seen many families improve their relationship through dream work.

WHY DREAMS ARE IN CODE

In contrast to the soul-mind which wants us to take risks, make changes, learn and expand, the brain is fearful of too much change. It likes things that are familiar and non-threatening, things it already knows and believes in.

It is important to be aware that as soon as we awaken and recall a dream, the brain takes control of the interpretation. Our brain has accumulated automatic defense mechanisms for the purpose of controlling fears. These controlling mechanisms will immediately begin altering the dream as we recall it, for the purpose of making the dream information acceptable to the belief systems of the brain. If the brain sees confusion, fear, threat of security and other destabilizing factors in the dream, it will change and distort the information. Because of this, the mind presents the dream in symbols, a language which the brain does not readily understand. This prevents the brain from distorting and changing the dream upon awakening. The symbolic information is less threatening to the brain, but it is also confused by dream events that do not seem to make sense and tends to dismiss the symbolic information as nonsense. Interpreting dreams requires an extended effort and commitment. The effort is in the daily record keeping of dreams and personal symbols. The commitment is in seeking understanding of what is happening in ones life and correlating that with the dream messages. The dream interpretations that have been used in the past in psychology leaves much to be desired. The idea that most dreams should be considered from a sexual perspective is misleading. I consider dreams to be the single most important tool for the spiritual seeker to attain self knowledge and balance, it is a form of divining and is a gift of the mind.

DYING & DEATH

When I was in my early fifties I had the usual ideas of death that most westerners have. Even though I had studied many writings about enlightenment and I was convinced that there was life after death, my old Catholic beliefs still had me in fear. Death was somehow connected to punishment for sins. Then, one day, one of my master teachers appeared and spoke to me about death: "It is time for you to have an understanding of death."

When I heard that statement from the master I immediately thought, "What now? Does this mean I have to die?" Not that anything I had been taught by them had been terrible, but death was another matter. I went into my altered state and found myself moving (in my astral body) through a murky darkness with the master beside me. I tried to take note of what we were passing through but nothing showed itself to me. Suddenly we stopped, and I could hear a muffled crying just before us.

The master's voice came to me, "We shall begin with this one."

As soon as he said the words I could see a person huddled on the ground. He looked frightened, and while sobbing, looked around as though lost. The master said, "This one has been in the dark since he died." I mentally communicated to the master that the man did not seem to see us. The master advised me that the person could not see through the dark, and that he was experiencing the dark world between the human experience and the place of light. He added that if someone dies violently, without having some preparation before death, being lost in the dark was the normal result.

I asked a question that I already knew the answer to, but it was answered: "As you know, there is no time and space here." For a second I felt my usual embarrassment as he went on, "Those who die in great emotional confusion must wander in the dark until they are released."

My next question was to ask how they became released. I was told that he and I were there for that very purpose. He would teach me how to assist those in the dark to pass through to the light, then advised me to just observe what he was about to do. I watched as he moved toward the man and called out his name, "William!" The man stood suddenly and looked toward us, "Hello! Hello!" he called, "I can't see you!"

The master stated: "You have been lost in the dark, and I have come to help you."

"Who are you?" His voice cracked fearfully. He looked as if he was about to run away. The master calmly said, "I am your uncle John, who passed on when you were a boy. Don't you remember me?"

"Uncle John?" the pathetic voice queried.

"Yes," assured the master, "look closer, and you will recognize me."

I watched as William squinted. Suddenly a look of recognition flooded his face and he exclaimed, "Oh, Uncle John! Thank God!"

Before he could say more the master told him to turn around quickly and notice the pinpoint of light behind him. The lost William turned and at first hesitated, then he said, "Yes, I see it. It's getting brighter!"

The master urged him to move toward it, saying, "You see?

Someone you know is in the light and is there to greet you."

William moved hesitantly toward the growing light, and suddenly his voice broke as he said, "Mother? Mother? Is that you?" Turning to me, the master suggested we move on and find another who was lost.

This process of learning about death and where we go after death went on every day for about four months. Some days there would be four or five that were lost, and other days there were as many as twenty to help through their fear and terror so they could find the light. After observing the master help a few into the light, he informed me it was my time to do the work of helping those who were lost in the dark to find the light.

One event that impressed me immensely was the occasion of coming upon a family of five who had died in an automobile accident. They were huddled together in total fear, and the mother grasped the youngest child as though something might drag it from her. This was a scene in which I was guided from moment to moment in what to say and how to project an image that was familiar and safe that they could trust and find the light through. Later I questioned the master about the validity of what I was experiencing, and it was this particular automobile death scene which convinced me that what I was doing was real. I was told to obtain a particular past newspaper, and on its front page was the story and picture of the accident scene I had visited.

That woman and her family was one of my first successes in helping those who needed to find the light. I cannot say I was a great success in the beginning, as the first man I tried to help became even more frightened than he had been, when I attempted to help him. It took me a few times of practice to be able to mentally influence the person or persons to believe that I was the image I was projecting to them.

Part of the process was learning to scan their minds to determined who they might trust. Once I was able to do that, it became simple to act out the part and get them to see enough of the personality to recognize who I was supposed to be. That image, of course, had to be someone they could trust and believe in. After I convinced them I was there as a trusted one, I could get them to see the light. Once I got them started to see the light there was always someone who came out of the light who would take them further into it.

These were my initial lessons about death and what happens after death. As the teaching went on I learned about the many conditions that one might experience at the time for death, not just after death, but what preparing for the death experience can mean to those dying slowly from old age or sickness.

Death is not painful physically; it can be a strain if fear is involved. There are many that die who linger between the material experience and the 'other side' - they need help of various sorts to make that transition.

Eventually I learned a considerable amount about dying, and if I were to give one word of advice about it, it is that death is more of a beginning than one can imagine. There is much to do after death, usually in preparation for the return to the material third dimension. Most of us fail to learn our soul lessons, and we return to work on those again and again.

For most people dying is a confusing and frightening idea, it certainly falls into the category of mystery and the unknown. Anything that is unknown, the brain is fearful of. The brain's thinking system is designed to suspect and be cautious of anything that is not understood. We get a lot of negative information about death and dying and most people would just as soon not think about it.

If we manage to live a life that has not driven us to consider suicide, we do reach a point of considering death in old age. When the idea of retirement comes, most people are at an age where body parts begin to malfunction. This is the rest home stage for most people in western society. When this stage is reached it is usually all 'down hill' until death overcomes the body. One can visit rest home after rest home and see those and feel the fear and pain of knocking at death's door, begging God to take them and end their misery. What can we do about this mental state? I pointed out earlier that the fear of death has its roots in the fact that there is little in the belief system about death except confusion, pain and misery.

During a period when I was working in nursing homes for the elderly, my guides instructed me to give understanding to those who were about to transition through death. The process was simple and was based on assuring those who were dying that there was someone waiting for them on the 'other side' to assist their transition. Also, that they could ask for whoever was waiting for them to appear and make themselves known before the death. In addition they could ask that someone to be with them while they make their transition.

It was always a heart warming welcome for me when I would visit one of those elderly and have them whisper to me that their 'friend' had come to visit and agreed to help them leave. I recall one woman who, as I entered her room I heard talking to someone. She immediately stopped talking as I entered. Then she said to me, "Oh, thank goodness it's you, and I can tell you!" I encouraged her to tell me. Then she asked in a happy way, "Can you guess who I was just talking to?"

"No," I urged, "who?" She answered like a young child with a secret, "Well, like you told me. I asked, and my sister who I love, who passed on three years ago, came last night, and she's promised to help me go. What do you think of that?"

I assured her that what happened was special, and it was important for her to tell her daughter when she visited that day, as her time to leave must be quite near. She died happy three days later, and her daughter took the time to let me know that she herself now had a completely different way of looking at death because of the change her mother had experienced. Her mother had gone from being fearful and crying each time she had seen her daughter to three days of peace and happy conversations before she passed on.

Someone once said, "We've all died many times, but it hasn't killed us yet." Death is not the end of life, it is merely a transition, but it is without doubt the most neglected and misunderstood of the many stages and transitions we go through as human beings. When we finally do come to death, most of us are ill prepared to face it, or deal with it, or appreciate it. For death can be a beautiful, painless and joyous experience. Many who have gone through the near death experience (NDE) describe this blissful state.

DYING & THE IMMUNE SYSTEM

Science these days is heavily engaged in trying to determine what can be done about restoring the immune system. Tests show that when a person's cell system is deteriorating, T cells' which function to eliminate mutated cells, fail to do the work. According to the tests, if the T cells are not doing their work, or if there is substantial deficiency of T cells, the person gets worse and dies. The supposition is that if science can create the right chemical to boost the T cell activity, the T cells will do the job and end the disease.

Other tests have shown that if the person has a sudden mental upturn in what we call 'spirit', T cells increase and attack the illness, causing the person to 'get better'. This has been shown to happen to patients responding positively to laughter and funny movies, certain kinds of music, certain types of visualization and sometimes through the visits of a person or an animal who can 'raise the spirits' of the sick patient. Unfortunately, those same tests more often than not reveal that after a while the laughing, the music, the visualization and the spirits raising cannot do the job anymore. Once again the T cells begin to stop doing their job as they diminish in number, and the patient gets worse physically.

What is it we are observing? What is going on? First the patient gets sick, T cells are lacking. Then certain positive psychological influences on the patient seems to correlate with an increase in T cells, and the patient gets better. Finally, the psychological influence appears to be losing the ability to maintain or increase the T cell level, and then the patient gets worse again.

What is happening to the so-called immune system cannot be measured by scientific testing. This is because the so-called immune system does not exist as a material process. The T cell activity is a response to the infusion of life force into the electro-magnetic/chemical body. The words 'immune system' were designed to give a name to what 'appears' to be happening in the body based on the seeming behavior of what is termed the T cell. What is being described as the immune system is nothing more than the body reacting to a change in the thinking of the person; this is as obvious as it can be.

Science has not yet learned what thinking is, what it does, where it comes from and how it effects all the cells of the body, including the T cells. Educators make a distinction between 'hard science' and 'soft science', psychology being 'soft' because of the lack of repeatability of tests. But for a long time now we know that there are exceptions to the rules of hard science repeatability. Many times tests have conveniently been swept under the rug and ignored because they don't fit the accepted equation. The 'spontaneous remission' is an example. Soon we will have to acknowledge that there are no true hard sciences.

Putting chemicals in the body can affect it in one way only, and that is in helping the body to balance its chemical composition. The immune system is affected primarily by the thinking of the person. Negative, fearful and depressed thinking robs the system of life force and lowers the effectiveness of the immune system (regeneration). For a restoration of the body's health it is not enough to use laughter and other temporary psychological crutches, but rather the personal reasons and beliefs for the continued attraction and use of depressed thinking must be found and altered.

DYING & SIGNS FROM THE INNER

Just as we get messages during our night time dreams which are in symbolic, coded form, so can we look at every single incidence in our waking life as a symbolic message from the inner. That wise, all knowing part of us is always busy at work, waving flags to get our attention, building roadblocks to keep us from hurting ourselves, or using a 'two-by-four' if all else fails. The mind uses thousands of ingenious ways to assist us in becoming wise and abandon the wayward ways of our sometimes primitive destructive, 'pea-brained' behavior.

Recently I received an 'inner' message about the cause of multiple sclerosis (MS). It said to use the opossum to explain it. What could the opossum have to do with MS? What is the opossum known for? It plays dead. Simply stated, this tells us that the person who has MS begins the disease by 'playing dead'. This does not mean they lay down and physically play dead. The action of the opossum is symbolic. But anyone has heard it said, "When you think something often enough it will happen". If we think about 'not living' (playing dead) enough times, we begin to die.

What better way to die than to have an honorable disease like MS? Oh yes! We must choose an honorable way to do ourselves in. Collectively we reject the idea of suicide, so we cannot consider outright self destruction. However, there are many honorable suicide methods: MS, cancer, Alzheimer's disease and others. Death through suicide by disease has accelerated in spite of the tons of medication being consumed in our society. The words 'not living' are significant in all this. The primary factor in living or dying is making choices in the life. If we are not expressing life, we are dying. Our ego belief is that if we do not actually choose suicide we are OK. However, life is simple and exact; it can express outwardly only what is in the inner. The ego only facilitates what is deeper within us. If we are not expressing life openly and acting accordingly, then life automatically begins to dissolve (cells mutate).

Why do we die? We can blame it on old age or contagious diseases or even accidents. These are the simple surface explanations. Yet there are those situations where for no apparent reason someone simply wastes away and dies. What could be the reason for wasting away when you say you don't want to die? There is plenty of evidence to show that if someone retires from work because of age they often will go through a change which ends in early death. Why? Obviously the answer to unexplained deaths and unwanted diseases lies in something going on in the 'inner' of the person. 'Inner' of course does not mean physical inner, but psychic or spiritual 'inner', or what I call 'things of the heart', which are our true and often secret desires.

Since we are mental human beings, made of thought particles, we manifest our entire condition using thought. What we see manifested in the body, are the symbols of what is going on in that 'inner' part of our life. If something within us wants us to punish ourselves, then the body begins to die. When the soul-mind wants us to take a serious look at ourselves it uses the body to give us a message. If we are not supposed to 'go ahead' with something, but persist in doing it anyways, we may manifest a problem with being able to walk. If the mind does not want us to say something, and we ignore the subtile signs, it may arrange to prevent us from using the voice, maybe with a sore throat or even a throat cancer. In the case of MS and similar diseases we often find these persons active and seemingly busy in their work. It would seem that they would be the opposite example of those who made an 'inner' choice to die. Close examination reveals that they are highly involved in "playing out" the death process in a grand way.

This message about symbols of 'not living' is of great significance today, with so much confusion about survival, physically, emotionally, financially, politically, spiritually and philosophically. Staying confused and fearful is a certain ticket to not expressing life - not living. Death can come quickly, accelerated by anger and frustration or slowly, through diseases, if one does not express the self through life.

Several years ago I was asked to help a woman who was hours from death. Her body was racked with cancer. She was in a hospital and last rites had been given her by a priest, and she was expected to die momentarily. She was a prominent sculptress and her condition had been brought to my attention through a mutual friend. I had been previously advised by the masters to not be involved in healing practices while in my training. On this occasion they advised me to make an exception, if I so chose, after reminding me to be cautious of those who inwardly did not want to live.

I contacted her guides and received an 'inner' message that she had made a recent decision within herself to let go of her confusion and live. With this knowledge I made the choice to help. I also learned from her guidance that she had little life force left and did not have enough energy to reverse the cell process from dying to living. I was asked by her guides to share energy with her that she might heal herself. I provided the energy and she had a total remission (healing) of the cancer in a matter of days and left the hospital.

This had been a vibrant woman who had become frustrated and confused about her life as she tried unsuccessfully to help certain members of her family in their personal lives. Feeling she had failed her family she had quit her work and could do nothing productive. This amounted to a death wish. In a very short time she developed cancer and was at death's door.

On her death bed, her choice to ignore her family members and their personal problems and become involved in her artistry reversed her physical dying process. She had made an 'asking' of that which is greater than herself for help to live. Without having made that choice to live for herself she would have died. After her healing she went on and completed some noted sculptures.

Years later I received a call that my sculptress friend was back in the hospital with cancer again. I was told that she had completed her work and wanted to die but couldn't leave.

I again consulted with her guides who confirmed that she wished to transition. I went to the hospital to see her. Her husband greeted me and said he and the family were honoring her wishes to leave but she had been unable to die. He said the doctor could not understand, from her condition, how her body continued to live. She would lapse into a coma but would reawaken frustrated.

She was glad to see me, and when I asked why she had me called, she explained that on several occasions she had left but there was no one to meet her and she became fearful and could not let go. I asked her guides about the situation, and they told me that she had to realize that it would be she who would meet herself. I gave her the message. Hearing this, she said her last goodby to her husband, smiled and closed her eyes. In less than a moment we watched the last breath leave her, and she died smiling.

There seems to be a contradiction about believing in living or dying. Some who are dying from a disease are without motivation, they lay about as though waiting to die. Others who are dying are active in their work and will often tell you they are not giving in to the illness. They insist that they do not wish to die and are fighting to live. They can be emphatic and insistent on their will to live being real. The appearance is that they are involved in life, and they do seem to not wish to die. However, the truth is that if they are dying of the disease by medical standards, then they have an inner desire to transition from this plain. It is not usually the conscious brain which chooses to die. It is the inner (subconscious) of the being which makes the decision to transition.

NEAR DEATH EXPERIENCE

We now have reports from hundreds, if not thousands, of people who have been pronounced clinically dead and through modern medical technology were brought back to life. Raymond Moody's *Life after Life* is the best known source of such accounts. Nearly all of them tell similar stories of how they died and then had an 'out of body' experience. Often they would suddenly find themselves above their body, watching everyone working on reviving their body. They tell of moving through a tunnel and into a light where they were greeted by a departed loved one. On returning back to the physical body, they findtheir attitude and beliefs about life and death profoundly changed. Much of the medical profession wants to discount the 'realness' of these experiences as being merely chemical and biological reactions in the brain affecting the neural system and causing a dreamlike illusion. They insist it is nothing more than a reaction to body trauma, triggering a brain controlled synaptic process. They do not notice they have said 'dreamlike' in their interpretation. They use 'dreamlike' as if they know what dreams are or where they come from, and as long as they said 'dreamlike', they have answered what the Near Death Experience (NDE) is. Medical researchers know no more about dreams than they do about the NDE. Being at a loss as how to explain NDEs they make the error of saying 'dreamlike' as though that explained something. They are guessing at what the NDE experience is.

Well-meaning medical researchers are touting the greatness of the brain. For several decades they have sliced and measured the brain, believing it holds the last mystery of the human being, indeed the universe. To me all this probing into the brain looks like the search for some great key, and some day they expect to open a little chamber in the brain housing a tiny little man with a long beard sitting on a throne, and they announce, "Well, we have finally found him!" Science treats the brain as though it were God.

The brain is only a part of the thinking mechanisms of the human being and it is used by the soul-mind in the NDE. One may go through a NDE when life has reached a crisis and one part of the person wants to die and another doesn't. It is the soul's way of saying: "Its time to face facts." Those who have NDEs almost always report having to return to the physical life experience because something was left undone in the life.

The tunnel of light in the blackness reported by many is a path taken by their astral body to the 'other side.' It is your astral body that is up on the ceiling, watching doctors trying to save the life. This body, with its subtle energy ability to function mentally through the soul-mind, is what we use to connect the human material dimension and the non material dimensions. As long as we are still connected to the third dimension we have an astral body.

Some people are able to move out of their physical body at will and travel to other places and other times using their astral body. This is known as astral traveling. Robert Monroe's books *Far Journeys* and *Journeys Out of the Body* provide good information on astral travel and out of body experiences.

During my training with the masters (see section on DEATH & DYING) I was led, using my astral body, into the level one is in when first experiencing transition or death. In this dimension I was guided to experiences where a person or persons had died sudden violent deaths and found themselves surrounded by blackness and in great fear. They were unaware that they had transitioned and would either be near their dead human body or had wandered away from it in confusion and panic.

The training I was undergoing with the masters was helping these lost persons in their astral body to find their way to the next level. An experience of helping would go like this. The person who had died was usually in confusion and great fear. I would approach the person or persons who had died, calm their fears and lead them into finding the lighted tunnel. This out of body training went on daily for several months.

NDEs are not simply some neural or brain chemical responses. An NDE is the first stage of a human being facing transition and being informed of having to stay in human form for soul lesson reasons. The NDE thinking processes take place in the soul-mind of the person and are transmitted to the brain to be remembered for soul growth reasons. This can take place even while the brain is ruled 'brain dead'.

Recently, on national television, Diane Sawyer hosted a show called 'Near Death Experiences'. In one medical emergency room researchers had placed a sign which was visible only from above everyone's head. The purpose for the sign was to test whether or not a person experiencing a NDE, floating above everyone, would read it and report so. During that research there had been no reports of anyone reading the sign. It was determined that there was not enough opportunity to develop a valid testing condition of the sign reading.

Individuals trained in 'astral traveling' are able to read signs placed where they can see them while out of the body. This is similar to the NDE except that the person doing the out of body traveling is not in a near death situation. The point here is that we can travel out of the body for different reasons and while in different altered states of consciousness. We all do this far more regularly than most people realize. Out of body movements are always directed by the soul-mind, we can consciously choose to release ourselves to the mind experience, or it can take place when we are in an unconscious state.

HYPNOSIS

In the mid 1700s Frederick Anton Mesmer created a stir in the world of medicine when he applied his theory of 'magnetic fluids' to healing. In his 1766 medical dissertation he suggested that the two halves of the human body (right and left) are acting as magnetic poles. His position was that the will of the person controlled the fluids or gases and that hypnosis influenced the human being by influencing the will.

Mesmer treated thousands, and when his work reached a point where he was using magnetised water and different metal rods in the healing processes he was ridiculed and eventually disgraced. However, for a while hypnosis was the primary tool of the early medical doctor/psychiatrist/psychologist, and because it could not be explained and was a power easily abused, the medical profession eventually ignored it.

Hypnotism has been around for thousands of years, but because it was never accorded a rational explanation it failed to sustain its place as a healing tool. World War One, with so many wounded suffering from trauma, created a need for hypnosis to come back into the medical treatment process. Many soldiers were helped through hypnosis by those trained to use it.

Today, with all our sophistication, there are those who consider hypnosis an unworthy approach to treatment of mental problems. But the recent consciousness shift into researching the subjective aspect of the human experience has brought hypnosis back into an even greater role than it has had. Hypnotherapy is becoming a valuable tool in transpersonal psychology as the different forms of regression therapy are applied and investigated. As is usually the case, the masses of society are beginning to notice the importance of regression and hypnotherapy while those who should be advancing new ways of healing are ignoring the public interest.

Hypnosis has been with us for a long time and has not fully been accepted because science has not known what it is. In the chapter on TRANCES I explain the hypnotic state in the context of this mind paradigm. Here I will limit hypnosis to its historical evolution in the hope of its gaining greater acceptance for the benefits it has to offer us.

There are almost as many ways to induce hypnosis as there are hypnotherapists. This factor in itself points out that the human being is capable of moving into a hypnotic state under almost any condition. Observation of this phenomenon tells us that the hypnotic state is truly a *normal* state and that most people are going in and out of the hypnotic state many times during the day. Depending on their daily activity, people find themselves moving through daily routines in hypnotic conditions much of the time.

We cannot read very long, or watch a movie, without realizing we have placed ourselves in some automatic process which requires a conscious effort to change. The difference between the automatic, every day habit of falling into semi-trance states and being hypnotized by a hypnotist is very small. Whereas our self-induced trance is purely habitual and non-specific, the hypnotist is taking the subject, client or patient through a specific process to induce a trance state with a specific goal.

Let us return to Mesmer and his theories about magnetism and the permeating gases and fluids. In his day the ideas and theories about healing and medicine were in a turmoil. Scientific understanding was shifting and settling consciously into the mechanistic paradigm, and ideas of gases and fluids and planetary magnetism were suspect. Mesmer was what is called a 'forerunner', a person who has truths to share that are seemingly ahead of the times. Forerunners suffer the burden of judgement from those in social power and often die degraded and impoverished. Mesmer fell into this category. The gases and fluids (energy sources) he was trying to describe are the energies acupuncturists of today influence using metal needles and specific pressures.

Mesmer was into healing. He was mixing hypnosis processes with material influences on the life force energies of the body. Using hypnosis, Mesmer was able to get patients to mentally accept the shifting of energy patterns in the body. Healing was effected because he was helping the patient to access the belief system and activate the cellular memory fields related to the part which needed healing.

Mesmer's physical tools, the magnetized water, the metal rods and other paraphernalia, had some influence on the electric-magnetic system of the body and the thought processes, as they also supported the idea of faith. If the human being finds s/he can do something physical to support the mental process the healer is using, then s/he reinforces the belief of the asking, giving greater emphasis to the willing powers.

TRANCES

Accepting for now that thinking is done through two systems, the brain and the mind, we need to consider what is happening in the thought processing when a person is in trance. I have stated that there is a constant stream of thoughts (mass thought) being delivered into the mind from the planetary fields. Those thoughts stream through the individual without interruption. These are the thoughts that one can call subconscious because they do not register in the brain except in certain processes. Those thoughts are available to the conscious level but usually they are not brought forth.

The normal condition of the average brain is that 1) it seldom deliberately examines the thoughts streaming through it, and 2) is in the habit of reacting to events that come forth. During the day, while in this neutral, non-choosing of thoughts state, the individual is in a semi-trance. This makes us susceptible to any suggestion that arises out of habits or traits. It is this condition we are in when we suddenly realize that we have been driving our car for miles without being conscious of where we were. When we cooperate with a hypnotist we give over some or all control of that semi-conscious state we are often in. When we do this we let the hypnotist join our thinking processes at the fifth chakra (throat) and at the eighth chakra (transpersonal). This allows the hypnotist to manipulate the thinking process so that the information in the mind can be accessed.

The mind has the ability to access all past, present and future information about the client and anyone connected in any way to the client. Levels of trance are simply the reflection of the degree of interference in the conscious mechanism of the brain. The deeper the trance, the greater the dominance of the mid-brain activity. The deepest trance can cut off all connection to the hindbrain, and consequently the motor mechanism of the body will not function, except autonomically. The lighter the trance the greater the left brain control, meaning conscious awareness

For the hypnotherapist it is important to decide what depth of trance is ideal for the kind of treatment intended. If the goal is to assist the body in healing, a deep, somnambulistic trance which isolates the hindbrain would not be desirable. On the other hand, if there is a need to avoid body interference in the process, such as in examining the future life, it is advisable to use a deep trance.

The brain has four major parts, the forebrain, the hindbrain and the left and right hemispheres. Their function and involvement in the trance state must be considered for a successful outcome of the hypnosis treatment.

The forebrain manages the intellectual and cellular levels of thoughts (memories), and if these areas are important to the process they should be kept accessible, and a light trance state is desirable for this work. The hindbrain manages all that has to do with healing (cellular physical memories), and a deep trance state is more desirable when doing healing work.

The ideal level of trance for most therapy is a state just beyond mid-range of depth. Testing trance depth can be done by simply asking the client how deep s/he is on a scale from one to ten. This permits the client to participate in the healing process with the guidance of the therapist. All people can be hypnotized; it is merely a matter of the client feeling comfortable and trusting enough to give up left brain control. In some cases if the left brain of the client is temporarily blocked from control then a trance state can be induced. When the left brain is in fear it will block the trance process in an effort to protect the belief system from being altered.

9

Illness
& Wellness

MIND/BODY CONNECTION

The phrase 'mind/body' has been used in many ways recently, usually implying that healing is done through the mind/body connection. Since there is a confusion about what the mind is, with some people believing the mind is the brain and others believing the mind is what the brain thinks, the body connection is vague. Failure to understand what the mind is and how the mind connects to the brain creates confusion and blocks healing.

Healers, such as Deepak Chopra, *Ageless Body/Timeless Mind*, who have a good grasp of the fact that thinking can affect wellness or illness, sometimes confuse some aspects of healing because of the misunderstanding of brain and mind roles in the healing process. Closer examination of their theories would reveal what part the brain is playing and which part the mind is playing in healing and illness. If we take the position that the physical brain is responsible for the condition of the body, and the mind is responsible for the care of the soul-being, we can better understand what is going on with the body.

The body is not conscious and aware of what is happening to it. When we inflict a small wound upon it, the hindbrain will heal it without the conscious attendance of the persons thinking. This means that the physical mechanisms of the body automatically heal wounds. If we wound an unconscious person, and after awaking the person inform him/her of the wound being nothing more than a small scratch which will heal normally, the wound will heal. It will heal much the same as it heals if the person is unconscious and unaware of the wound.

If we wound an unconscious person and after awaking the person inform him/her that they have a wound which is mysterious, they begin mentally involving themselves in the wound. They may wonder who did it. They may suspect that it was perpetrated in a way which could be disastrous to them, such as with an object tainted with AIDS blood. The more secretive those involved act, permitting the person to think there may be a major problem, the more aggravated the wound will become.

What this says about the two ways of handling the wound is that there are two different processes involved. In the first example, the physical body and hindbrain are involved in the healing process and the healing is automatic. In the second example the soul-mind has entered the situation as well as the left brain, resulting in imagination, fear, soul lessons, soul tests, etc. becoming involved.

If we look to the human body only as the animal, with respect to healing, we can see healing happen automatically as it does for any animal. The hindbrain and the cellular memory field of the animal body recalls the creative process and acts accordingly, and if the necessary chemicals are present in the blood the wound heals.

Since healing is taken care of by the hindbrain, the biggest interference in this natural process comes from conscious, intellectual thoughts. Such thoughts are usually doubting and confusing and fearful. They are reinforced daily by news reports on health issues and statements by authorities. What can we do to remove this interference with our natural healing process? How can we stop the destructive, confusing thoughts from influencing us?

First, we must understand, without question that the body heals itself. Second, we refrain from intellectually dwelling on thoughts about the injury or sickness. We do not think about what might happen, and we do not talk to others except those who we want professional opinion from. Third, we find the symbolic meaning of the injury to the body so we can understand and resolve the soul lesson related to the distortion of the body.

When the lesson is understood the body may have an instant healing. If any mental reinforcement is needed for the healing, I recommended the study of the particular body parts involved to gain total understanding, their healthy functions, their material makeup. One should be able to draw the body parts in question from memory.

The key to sustaining healing is to keep thoughts of concern and doom out of the thinking. Should such thoughts creep into the thinking, interrupt the pattern of thinking by doing something to shift to the right brain. An example of this would be to turn your eyes up into the forehead. When we do this we can no longer think or stay in a thinking pattern. The Ener-Pulse meditation described earlier can assist the thinking change and the healing phase. Sleep is another way to stop the thinking pattern because during sleep the left brain is neutralized and the hindbrain is able to function free of the thinking interference. Sleep allows us to break the draining thought patterns which allows the hindbrain to regenerate the body.

When we connected the thinking mechanism of the soul-mind to the body, we have created interference in the life process at the thinking level, and the brain processes have become more intricate. This results in thinking directly influencing the healing of the body. If there is an opportunity for soul learning the soul-mind will interfere with the natural healing process.

The common idea behind the term 'mind/body' is that the brain's thinking somehow influenced physical healing or illness. The idea has merit, but it is vague. Today it is important to understand the mind's intent, which is often separate from the brain mechanism's role as far as healing goes. Through a grasp of the different roles of the primal brain, the ego, the cellular memory field and the soul-mind, the process of healing and illness become clearer.

ILLNESS

As long as we are applying rules of hard science to the examination of illness the origin of illness will not be found. However, if consideration is given to the thinking that came before the illness or symptom, then the cause of the illness may be found. All that exists is the manifestation of thought. This means that all that exists in the life of the individual is a reflection of that individual's total consciousness. If one has cancer, or AIDS, or muscular dystrophy, or any illness of any kind, that is a reflection of the consciousness. We look upon illness humanly either as chance accidents or as some kind of punishment, as though God or something were punishing us. We find it easy to look outside of us for the cause.

Illness is not an accident, and it is not meant to be a punishment. It is simply a reflection of our thinking. What manifests on the body as some illness are the thoughts that were used, and they manifest to tell us that we have an incorrect use of thought. Note that I stated an 'incorrect' use of thought, and that is the cause of the illness. Incorrect does not mean bad. Incorrect means that the use of thought was not correct in the sense of a greater truth. For example: one of the greatest incorrect uses of thought is the idea of self punishment. This would be anger at the self for some thought or deed which resulted in guilt; it is the guilt which turns into illness. Thoughts laced with guilt actually have a draining energy which depletes the body of life force. If enough life force is drained (according to the impact of the guilt) the body attracts the form of illness which reflects the level of energy lack, and the body begins to distort and possibly die accordingly.

Cancer has been under investigation for a many decades, and researchers have been using the principle of the examination of matter (biology) to find its source. Researchers are looking for some kind of matter which is at the root of the cancer. They have gone from suspicion of one kind of matter to another kind of matter, including examining the building blocks, like chromosomes for example. They are always amazed to discover another or new type of cancer when they get close to what might be the source or problem. The so-called culprit particle (or whatever) has eluded medical science from the beginning.

Cancer is a good example of the failure to find origin in biology because so much work has been done looking for the material answer. The answer has not been found in matter, in fact it seems the more we examine cancer, the more cancer we find. If thinking about something is a factor in whether it is created or not, is there a message in the statement that the more we look for cancer the more we find of it?

Let us examine illness from the perspective that thinking has something to do with cause. This leads us to the following premise. thinking causes illness, and thinking consists of minute thought particles that carry positive/negative energy forces that feed or destroy life matter. In cancer, as in any disease, we are looking for the origin of a negative physical condition. If we are to accept thinking as a cause of illness it follows that we have to look for negative kinds of thinking for the cause of illness.

Using thoughts and thinking as a method of research, imagine thinking happening at the center of the body. Imagine thoughts as little bursts of energy exploding in that center and bursting throughout and beyond the body. As thoughts are willed, the little thoughts burst outward, pushing energy in every direction through the body and its parts. As long as the bursts are constructive energy bursts of thinking, the energy is bathing the body in waves of harmony.

Let us change the thinking and imagine that suddenly some of those thoughts are destructive and are bursting destructive energy through the body. Let us say the destructive thoughts are bursting out in the direction of the lungs. As those destructive energy rays move through the lungs they starve and distort the cells. This distortion could then be the beginning of cancer in the lungs. The body would attempt to readjust the cells, but if the destructive thoughts kept spraying the lungs, the body would eventually fail and cancer would be the result.

From a behavior perspective we have to ask why someone would think destructive thoughts to form cancer? First of all, destructive thoughts do not always mean angry or violent thoughts, they may simply be thoughts of hopelessness, despair or self pity. Such thoughts are destructive to the body since they drain it if life force. Second, if we could find evidence of any changes in their thinking from constructive to destructive thinking before a person developed cancer, this might lend support or evidence to the idea that thinking caused the illness. But, may appear that the person who has cancer has been thinking no differently than s/he has for many years. We even have research which reports that some cancer patients seem to be easy going and cooperative in their natures, certainly never displaying any conscious destructive thinking. This type of patient fits the user of unconscious self destructive thoughts.

Why would people create cancer in their bodies? Certainly if you ask the patient s/he insists that they want to live and not have the illness.

I have already said that we do two kinds of thinking. We do conscious thinking of which we are aware. We do unconscious thinking constantly (fed to us by the planetary thought streams) which far exceeds the amount of conscious thinking. Most illness creating thoughts are at the unconscious level. This is a long drawn out method of creating disease. Illness thoughts used in the conscious state are just as lethal as those used in the unconscious, except that they are far quicker to form diseased cells.

If one angrily and consciously blurts out a statement, and in the unconscious thinking there is a stored program of thoughts which reinforces the outburst, one can expect immediate manifestation. I am reminded of a time when I was too busy in business, and as an executive I had all kinds of people making demands on me. For some time I had been resenting all the little demands and secretly wished I didn't hear them (see WORDS & INTENT AS FORCE). One day I entered the office to hear from my secretary that someone was insisting I do something for him. I lost my temper and stated, "I don't want to hear another goddamn thing from anyone." I left the office, went straight to my home and took a nap. When I awoke I could hear nothing. My hearing was 100% gone. An hour later an ear specialist informed me that 'strangely' all the blood vessels on the tuning forks and around them had atrophied and that I would never hear again. I had received my wish: I was stone deaf and could not hear anything.

Fortunately, I was trained in the use of thought by the masters, and I discounted the doctor's final statement of, "You'll never hear again." I demanded an appointment within two weeks for the purpose of measuring how much hearing I had regained. The doctor was reticent to make the appointment, and I could tell that he was feeling I was in denial of the severity of my condition. He finally humored me by giving me the appointment to measure my hearing. I went home and immediately started working mentally to get my hearing back. The end result was that I restored the blood vessels and regained the hearing (to the utter amazement and confusion of the doctor). The point of this is that I had built up an unconscious stream of thought against hearing, and I consciously activated the mental demand with my emotionally loaded statement.

Illness is looked at many ways, however, from a soul perspective we need to face the fact that illness is telling us something. It can be a message about some specific aspect of our soul learning which can be temporarily treated into remission if we do not face the lesson, or it can be final and is the way the soul gets released from the body through death. This is a personal soul message to the individual.

Illness can also be a soul message to the human species; we see this when there are plagues and other mass forms of illness. AIDS is such a soul message to the masses. On the surface AIDS seems to be an illness directed toward those who are labeled 'gay'. When we examine what AIDS does, we find it causes a total breakdown of the immune system. An illness manifests as failure of the immune system has to be a message to everyone. It is a message saying, "All human beings are now physically subject to an immune failure."

Although the gay community seemed to be the focus of AIDS, it is not a 'gay' disease. AIDS affected the gay person because the gay person has a major mental disturbing factor that causes their bodies to be more vulnerable. That factor is mental confusion of identity. Mental confusion of identity causes the basic thought particles of the body to destabilize the energy of the human body building blocks. Those basic building blocks of the body normally contain a certain level of yin or yang energy. That formula of energy becomes disturbed when the person questions their gender identity. If the doubting of gender identity continues, the basic building blocks of the body lose strength, causing the body to be vulnerable to disease.

In the past the basic energy condition of the gay person, although not stabilized, was not so easily affected by disease. However, in recent years the planet itself has become highly toxic on every level - air, water, soil, weight, sound and thoughts. This toxic condition has accelerated and is affecting all immune systems. The gay element of society is naturally the first to feel the inability of the immune system to fend off these dangerous levels of poison. If world toxic conditions continue to increase millions of people will suffer what we call AIDS.

HEALING

In western societies we get interested in healing when we get injured or sick enough to want to get healed. As westerners we want a 'quick fix' healing because we are used to getting things either out of the way or fixing them quickly. We apply this philosophy to everything, whether it's the bicycle, the car or the human body. We are wise enough to know that maintenance and care keeps the bicycle and the car efficient, but for the human body it appears we can't take the time for maintenance.

Actually we are smart enough to understand that the body needs maintenance also. What prevents us from using proper maintenance is the belief that we are invincible. Nothing short of a serious death scare will wake us up to the vulnerability of the body. Unlike the car which has a list of parts we can easily replace, the human body is far more complex. We know many of the parts of the body, and some, we know, can be replaced. We are also discovering there are aspects of the human body which we do not know about. We know now that thinking affects the body. We can use a bio-feedback machine to watch how we can manipulate the body's process. To date we have done much research and made a lot of discoveries about the physical body. What we need to learn more about is how the thinking can heal a part of the body, or the whole body, for that matter. There is no question that the biology of the person is a factor in any illness, however, before the material form exists there are thoughts involved in the formation of the material form. Thinking makes up the blueprint behind the genes and the DNA formula.

The body heals itself as we witness time and again by observing the simple scratch or cut. The healing of the scratch can be accelerated by managing the thoughts about the condition. We have all heard reports on how laughter has had a healing effect on some illnesses. There is even the saying, "Laughter is the best medicine." Healing through laughter has its source in the thoughts used. When the body heals itself it uses the cellular memory field of the human form to draw on for information to heal. It is this field that direct thought intervention acts upon to either deter healing or accelerate healing.

Ultimately, to me, all body failure is connected to the learning of soul lessons. You only need to talk to people who have overcome cancer,and usually they will tell you that the illness totally changed their life and that it was the best thing that ever happened to them. The soul lesson ignored will work on the body through thinking processes, eating at the human expression, either quickly as with a seeming accident, or slowly as a cancer.

We can assist the process of healing by uncovering our deeply rooted beliefs and self destructive thinking. Regression therapy is especially suited to this kind of examination. Complete understanding of the cause of our inner distortion, along with clear choice of healing at all levels can result in complete healing and at times instant remission of the illness.

PLACEBO EFFECT

We need to look at phenomena such as the 'placebo effect' to understand how medical science accepts subjective thinking while at the same time denying that the subjective is scientific. I say this not to point fingers at science for discrediting events humankind calls 'miracles' and instead calling them 'spontaneous remissions' so they can use the phrase in research, but to point out that science is beginning to accept the idea of thinking as an influence in healing. Like the term 'spontaneous remission', the 'placebo effect' is a subjective event. What 'placebo effect' means is 'thought influence'. Instead of saying, "Let us measure the thought influence in this experiment," researchers are trained to say 'placebo effect' without understanding what is being done to the taker of the placebo.

If science looked closely at what they call 'placebo effect' from the perspective of 'thought influence,' perhaps science would begin to unravel the role of thought in the healing and illness condition. If a sugar or chalk pill (placebo) is given to an unsuspecting patient in place of the 'real' medicine and the patient gets well because s/he believed it was a medicine to make them well, is it not reasonable to assume that we could all heal ourselves with our thinking alone? This implies that medicine and diets in themselves are much less effective as healing agents than what science leads us to believe.

This observation of placebo healing also ties in with the idea many doctors expound about not giving false hope. There is no such thing as false hope. Without hope a patient will not recover, no matter what medicines are given, and yet the patient's hope alone has brought back many people from the brink of death after the doctor had given up entirely. The worse thing any doctor can do is 'condemn' the patient by taking the hope away which might be the very ingredient needed most for recovery. The word 'terminal' should never be used by an attending physician. Many people have overcome so-called terminal illnesses, a record usually ignored by researchers and the medical profession.

If we can increase the effect of the placebo pill - the expectation, faith and trust that healing will result - we will see more spontaneous remissions (miracles). It matters not what the person places their faith in - the doctor, the medicine, the diet or God - as long as we (the brain system) believe, and as long as we truly wish to be healed, we can be healed.

FAITH

When we consider faith, we consider belief and usually belief in the religious sense. Faith is a very powerful energy for creating manifestation in or outside the human body. Although faith can be in many things, faith healing usually has its roots in a religion. If mass thought is considered, the religious power or energy is tremendous. This mass energy can act to heal the body or in some cases alter the physical condition as in the experience of having wounds (stigmata) appear on the body. Such wounds are the result of mass thought from those in the religion connected to the person with the manifestations. The person who attracts these thoughts from the masses has an essence containing the need to express martyrdom.

We see the power of faith in the thoughts followers have in those they believe in. There are many saints in the Christian religion who have been dead centuries and their bodies are expressing some kind of life force to this day: they heal, they bleed and they often do not disintegrate. Some of these bodies have been stored for centuries in glass cases with no preservatives. If this were the case with one or two bodies we might ignore it, however, there are many of these bodies which are incorrupt. They have one common denominator: they are revered as special by masses of people of a particular faith. There incorruptibility is directly attributable to the power of thought through faith. The prayers of thousands of believers sending their thought of well being to these 'saints' creates the life force in those dead bodies, keeping them intact (see The Incorruptibles by Joan Carrol Cruz).

271

AGING & DEATH

From the time the body is born it is replacing itself automatically. All parts of the body are periodically completely replaced as cells cycle through the manifestation process. This means that the body is capable of reproducing its own image as long as it contains life force. What gets in the way of the body reproducing itself forever, one might ask.

In *How and Why We Age* by Leonard Hayflick we are treated to a thorough examination of the process of aging presented from the accepted scientific view. Hayflick also discusses the biological clock that science is certain is in everything, in this case the biological clock of self destruction of the body cell. Science sees this biological clock as being in the way of the body staying young forever.

Among researchers the term 'brain drain' is used, referring to a loss of nerve cells related to aging. This reference is a good clue to what is behind aging. The diminishing of neuron cell reproduction is directly caused by the mass thoughts attracted into the thinking system. The intellectual clock that human beings have put on their life process through habits attracts thoughts of aging. In the mass thought streams of the planet are aging thoughts which actually infect the cells of the body with information to begin the dying process. There is a mass expectation of aging and the acceptance of the belief of aging is an automatic mental order to deny the cells the necessary life force needed to sustain a lasting life.

When we view the process of life in this dimension from a mass perspective we can easily see that if the material form is not growing and regenerating, it is disintegrating. We see this process ongoing, no matter what the material form, it can be an animal body or a section of highway. Simply take note of a section of highway that is bypassed and in a short time the piece of highway that is no longer being used shows signs of deteriorization. The old section which is not being used is often right beside the new section that is being driven upon, and although they both may be solid concrete we soon see cracks and a breakdown of surface on the one not being used.

What causes the old highway concrete to age quickly and die?

The answer is that the old highway is no longer being kept in materialization by the thoughts of those who pass over it. When and as human beings use the highway they are mentally nourishing the 'illusion' of the highway, feeding it thoughts of materialization.

Elsewhere I have mentioned that we have two thinking systems, a conscious and an unconscious. As you drive over a highway you may not consciously think about the highway but that unconscious system is constantly connected to the highway, making certain it is in a condition to be traversed. Those thoughts bombard the highway, as we move along it and are emphasized by the vibrations of our passing over it, all of which feeds energy into its existence.

Whether we know it or not, we are constantly affecting the condition of that which is material in our existence and that includes the human body. We have the choice and the power of thought to stop using the body at any age and let it disintegrate. If we stop using the body to express life it begins to age and die; just like the old highway.

We fail to recognize that aging is a part of the dying process. Just as we fail to recognise that sickness is a part of the dying process. Most deaths fall into certain general categories such as cancer or heart disease. Both of these usually are connected to aging in the sense of 'time to die'. One method (cancer) is a lingering slow death process, the other (heart attack) is usually a fast process of dying or leaving. Both kinds of death are acceptable socially. Like so much that we do in our lives, we have to die in a manner acceptable to society.

'Time to die' is a powerful phrase. I have mentioned the power of the word, and when someone says, "t is time to die," they unconsciously give mental power to the aging process. We witness these kinds of statements about dying in many ways, we hear words like, "I can't stand it anymore!" (meaning they can't stand what they are experiencing in life) or, "I wish I was dead!"

By virtue of the fact that we are using mass thought from the planet to conduct our lives, we are all processing thoughts that tell us that it is time to age and die. The average mass thoughts which reflect limitations on living, such as aging thoughts, influence our physical condition. Besides our personal reasons for aging and dying we prematurely inflict on ourselves, we are also exposed to the mass influence of the average belief about aging and dying of all humans that is fed to us through mass thought streams.

The diseases are our methods of leaving the life experience. In addition to the 'natural' deaths from cancer and heart ailment there are the mass 'suicide' methods of death human beings inflict on themselves by drawing the information from the planetary thought streams. War is one such method of death that is not only classified as being tragic, it is also classified as heroic. When we classify and label diseases we lose the connection of the energies and vibratory causation between body tissues and mental/emotional states.

Death by AIDS is a self fulfilled wish attracted through the energies of guilt, rejection and confusion. Death from Alzheimer disease is the result of not wanting to think anymore about what life has to offer or what it is about. This causes a lack of energy from thoughts coming into the skull brain and dehydrating the brain tissue. All these varieties of unnatural premature deaths are a result of specific types of thinking.

DISEASES

Disease is dis-ease, meaning disturbance or change from the normal state. All diseases have to do with imbalances in the thinking processes of the human being. There is no question that cancer or AIDS are a very real destruction of the human tissue, however, their source is in the thinking of the person. Yes, there are genetic and physical influences. Medical science can prove that a father and a father's father had a specific gene combination determined to be related to a specific illness. Interestingly enough, medical science can also prove that a father and a father's father could have the specific gene combination without the descendant getting the disease. What is the scientific insight here? The ultimate insight is that although some human lineage shows a succession of disease, the descendant need not be diseased. Unfortunately, with the consciousness of medical science of today being what it is, the tendency is to point out the negative reality. The descendant is told, "If your father and your father's father had it, most likely you will get it". In the thinking of the average person, if someone of authority (who knows) says, "You most likely will get the disease," this is enough mental influence to create the condition feared.

Professionals should be saying, "We have proof that even though someone's father had a disease, descendants do not always get it."

All disease is the slow death of the physical state of the human body. The disease may be a distortion of the body, but in any case, cells mutate and die. Why? As a teacher of thought and thinking I could simply state, "If one has a disease one desires the disease." Why is this statement not enough for the diseased person to reject the disease? The answer is two-fold and simple. First of all, there are many more doctors saying, "It's not your fault you have the disease, you got it from your father (or from a transfusion)." The statement allows us to blame someone other than the self for what is happening.

The second aspect of not wanting to believe we create our own disease is the conscious ego belief that we want to be healthy and live forever. We each have created this clever ego which operates from a set of surface beliefs that attempts to manipulate our life and those around us. We are all aware that we have two opposing mental forces; one part soul-mind) of us knows we are eternal, and another part (left brain) believes we will die. When we openly want to die, we call on the part that believes we will die. When we don't want to die we call on the part which knows we are eternal. Unfortunately, the thinking process is designed in such a way that the part which believes we will die has the last word. Any thoughts used by the thinking system of the eternal part of us has to pass through the thinking mechanism which believes that we will die, and most of the time it will deny the eternal thoughts any power in physical decisions.

IMAGERY

Many practitioners in the alternative medicine field use imagery for healing of the body. There are several approaches of using imagery for healing. Those with illnesses are asked to concentrate on creating images for the purpose of destroying the illness. One individual I am aware of healed his brain tumor by envisioning the tumor as a dark glob of energy and the healing method as of electricity showering the mass. In time, in the images of the patient, the mass began to diminish in size and shrivel from the electrocutionary bombardment. Subsequent x-rays showed calcification developing around the tumor, this without any

death wish

chemical medical intervention. Eventually the imagery process seemed to dissolve the tumor completely. X-rays finally confirmed that the tumor had disappeared.

There are other methods of imagery being suggested to people with life threatening ailments. I observed one group process in which the group was told by the facilitator to go into a meditative state and visualize the body being bathed by soothing energy to alleviate stress on nerves, muscles and all body parts, and to allow the immune system to function without interference and do the healing.

A number of people have reported total and partial remissions due to imagery processes. Unfortunately the success rate reported is not as spectacular as the idea which is founded in the belief that thoughts can destroy tumors and illness.

Having had several experiences with total remission for myself personally, I can definitely say that thinking, in and of itself, has the power to heal. Imagery works for those who have certain mental beliefs prevailing regarding their life experience. Of utmost importance is that the person with the illness does not have a death wish.

A death wish is not an idea of the conscious state of thinking; it has its origin in subliminal or unconscious thinking. The inner decision to terminate the life of the body can be deliberate, based on the conclusion that the life is not serving the soul need. If the person refuses to change and learn, or if the life chosen does not offer the opportunity for learning the soul expected, it may decide to withdraw from the body by creating illness. Death can also be a prearranged situation (arranged on the other side in the astral level by those to be directly involved at the time of death), for the learning benefit of those who are to be bereaved as well as the one to transition onward.

If there is to be a death that is automatic or planned, imagery can have no effect on the illness. However, if during the illness the inner (unconscious) death wish is cancelled, then imagery has a very good chance of directly influencing the cells to live and not mutate or die.

If there is no death wish, the message to get well has a good chance of success when certain steps are followed in using imagery. The first step is to reinforce the belief system against being influenced by others who believe that the illness is terminal. Anyone who has influence on the belief system of the sick person and who believes there is no hope, will work against the imagery being successful. Outside influences should be examined carefully because even though the person who doubts success does not verbalize negativity, on a psychic level the influence can prevent cure.

Second, an environment which contributes to mental and physical wellness is vital. In addition to positive thoughts, sounds and speech, there should be lightness of heart, lightness of space, and lightness of behavior.

Thirdly, understanding the function of physical organs or tissues directly connected to the illness is vital. If there is a tumor then the exact location of the tumor and its relation to vital parts of the body should be clear in the thoughts of the sick person. A mental picture of a clean, healthy organ or part of the body where the disturbance is located is important, as is understanding of how the body rebuilds a damaged part or organ. Understanding what cells have to do to reverse the degenerative process they have become set into is vital. The patient should be able to draw the perfect organ in its perfect working condition and anatomically correct. The drawing should be treated as the blueprint the cells are to work from. Thoughts of nourishment oxygen, blood, minerals, etc. needed to restore cell growth should accompany images of the blueprint.

Having more knowledge of how the body works, especially those parts that are diseased is important. It is the belief structure that one must work with. The more knowledge of the body's anatomy and of the proper function one has, the more acceptance of the healing processes takes place.

The body knows how to reproduce itself cellularly from birth, however, as we grow we acquire certain beliefs about health that are intellectual. Those added intellectual beliefs interfere with the cell's natural memory process of body regeneration. By giving the self understanding of the structure of the body and its parts we can realign the belief systems with the natural process of regeneration

Step four, when imaging requires that use of thoughts and words be limited to happy words and thoughts which attract life force. This is especially important. Filling the waking hours with happy thoughts is vital.

One should relive and experience all happy memories of childhood experiences. Such happy events should be so clear in memory that one can relive the excitement in the body at the time of the happy events. It helps to carry a list of such events so that the ill person can pick one out to share with others in a way that arouses the enthusiasm of the original feelings while a child.

It is important when working on physical regeneration to understand that life force comes to us through happy thoughts, not food. Advertising influences us greatly and those who have food products to sell are constantly affecting our belief systems about nutritional needs and values. From early life on we are

told to eat some particular food to get energy. That food is usually the most advertised product. In addition we are always told by researchers about the latest and the best thing for getting energy. Our belief systems get confused because we are always being brainwashed by companies and health experts that a certain food is best for us. Shortly thereafter we are told that food is not good for us any more. The average belief system is totally confused about what keeps the body healthy, and this interferes with the natural process of regeneration.

The major confusions about energy and the body is our intellectual conditioning telling us that we get energy from eating particular kind of foods. Food supplies us with very little energy. If you are using imagery for healing you need to have the right chemicals to help the body heal. We eat foods for the purpose of getting those right chemicals, minerals, enzymes, vitamins, etc. We eat the food (chemicals) to keep up the material compositions of the body. We must replace the chemicals we have used. This of itself does not supply energy or life force. Energy comes to us through a mental 'feeding' system between us, others and the planet. Our primary source of energy is the thoughts we use. If we process streams of thoughts through our systems that are happy and energizing we feed the body life force.

There is a difference between the intellectual belief structures and the natural memory processes of the body that have the responsibility for body regeneration. The belief structures can override the natural process and this is why most people cannot get results from their imagery efforts to heal the body. Medical science has discovered that when a person is injured and unconscious, and stays unconscious, the body takes over and begins to create natural splints and other measures to regenerate the body. This tells us that the body knows how to rebuild itself.

Imagery is a powerful method of healing when the principles are understood and opposing beliefs and thoughts are not interfering. If results are slow or not coming when applying imagery to a problem then look to the soul lesson the person is involved in and work to resolve that.

LIFE FORCE & DEPRESSION

Depression is the result of the prolonged use of kinds of thought particles which drains life force from the body. I call these 'falling thought'. This process is compounded by the law of attraction. Since such thoughts have a strong content of attraction to one another, causing the person to unwittingly use more of the same kind of thinking, the depression increases. Continued use by the person of 'falling thought' particles eventually leads to a draining of life force from the body cells, thereby creating a 'starving reaction' in the physical body at the cellular level. This is often experienced as a physical discomfort which causes the person to behave as though they are plagued by an inner itching sensation. The sensation is the reaction of the physical senses to the distorting of the cells as they begin to mutate and gravitate toward one another, forming pockets of dis-ease. At some point the person in this condition will act in desperation, oftentimes doing things to stimulate some kind of sensation. Engaging in excessive masturbation and other sexual activities would be an example.

Nearly everyone slips into depressive thoughts at one time or another. The sooner we recognize this and decide to stop the flow of draining mass thought particles, the easier it is to come out of our depression. To stop the constant flow of falling thoughts it is only necessary to turn the eyes way upwards into the skull; this stops the flow of all conscious thoughts immediately. When this is repeated several times the flow of draining thoughts recedes and stops coming.

A rubber band on the wrist which is comfortably loose can also be an aid to the stopping of falling thoughts. Each time it is realized that the thoughts are ongoing and draining, a snap of the rubber band, causing a slight sting on the wrist will stop the flow of thoughts. This can be followed by the eye excercise.

Every effort should be made to develop a flow of happy thoughts after the draining thoughts have been stopped. This can be facilitated by keeping a personal log of pleasant experiences handy. Keep a log of ten or more memories about happy childhood events in your book. When reading a happy event make the effort to relive the happy experience mentally.

These are some simple but effective ideas to help the brain stop attracting from mass thought the draining particles which suck energy out of the system. The importance is to understand that depression is caused by the type of thinking the brain is caught up in and there is a need to reverse the automatic attraction process going on.

The reason why electro-shock therapy often works for the severely depressed is that the electricity actually burns away the thought particles passing through the thinking system. The draining mass thought streams are stopped, and the thinking system is disrupted from attracting more thoughts for a while.

My training tells me that regression hypnotherapy is by far the best method for dealing with depression and eliminating it. This is true for those who are willing to take responsibility for their life and their thinking. With regression work the source or reason for having attracted a continuous flow of draining thought particles can be revealed. Once the source of the falling thoughts is found, the therapist can assist the person to alter the thinking into a constructive healthy pattern. Thereafter it is vital to make choices of the thinking, choices that include positive ideas and happy thoughts.

There are many kinds of energies connected to the thought particles being attracted into the personal thought systems. Chronic states such as depression, anger, withdrawal, hyperactivity and others all have their own quality of thought particles which are attracted according to the emotional condition.

I am reminded of an article I recently read which was titled: *Psychologist Links Passivity To Cancer.* In this article psychologist Lydia Temoshok, author of *The Type "C" Connection,* states, "Those with passive behavior are more likely to get cancer than those who are not passive. Such behaviors invite the development of cancer by somehow lowering the body's ability to fight off disease." Temoshok is correct up to a point. What occurs is that those who stay passive (the dictionary says passive is lacking in energy or will) fail to do the thinking necessary to attract thoughts which carry life force to them. The thought streams they have been attracting have a like- attracts-like quality which was set in motion and sustained through some psychological self destabilizing circumstance.

I do not want to leave you with the idea that simply using the correct thought which attracts life force to you will completely heal you. Life force energy can help heal, and if all the mental conditions are what they need be, healing will take place. One does not heal if one is not getting life force energy. However, life force by itself is not enough to cause healing. There are some other factors involved in healing, including, but not limited to, soul needs being satisfied. If all these other factors are taken care of and all that is needed is the life force energy, then healing can take place rapidly when life force is received. I have witnessed several healings which some would call miracles which were simply the result of the other factors mentioned being resolved. When the diseased person had received an infusion of life force from an outside source, such as a hands-on healer who projects life force energies to others , the healings were instantaneous.

DRUGS

When we consider the role of the soul in the human experience and the idea that the soul attains its growth and balance through the person learning to live harmoniously with others, we can see the probable interference drug taking has on personal growth. From my perspective, the greatest challenge the human being has is resolving soul lessons. This is done by facing those things that cause us to become emotionally upset to the extent that we make poor choices in our life. Mood elevating drugs can be essential to saving the life, however, drug taking has become a way for many to avoid life. Drugs like Prozac are now ingested by millions of people who are concerned with mood swings and various levels of depression.

I was visited the other day by a friend whom I had not seen for a year. A year ago she was involved in resolving family difficulties by taking classes in how to relate with family members. She appeared to be excited about resolving family problems in a holistic manner which involved discovering herself and understanding the behavior of the other family members from an ethnic and transpersonal perspective. Then she moved to another area, and as I stated, I did not see her for some time.

When she visited me the other day she seemed happy and 'up' (excited) about her life. On the surface she appeared much improved. As we talked I began to see the signs in her speech and body language of a person on drugs ('uppers'). She soon related her concern about divorce, was disappointed about where she had moved to, and financially she was near crisis.

When I commented that she seemed awfully 'up' and happy considering the condition she was in, she told me: "Thank God for the drugs! You know, Joe, we had to move and things got worse, and I had such headaches. I couldn't take it anymore, I had to get something, now I do much better, this stuff really works. Yes, my problems are still there but now they don't bother me." I asked her about her self improvement efforts. Her several comments about all she was going to be able to do now that she was no longer feeling pressure made it clear that self improvement was something in the future.

From the soul lesson perspective it is that 'pressure' we feel about things that is a sign there is something that we should be resolving in our thinking. If the pressure is artificially released by a drug and we cannot function normally, facing 'our lions' and working through them, the soul is cheated. In the case above I know this person well and as I talked with her I was happy for her light hearted air but I was concerned for what was happening in her relationships now that she was no longer dealing with them directly.

Drugs can make it possible to escape dealing with soul lessons for awhile, but after the drug period has run its course and distorted all the connecting relationships, one must then face the greater problems accrued, which will seem insurmountable. Time does not exist for the soul, and it will always be knocking at the door, expecting the ego to eventually wear down and face the 'music' (the need to be one with all).

LIFE FORCE & SEX

There are many connections between life force and sexual behavior which need to be understood. By being aware of the link, we can understand why the sex act and activities related to it have such an impact on the human experience. Everything, from young, happy love to violent rape and heinous mass killings often are connected to life force and sex.

In commenting on depression I mentioned that depressed persons often excessively masturbate. This is because the person is associating the feelings of masturbation with experiencing pleasure. Pleasure is connected to joy, and the feeling of joy is a state of attraction which brings life force to the person through their thoughts. Through masturbation, in this example, the depressed person gets a momentary infusion of life force which temporarily relieves the depressed anxiety condition. It does not last very long, but it does supply some relief. It is like the temporary fix, or high, the drug addict gets when taking a drug; it gives relief but only for a short period.

When a male and a female are angry with one another and verbally abusive, they drain one another of life force. Often, when the argument is suspended, or there is a collapsing of confrontation, the two will often engage in an intense physical sexual experience. This results in a feeding of life force energies back into the bodies of the two. The intense creative, passionate, joyful feelings exercised in the sex act can attract considerable levels of life force. Because of the anticipation and experience of exciting, erotic, sensitive feelings in sexual contact the individual 'sets' him/herself up for an inflow of exultation and power.

Besides the memory of past sexually exciting encounters, there is the memory of the orgasmic experience. This combination not only attracts life force to the participant, but in the case of the male there is the inner knowing that the orgasm is going to give him a release from all things. The moment of orgasm is the only time the male escapes the continuous demands made on him by his left brain while he is in the conscious state. Immediately after the peak experience at orgasm the male ceases to think and is temporarily free of all pressures. This being free temporarily after having received a jolt of life force can be a state of escape.

Having understood that life force is low in older people and that young people have an excess, we can see why a young person can become attractive to an older person.

Children automatically feed life force to grandparents, and when there is play and excitement in the relating, more life force is transferred to the grandparent. The grandparent, when playing with the child, finds him or herself energized by the experience of playing with the child. This infusion of energy feeds the cells life force and assists in healing body ailments. Grandparents today are not aware that they are being fed life force by their grandchild. It simply 'feels good' to have the grandchild around. If we add sexual energy to this combination, we realize how the life force content can be increased in the older person simply by having sexual thoughts when around the younger person.

The grandparent who has a body which has been starved for life force and is a cellular anxiety state becomes intoxicated with the life force fed by the child. This is sometimes the point in the relationship with the feeding child when the grandfather makes a crucial error in judgement. In physically playing with the child, the life force connection between his hands and the body of the child can create a magnetizing sensation which is exhilarating to him. This can cause him to be more exploring with the hands. It is at this point in his excitement that he automatically attracts mass thought which tells him to explore a little further. It is also at this point that he is crossing the line between life force transferring on an accepted social level and a non-accepted social level. Mass thought will feed him the thinking to cross that line and stimulate sexual feelings, causing an even greater increase in the life force feeding process between him and the child. At this point the mass thought streams dominate his left brain process and they may override his moral social training.

In such a case the grandparent has made a blunder and created abuse, however, he has received a major life force injection, and his body benefits as the cells receive energy. When some time has passed and his life force level is low enough to starve his cells, he will be driven to repeat the play and possible abuse of the child - a similar condition as that of the addict. This is the situation of the 'kind' and 'gentle' old man who finds himself exposed for having abused a child.

284

What we call 'old age' involves more than the number of years someone has lived. It means the body is not nourished as it was when young. As years go by, our belief systems, reinforced by our social structures, compound the dis-ease kinds of thought processes we use at different stages of our lives. These thought processes guarantee the starving of our bodies, keeping the life force needed for perpetual manifestation at the low levels which cause the body to dematerialize itself.

Many males unwittingly cross the line and gain some life force from children through sexual thoughts. Many do not act out those thoughts, but because of circumstances and self control manage to find other ways to satisfy their need for life force. Fortunately (or unfortunately) the changes of life force attracted from extreme behaviorist abuse is not sufficient to sustain an acceptable level of life force.

The rapist is often the person who went through a psychological process of gaining life force to feed his body through some sexual experience. In the beginning the rapist might have added more life force by fantasizing during sexual experiences with a female. At some point he may have unknowingly increased his level of life force by having a sexual experience which was awkward and as a consequence was exciting. His next stage might have been a forced sexual experience with someone he knew. The next phase after that may have been discovering that the anticipated forced sexual encounter fed him some strange power (life force). After that he would broaden the concept of excitement in the experience through elaborate stalking or preparing for excitement. He might add physical harm and excessive threats to increase the infusion of life force he is unknowingly getting. From there he could increase the level of momentary power pleasure through further acts of violence, upping the level of life force he would receive, giving him more power. After each experience the need to use force becomes greater in order to sustain his life force, excluding other ways of getting it naturally.

Much of the sexual depravity and abuse that is perpetrated on others could be eliminated through education about the energies involved. If an understanding of energies was taught to children at an early age and that education included recognizing feelings of life force in the body, people would grow older understanding the energy needs of the body. If the energies are explained as more than what has been referred to as the libido, but includes understanding the difference between sexual urges and life force needs, sexual abuse would not be rampant as it is now.

As for the adult abusers, it is important that they receive education as to why they feel driven to involve themselves in extreme sexual behavior. This may not be a complete deterrent to extreme behavior for all abusers, but it should help many to divert their attention to more acceptable ways to energize the body. Research and therapy should be undertaken to discover what methods of education would help those who are already infected with the wrong kind of thinking as to supplying body energy needs.

AUTISTIC OR MIND CHILD

Robert Schwartz, at the 1992 International Transpersonal Association conference in Prague, mentioned a man named Peter who was near forty years of age and suffering from autism. Peter is a good example to show what can go wrong at birth in the union at birth between soul-mind and animal brain. Peter was described as having an unusable body, confined to a wheel chair when Robert met him. Peter could not talk nor move much. His head was twisted, and he could not focus his eyes. Peter is a member of a wealthy family who had invited Robert to attend a meeting at which endowments would be granted. It was not expected to be a healing meeting of any kind. However, at that meeting a researcher of autism got Peter to type on a computer by supporting his hand and asking him, "How is it in there, Peter?" Peter, who had never been able to do anything, let alone focus on a computer, typed the answer, "Its terrible, I've been trapped in here for thirty-eight years." That started a whole new way for Peter.

Let's look at Peter and what was going on in his life to cause him to be autistic. When Peter was born, the soul-mind joined to the body, and the two thinking systems connected. There are different degrees or levels of connection between mind and animal brain due to many factors. The ideal melding would result in a balanced situation, meaning that the brain and mind would have equal input in the overall thinking to be done by the human being. This did not happen for Peter.

In our present primitive state of consciousness, it is the norm for the left brain to control most of the mechanism which allows thought to express into the human reality. We might say a 'veil' is dropped between the soul's mind and the door to the human reality, and the guard at that 'door' is the animal brain. Occasionally, due to various kinds of conditions, the mind is able to dominate that doorway and drop the curtain on the animal brain side of the door to reality. This causes the human being to have limited use of the body. In Peter's case, the mind dominates the physical human brain, which is the opposite condition of the norm.

As I have mentioned before, in this realty mind thoughts must be expressed through the animal brain. In Peter's case, that function became limited and he was trapped inside the mind ball and unable to use the animal brain for motor purposes. He also had no way to use mind thoughts until the researcher placed a computer board in a position where he could access it.

How did Peter get to use his hand? Why did he suddenly start typing on a keyboard after all these years? What happened that allowed him to get momentary control of his fingers? Human beings connect through a subconscious mental cross feeding process using the eighth chakra between them when they have like desires in their consciousness. Peter was able to draw on the energy forces of the man who wanted him to communicate. That energy was transferred to Peter's hand by telepathy. There was not the normal transmission and energy projection from the animal brain through the nerves to the hand.

How did Peter see the keyboard letters? Peter's soul-mind (not brain), using the eighth chakra, connected to the mind of the man helping him, along with the minds of the others in the room, and used their senses to see and use the keyboard.

As Robert Schwartz disclosed, they discovered Peter had knowledge of things which the average human being does not seem to have. Was Peter able to read a whole library of books without seeing them? When asked how he read the books, he typed out that he had 'peripheral vision'. What is that which can read volumes without physically looking at them? All minds are capable of doing this. Many seek this mind connection. It is the state yogis and adepts search for all their lives. Peter had it at birth. Unfortunately, instead of him controlling it, it controlled him. Whereas the yogi learns to access the eighth mind chakra by temporarily circumventing the left brain control (lifting the veil), the autistic is unable to make use of the left brain while using the mind chakra. Once the connection at birth is made, the individual fixated in autism then struggles to physically surface, to have full use of the animal brain and the bodily controls.

The extraordinary mental abilities or talents displayed by many autistics are all capabilities of the soul-mind without the restrictions of the left brain. Peter managed to use his fingers after all those years of non use because his mind gave up some control. Material thoughts were allowed to pass into the hindbrain and the shift was made.

I suspect that the timing of Peter's breakthrough had to do with the timing of events on the planet and the mass need for consciousness raising. Schwartz told the conference audience in Prague that he likened Peter's being 'trapped' to the trap all human beings seem to be in today in thinking which is limited and destructive to the earth and fellow human beings. Schwartz is correct about us being trapped, but unlike Peter, most human beings are trapped in the constructs of the animal brain which does not want the soul-mind to share any of its power. More than just trapped in the animal brain, most human beings are trapped in the left brain hemisphere, which has been conditioned far beyond its optimum relationship to other parts of the thinking systems.

Since the time of Peter's breakthrough several discoveries have been made about autism. Through the use of the computer autistic children are able to communicate with the world and even get involved in schooling since it was discovered that someone could hold up their arm and they could type.

Recent articles about autism have also revealed problems arising for those directly involved (see SOUL LESSONS) in the autistic child's life. Some insist the assistant, the arm holder, is manipulating messages typed by the autistic. Others are concerned about the messages themselves. There are some messages from the autistic making accusations about those around them. In regard to those messages we must make an effort to understand how the right brain and the soul-mind use thought.

The autistic does not think in the same context as the so-called 'normal' person does. The normal person has a human animal ego constructed through left brain conditioning which has built-in self protective mechanisms. The autistic does not have the use of these mechanisms. The autistic ego is soul-mind and right brain oriented which is vastly different from the animal left brain ego orientation.

The thinking of the autistic is dominated by the soul and contrary to what most people understand, the soul is an emotionless demander of lesson learning. The soul's primary interests are having a body to learn lessons through and to develop the needed lessons of the heart.

When we examine the world of the soul-mind we realize that it sees everything from the perspective of thought particles and energies; it does not see material of any kind, only the energy of the material. Neither does it become involved in good, bad, moral, unmoral, pain, no pain, duty or any of the thinking that has to do with the human world of illusion as we understand it. The soul-mind is aware of these human ideas but it sees all human things as tools of learning to balance its forces and energies.

In the instance where an autistic types out that someone has sexually abused him/her, one needs to understand that the accusation is not personal. It may even mean that the actual physical act of sexual abuse never took place (although it could have). Perhaps I could give this example: Let us assume a parent of an autistic child is involved in a normal sex act with the spouse. During the act, or when thinking about the act, imagine that the parent, for a moment, thought about his/her autistic child and wished it could someday experience the emotions and feelings s/he is experiencing in the sexual act. That imagined hope for the child could be projected to the right brain and soul-mind of the autistic child, creating a memory it could someday draw upon and relive or experience mentally. It is probable that at some point in the future, when the autistic child had occasion to think about something sexual, or even see something referring to sex, s/he would attract the memory of the sexual fantasy of the parent and the autistic would re-image the sexual experience of the parent as though it were his/her own experience.

There is also the ability of the soul-mind to bring forth sexual experiences from past lives integrating such thoughts with today's thinking. We are mental beings, capable of projecting our images and energies onto another being. Sexual energy itself is a powerful force made up of yin, yang and life force energies. These energies are easy to will upon another, and the soul-mind and right brain are capable of holding and projecting these energies as illusory form. Jesus said simply, "If you think it, you have done it," and this is something the autistic child has easy access to and has difficulty in distinguishing fantasy from reality.

TO PROFESSIONALS

I am aware that there are many who have searched for answers to the brain and mind question. There are also many who have presented insights into various paradigms involving the idea of consciousness. What I am sharing about thought and thinking has to do with the consciousness (mass thought) changes we are facing on the planet today. We are now living in the quantum age (fully three dimensional) and answers must be found to assist the consciousness raising and solving of problems that are manifesting around the globe. We need to get enough answers today to take human beings off the 'hot seat', and to satisfy the entity 'earth' before it decides to give us some answers the hard way.

There are no accidents in this universe, and it is no accident that over the past few years, by evolutionary standards, many insights and discoveries have appeared involving the brain, the soul-mind and aspects of thinking or consciousness. Researchers in all fields are looking for answers and solutions to the need to marry hard science and subjective truths. There has been and still is, an air of expectancy among researchers. Karl Pribram has been stewing over the evolutionary flame for some time with his 'holographic' idea. Pierre Teilhard de Chardin's idea of the 'noosphere', Carl Jung's 'collective unconscious', Karl Lashley's 'engram', David Bohm's 'holomovement, Rupert Sheldrake's 'morphic resonance' and many others, all have been cooking the same stew, that stew is called raising of consciousness.

I have been cooking that same stew, and I can remember laughing at a cartoon years ago about some neuro-scientists who were looking for the 'source' of consciousness. The cartoon showed several doctors surrounding an operating table and the senior researcher, pointing down inside the opened skull of a patient, saying, "There he is! I knew one day we would find him!" An insert of inside the skull showed a tiny god sitting on a throne behind a peeled off layer of brain matter. All the other researchers were smiling in unison.

I was reminded of that cartoon when I read in Marilyn Ferguson's *Brain/Mind Bulletin* that Karl Pribram might be haunted by the question, "Who was the little man inside the little man?" I was humored then and now because scientists are still looking to the brain in the mad search for answers about consciousness and the mind, only today they have lasers and other fancy gadgets to do that with. There is no beginning spark of consciousness (God) to be found in that group of muscles called the brain.

The holographic idea is as close to the answer about thinking and the mind as is the morphic resonance theory. Astronomer James Jeans was close when he said that the universe is more like a great thought than a great machine. As human beings we are too unenlightened to be given all the answers at once. We are still warlike and would destroy ourselves if we were to actually discover the unlimited use of the power of pure thought. We are finding answers now about consciousness raising as that is the vital need of the planet and its beings today. Up to now the holographic idea is about as far as the brain has been able to reach toward understanding thinking and thinking systems.

Psychic phenomena (channeling, visions, voices) has a role in the raising of the consciousness of the human being. What is transpiring around the globe has to do directly with unveiling the relationship of the brain to the soul-mind. Psychic phenomena plays a primary part in getting information to those 'forerunners' who are paving the way for humankind to get an understanding of consciousness raising.

Today the brain is in charge of the material third dimension and it is stumbling along at a primitive second dimensional level of awareness. Connected to it, but patient with the brain, is the mind, a separate entity, bonded to the material being. Both brain and soul-mind have their different roles and levels within the framework of the thinking systems of the planet and the human being.

CONCLUSION

In all societies and throughout history human beings have looked to divining tools, prayer and meditation to connect to the non-material world, seeking answers and guidance for the self and for nations. That kind of inner searching resulted in visions, guidance by spirits and entities from many places.

Humankind has a mass inclination for going too far when looking for answers, and in looking for truths has often ignorantly turned to extreme right brain measures. Religious fanaticism often abandoned all reason in its righteous fervor to determine the will of God. Such was the practice where suspected offenders were bound hand and foot and then thrown into a deep pool of water. If they drowned, the 'word' (from God) was "guilty and unworthy of divine acceptance." If they somehow managed to survive, the 'word' was "innocent and worthy of divine acceptance." Such primitive use of non-material thinking escalated in horrendous mass extermination of human beings by religious leadership.

The misuse of right brain non-material mass thinking had its peak during the great Inquisition and punishment meted out under the guise of divine justice became intolerable. Right brain use by the masses had become distorted to the degree that the world needed a major change in thinking. World mass right brain influence had gone from its most creative period, which was before the advent of the Israelites, to its most downward destructive period during the Inquisition.

What I share about right and left brain influences is understanding gained from my many years of experiences with masters on the other side. It is my understanding that for eons, legions of master souls have reincarnated to guide human thinking toward adjusting with the planet's need to balance its forces. Again and again they have returned to write the books and create the discoveries that would shift the human masses toward enlightenment and change. At the height of the Inquisition it became necessary to guide human thinking into the left brain, and the Age of Reason was invoked into the human consciousness to make the changes. This, of course, took centuries to establish. After a relatively short period of left brain dominance scientists gained left brain control of the world with the paradigms of mechanics and evolution.

Because human thinking by both the male and female has accelerated to an extreme left brain (yang energy) use and influenced the planetary mass thought streams in a relatively short period (only a few hundred years), consciousness today, once again, requires a major adjustment. This time, the world needs an input of right brain, non-material thinking into the planetary mass thought streams. This is another attempt by the guiding masters to bring balance back into world and human consciousness.

This universe and our world is a school for souls to learn to balance energies. This is why I call it the 'University of Thought.' Through our thinking we are supposed to learn to balance our lives. In this simple third dimension where there are only two forces, yin and yang (negative and positive); the answer to harmony is in the middle. The right brain represents yin thinking, the left brain represents yang thinking; the opposing forces. When the two halves think in unison there is harmony. When one half dominates the other we are run by mass thought, and there can be no harmony for us, either individually or collectively.

Because of the long period of dominance of left brain thinking (scientific control) today the planet needs a strong move in thinking by the masses toward right brain influence. It is the right brain now which brings to the thinking change and expanded awareness. The last global change toward material (left brain) thinking took two hundred years to totally influence world mass thought. Because of the acceleration of consciousness during that period a change toward right and left brain balance can now be affected in a very few short years.

The masters have guided individuals and human kind into a strong right brain use of thinking in the last few years. This has been done mostly through the reincarnation of those who have strong right brain abilities. Already we see a veritable explosion of interest in things of the right brain. The world media on all levels is flooded with right brain thinking. We see it in the news, movie theaters and in books and magazines. Interest in phenomena and alternative ways of living in every area is flourishing. New-age books are making the best-seller list consistently.

There is of course a backlash to all this movement toward right brain thinking. Any threat to loss of control and material benefits causes the left brain great fear. The left brain feels threatened and is reacting culturally through left brain organizations. The more intense the left brain thinking in any organization, the more reactive and violent that group becomes in its opposition to change toward right brain thinking. It is natural for left brained people (yang) to move physically and violently against right brain thinking people who are less materialistic and more idealistic.

We are in a time when it is imperative that the world's political leaders and educators recognize the need to balance right and left brain demands in our societies. We are greatly in need of wise educators who can bring a balanced right and left brain teaching approach to students.

At this same time of struggle between left brain users and right brain users the planet is in dire need of balancing its own material forces. If human thought had not polluted the thought streams of animal, human and planet, humankind could move fully into third dimensional awareness without chaos.

We have been living in third dimensional vibrations using primarily a left brain mental approach, and the result has been that the left brain views everything two dimensionally and is continually stressed. We automatically focus on whatever we look at with the left brain. The left brain by itself can only perceive a two dimensional perspective. It requires a concentrated effort to avoid focusing and involve both brain hemispheres to see three dimensionally. The strain on the left brain is becoming critical and right brain integration is necessary.

Many episodes of so-called abnormal behavior relative to illusions has its roots in the person slipping into temporary third dimensional viewing. When this occurs to a left brain functioning person it causes anxiety and panic. The left brain holds no reference for actual third dimensional visions, and any head movement during such 'visions' increases the mental distortion and accelerates the fear sense. Most schizophrenic illusory experiences are nothing more than third dimensional sight distortion due to the imbalance of the two brain

294

hemispheres and a fear reaction to the circumstances.

Norman Friedman in his *Bridging Science and Spirit* (1990) hits the nail on the head when he knits physics, psychology and mysticism together as a fabric of a new paradigm. He makes it possible to see the subjective meld with the objective. Fred Allan Wolf in the foreword of Friedman's book, pinpoints the key to finding the catalyst to the answer to a new paradigm when he quotes Mr. A. Square in Edwin A. Abbott's *Flatland*:

> An unspeakable horror seized me. There was darkness; then a dizzying sensation of sight that was not like seeing; I saw . . . Space that was not Space: I was myself, and not myself . . . . I shrieked . . . , "Either this is madness or it is Hell." "It is neither," replied the voice of the sphere, "it is Knowledge; it is Three Dimensions; open your eye once again and try to look steadily."

> I looked, and, behold, a new world!

This is a description of the dilemma humankind faces today. It describes the terror of the left brain when faced with third dimensional viewing, an awareness that should be natural to human beings who are living in the third dimension.

It is the failure of humans to adjust their fears to permit integration into the third dimension that keeps us primitive and suffering paranoia. The quote above is a cry from the left brain when it unexpectedly slips into what we call an altered state. In reality we are caught in an altered state now (partial second dimensional perception) which is out of step with our true third dimensional existence.

Wolf's comment in the paragraph following the quote above: "For many of us, the new landscape we see from the bridge built by Norman Friedman may seem as strange as the third dimension did to Mr. A. Square. . ." points up how 'strange' and unfamiliar third dimensional viewing and living is today to the human race. Does this not show that we are not where we are supposed to be mentally today? Shouldn't we be striving to learn and teach others how to sense and act three-dimensionally in our 'new world' (consciousness raising)?

I have said much about the need to balance the brain, and the greatest opportunity for anyone coming to this planet to learn this is

Balancing the brain

through human relationships, specifically the relationship between man and woman. Soul lesson learning is everywhere, and it becomes more intense as we relate to someone on a personal, emotional level. The more intense the relationship, the more immediate the soul lesson and the opportunity to practice balance.

We can learn soul lessons with and through friends with whom we have emotional ties. We can learn with siblings and offspring where emotions are easily triggered. But it is in the facing of the opposite sex in an ongoing emotional environment that we can grow quickest spiritually.

I am focusing now on that relationship where the male is primarily of yang power and the female is primarily of yin power, for it is in the balancing of those two powers that we resolve soul lessons. The male yang and female yin marriage is the courtyard of major lesson learning. When one attracts the other they each have come face to face with their individual prime soul lessons. Each has attracted to him/herself the lesson most needed for spiritual growth in the form of the other person.

Today we have a great confusion of roles in marriage. Marriages are dissolving rapidly because of the misuse of powers. It is the powers, yin and yang, and their correct use which should be understood to create harmony and success in a relationship. In the past the male had a distinct role and the female had a distinct role. He went out and challenged the world for their piece of it, and she nurtured the unit, including the offspring. Such marriages were a good soul arrangement for lesson learning, except for one major flaw: the male failed to realize the value of the female's contribution; he not only has failed to see it, he failed to understand the dynamics of the yin and yang powers coming together for a purpose. In his typical 'animal' nature (being of denser vibrations) he understood himself to be the all powerful partner who conquered the world and owned what was in his experience at home. The male in the relationship does not understand that it is the power the yin female gives him that makes him successful in the correct, lasting manner.

When a yin and yang unit (relationship) melds to accomplish things together, it is the psychic aura of magnetic power generated by the unit that makes it possible to have and accomplish things. Bonded together, the man and woman have a power that is far beyond the power of two separate individuals.

After the honeymoon the male ignorantly gives all his attention to where he wants to go. The female's contribution of yin power is ignored. If she is a home maker and mother she is judged as not contributing financially which is far from the truth of the laws of psychic material manifestation. If the male fails to include her essence in his thrust for accomplishment, the female soon realizes he is going into the world without her essence. When her realization sets in that he does not honor her power in the unit, she unconsciously withdraws the yin force. Not knowing that he has alienated her and does not have her powers, he flounders in his projecting himself forward in the world.

As soon as the result of the energies to compliment one another as an attracting force stops working, estrangement of one another takes place. If there is no effort made to harmoniously rejoin the energies on the psychic level, divorce is inevitable. If there is an effort to come back together there is the usual phase of arguments in which one blames the other intellectually. This results in a raising of emotional temperatures and thereafter the arguing is set in a doomed process because negative thinking is automatically being fed to each of them from mass thought. As a natural process the quality of words used by each is destructive to the effort to build the relationship. I say 'natural' because automatically, through their emotions, each is attracting thoughts that contains the average kind of argumentative wording in the mass thought fields. The quality of that kind of mass thinking is negative and destructive to harmonious relating.

The answer to bringing harmony into the unit is for each to understand the other from the point of view of the power of each. If the man can fully understand the value of her yin power melded to his yang power he will honor her. If she has his respect she can once again choose to be bonded with his yang power. This is done by the two of them learning that they are different kinds of powers and act and behave differently because of these powers.

In confrontations the woman needs to talk through what is presented as a problem; the man needs to listen to her attentively and respectfully. He needs to think quietly about the problems, and she must honor his silence and respect that he is not like her and does not think, feel and express as she does. Male power cannot be female power and visa versa. Far in the future men and women may talk and think alike, but at this stage of evolution that is impossible, and ignoring this truth and demanding change usually ends in separation. Respecting each other for who and what each is and honoring one another's contribution to the unit is the answer today.

If the female chooses to accept the male after reconciliation, the unit can go on together in harmony. It takes considerable effort on the part of the male to release his ego ideas of possession of the female and all material things in his life while according to her an equal place of power in the relationship. If he can do this, and the female accepts him, he will readily observe what it means to gain back the yin force he had taken for granted in the beginning of the relationship. He will soon see that his efforts in the world gain far greater results materially with her essence.

Though there will never be a totally balanced human being, nor will there ever be lasting peace in our world, because this is a dimension of opposites, a school for learning balance, nevertheless we can experience relative peace and great joy through the accomplishment of our individual soul growth. It is my hope that this paradigm of thought and thinking will help smooth the way into our third dimensional lives.

To emphasize the importance of this need for the male and female to meld in harmony I end this writing with a transcription of a dialogue between myself and a master. This psychic meeting and discussion came as the result of my questioning of women moving into male roles in which they would become as destructive as males, such as soldiers and fighter pilots. As is usually the case when I communicate with a master, there is an awareness of my question, and without my asking it verbally, the master begins answering the question.

Excerpts of channeled dialogue, January 8, 1995, between a master and myself:

Master (in response to my mental question): "Take one moment to adjust the thinking process that comes about when faced with the realities of the living experience in the human male world. What transpires in the mind of the thinking male are oftentimes the greedy, self satisfying thoughts that alleviate and eliminate the thoughts of those around him. Man, if you will, the human man, is a self contained thinking unit that seldom allows any interference or involvement either from those around him or from the existing wisdom that comes in and goes out continuously. It is man's greatest folly to believe that he himself is responsible for controlling, shall we say, the environment in which he exists.

"Man's greatest lesson in the human male structure is to learn to adjust to that and those which come into his experience. Man is a taker but seldom a giver. Man seldom gives of his own being, for man is very closed, you see. Man is a closed unit. Man does not extend himself beyond that which he is. That is the greatest lesson of man, you see. Man constantly fights the environment and fights with those around him to keep safe, shall we say, havens for all that he is or has.

"When one comes into the human experience one comes in to blend and one comes in to become one with. For in the human experience all are a part of the whole. That is what the human experience is. It is not that all are responsible for what others do, but all are a part of what others do; it is unavoidable. Man, through his evolution, has felt the pain of that which others do, thereby closing himself off to the events around him. It is like enclosing himself in the safety of the bubble of his own existence and only allowing that in which he can, shall we say, comprehend and control. When man's environment is invaded, man thereby gets angry. Man's anger is out to destroy that which has invaded his environment.

"You say, what is the anger that is invading the planet? It is the maleness, it is the maleness in protection of his own environment. It is the maleness refusing to blend with the femaleness which is the balancing factor of the maleness. But man too, does not let the femaleness in. For the femaleness is the enemy of the maleness as man sees his structured environment. His structured environment must be in his control.

"When man allows the female to become a part of what he is, there is a part of the control that he must relinquish, and he does not do it willingly. When that within him is beyond his comprehension, beyond his control, and beyond his ability to, shall we say, build or destroy, he immediately annihilates that which is the cause of his discomfort.

"Man's power is far out of balance to the ability of woman to adjust. If I were to view your planet from afar, I would say, the male vibration is incredibly powerful. The female vibration is very weak. And yet it is the female vibration that brings the love and the peace and the gentleness and the adjust-ability.

"Your planet is rapidly going into a phase of protective survival which is the maleness, the male dominance. What is needed is more of the female and less of the male. If more of the female were in power, the planet would balance again. In the relationship, if more of the female were in power the relationship would balance again. In the health, if more of the female were in power, the health of the body would balance again. But man, once again, controls the money. Man controls the earth; man controls the thought; man controls all that is. And man feels constantly threatened by the presence of the female. He does not trust that the female does not want his power.

"The female is a much wiser vibration. The female wants nothing of the male's power. It is the foolishness of children that the female sees. And yet to speak is to obtain the wrath of the maleness of the planet. For man sets the woman aside when he does his maleness and that very action is the destruction of the human experience.

"You may ask me."

Q: "Why is it that we see this move of the female to become the male?"

A: "The female in reality does not want to be the male, my friend. It is the male that thinks the female who chooses to speak is looking for maleness. In reality the female wants not to be the male. For who would want to be the foolish child that is called the male, the aggressive one, who is the destroyer of all that is in the human experience, the angry one, the one who has no love for himself."

Q: "I am speaking of the women who are taking up arms, who insist on the right to kill as men have the right to kill. I am speaking about the women who have become male aggressive. Where is that coming from?"

A: "There are so few of those. The women who take up guns take up guns to stand beside the male. It is not of their choosing; it is never of their choosing. For that which they are as female is not male, you see. It can never be, it will never be. And the reality of it is, the female does not want to be male anymore than those who are male wish to be female, you see. There are those who play the part, but in the heart of hearts that is not the way it is."

Q: "I see women demanding the right to fly planes with bombs to bomb the enemy. What kind of woman is it who is doing this? What part of the female is doing this?"

A: "That is the woman who says, 'See me, see me, feel me, I am as you!' It is not that the woman wants to be male. The woman wants to be acknowledged, that is all. And if man only acknowledges man and those who do the deeds of a man, for the woman to be acknowledged the woman must do the deeds of a man. If man would acknowledge woman for her womanness, then woman would be womanness. But when woman receives no acknowledgement in her womanness, she shall be as the male to get the acknowledgement. Do you understand what I say?"

Q: "No, I do not understand what you say, because she is not going to get the acknowledgement. What she is doing is putting herself in a position to prove that she is as ugly as the man. There is no acknowledgement by the male for that kind of femaleness."

A. "The stronger the male, the stronger the resentment there is of the female. You are a strong male. That within you that views the female, views it much stronger, much stronger, according to the strongness of your maleness."

Q: "There is that within me which from observation and wisdom says that the woman does not serve her purpose in her role of balancing the male by becoming like the male."

A: "The woman is not perfect, my friend! You use examples of very few womanness. There are not many that fly planes and drop bombs. Woman's way is to balance man. The woman brings forth the balance in the male. What must a woman do for a man to say, 'Ah, this is a being!' When the woman reaches out to gain recognition by standing in the path of the man, the man says, 'Here is a woman that wants to be a man. That is not what is. What is, is the woman standing in the path of the man saying, 'Acknowledge that I too am.'

"Do you understand what I say? The planet must be balanced, must be balanced. If you look, men are in power, men are in power. The more empowered men are, the angrier they are. The angrier they are, the more imbalanced the planet is. The more imbalanced the planet is, the more violent the actions. The more violent the actions, the more anger surrounds the planet. And I say to you, the answer is in the woman, not the man. Do you understand that?"

Q: "I fully understand that. My only comment here is, does it serve woman's purpose to be out there doing what the man does, acting as the man, being destructive as the man. Does that serve the woman's purpose?"

A: "The woman's purpose is to balance the man."

Q: "Well, she is not going to do it by killing."

A: "You speak of so few, my friend! There are so few that do what you say! Woman stands beside the man she chooses. Oftentimes the man she chooses kills and demands that she do as he. That is more often than the woman choosing. Woman does not choose to kill. It is always the male vibration within that brings upon the killing. It is from the male. It is that the male vibration is so strong that it engulfs all in its presence. It controls all in its presence. That is what I say. It controls the female in its presence. It does not allow the female to think and be and do what the female is to think and be and do, the balancing point. He does not say, 'I am, as you are, we are as balanced.' It says, 'I am the man, do as I say!' and the woman does. For that is her role, you see, that is her role with the aggressive male. That is what she sees. And yet, it is not her role. In the respect that the male is aggressive and brings the female along, the female shall follow. For if the male does not listen, the female cannot balance. And if that is her role then she shall do what she shall do to bring about balance.

"I say to you, male thought is dominating the planet. I say to you, male thought is creating an overabundance of anger. That is what I say to you. And you say to me, 'What of the female?' That is not what I say. That is not even a part of what I say. That is so minute to the role of the male. It has nought to do with it. The female who kills, my friend, obeys the male who says, 'Kill!' That is when the female kills. The female obeys the male."

Q: "The female is not obeying the male when she insists on the right to kill. The male says, 'Stay home!'"

A: "The male does not tell her to stay home. In the war zone the male tells the female to kill."

Q: "We have no war zone here."

A: "I do not speak of your country. I am speaking of the vibration of the planet. I speak of the entire planet. I say to you, the female follows the male. The male is out of balance now for it has no femaleness to bring it back into balance, you see. The female must become aggressive, stand in the path of the male and say, 'Stop! You must stop!' And the male destroys that which says, 'Stop!' Then five females stand in the path of the man and say, 'Stop!' Fifteen, twenty, fifty, five thousand! Woman must help man to see the folly of his destructive nature before the planet is destroyed. Do you understand what I say?"

Q: "Well, thank you! That is my answer, that is what I was asking for, thank you."

A: "You, my friend, are male. You see the female as a threat to your environment. You too do not trust the female. You do not trust the female to not want to be as you. You see, that is the ego of man that says, 'I am, therefore all want to be me.'

"Woman does not want to be man, do you understand? It is very important that you know that. Woman does not want to be man. She views man as a foolish child, foolish, foolish child. That is the intelligence of the woman brought upon the planet to balance the male factor. It is a gift! It is a gift, and yet the male sees it as a threat. Why can men not see this as the gift of balance? Why must men constantly destroy that which is there to balance him? And yet he does. He verbally destroys it, he physically destroys it; he abhors it; he annihilates it; he belittles it and yet it is the greatest gift.

"In your book of books, in the beginning, man was given a gift, the gift of woman. And before the next page man had turned it into the enemy. Do you understand? The enemy. It is not the enemy, it is the gift. Man cannot survive without the gift. Man will only destroy himself and all that he is and all that is around him, and then he will destroy the gift; and then he will stand alone in his anguish and demand understanding and he has killed the understanding, he has killed that which is his balance.

"That is the folly of man and all men are of the maleness. All women are of the femaleness. Man does not wish to be woman. Woman does not wish to be man. Man is the creator, woman is the balancer. Man creates, woman balances. But woman cannot balance if there is not the desire to be balanced.

"Let me say it to you - and you may accept what I say or not, that is your choice - woman has no cause. Man has cause. Woman has not cause. Woman has no bonding with woman. Woman only balances. Woman balances. Woman does not form marauding bands of women to kill. Woman follows man. Woman follows man to balance, to balance. Man says, 'Kill, or I kill you! Kill, or I leave you! Kill, or you shall not be with me!' Woman kills. Woman balances, that is what woman does. Do you understand?"

Q: "Yes, I understand. I had the impression when you were talking to me you were feeling that I do not understand that, but I do understand that. I have understood that for a long time."

A: "You are maleness, my friend! You are viewing from a male standpoint. You, too, do not allow the balancing nature of woman. Only when it suits that which you do, you see. For it is very difficult for man to open his heart to the gift. We have said many times, it is the gift. It is not that woman is greater than man, for that would be to say that man in his accomplishments is greater than woman. That is not it. That is not it. That is not where it lies. It lies in the gift. The gift is the gift. It is the gift. And it is the balance. It is the humanness. That is what you seek. You do not seek to be greater than woman, nor does woman seek to be greater than man. I say this to you because man's power is far, far out of balance, and it needs to be brought back into balance for all to survive. I see much destruction, I see anger, I see much chaos if man continues on the path that he is on, seeing woman as choosing to be man."

"You must listen to what has been given, then ask on the balancing. That is all."

Q.: "I will do that. Thank you."

End of message

Illustrations

References
& Suggested Reading

(* literature recommended by the masters)

*Adamski, G. & Leslie, D. (1953). *Flying saucers have landed.* New York: The British Book Centre.

Alschuler, A. (1987). *The world of inner voice.* Unpublished data.

*Anon (1975). *Course in miracles.* Tiburon, CA: Foundation For Inner Peace.

*Asch, S. (1951). *Moses.* New York: G. P. Putnam Sons.

Assagioli, R. (1986). *Psychosynthesis.* Esalen, CA: Esalen Books.

*Beasley, V. (1975). *Your electro-vibratory body.* Boulder Creek, CA: University Of The Trees Press.

*Besant, A. (1903). *Thought power.* Wheaton, IL: The Theosophical Publishing House.

*Besant, A. and Leadbeater (1980). *Thought-forms.* Adyar,

India: Theosophical Printing House.

*Blavatski, H.P. (1888). *The secret doctrine.* Wheaton IL: The Theosophical Publishing House.

Bohm, David (1980). *Wholeness and the implicate order.* New York: Routledge, Chapman & Hall.

*Brodie, F.M. (1945). *No man knows my history.* New York: Alfred Knopf.

*Buckley, D.H. (1967). *Spirit communication for the millions.* Los Angeles: Shelbourne Press.

Buzan, T. (1976). *Use both sides of your brain.* New York: E.P. Dutton.

Chopra, D. (1989). *Quantum healing.* New York: Bantam Books.

Chopra, D. (1993). *Ageless body, timeless mind.* New York: Crown Publishers, Inc.

Costa, J. (1994). *Yeshu Hannosri: for god so loved the world.* Solana Beach, CA: Institute of Thought, Better Life Books.

Costa, J. (1992). A Dissertation. *A heuristic inquiry on channeling: an investigation of the source and meaning of hearing voices from the unconscious.* Solana Beach, CA: Institute of Thought, Better Life Books

*Crenshaw, J. (1950). *Telephone between worlds.* Los Angeles: DeVorss & Co.

*Crum, J.K. (1975). *The art of inner listening.* Wheaton, Il: Re-Quest Books.

Cruz, Joan C. (1974). *The incorruptibles.* Rockford,Il: Tan Books.

Davies, A.P. (1956). *The dead sea scrolls.* New York: Mentor Books.

Dennett, D. (1991). *Consciousness explained.* New York: Little, Brown & Co.

Dossey, L. (1982). *Space, time & medicine.* Boston, MA: New Science Library.

Friedman, N. (1990). *Bridging science and spirit.* St. Louis, MO: Living Lake Books.

Ferguson, M. (1980). *Aquarian conspiracy.* Los Angeles, CA: Jeremy Tarcher.

*Garrison, O.V. (1964). *Tantra, the yoga of sex.* New York: Causeway Books.

Gilligan, C. (1982). *In a different voice.* Cambridge, MA: Harvard University Press.

*Goldsmith, J. (1961). *The thunder of silence.* New York: Harper & Row.

Harman, W. & C. de Quincey (1994). *The scientific exploration of consciousness: toward an adequate epistemology.* Sausalito, CA: Institute of Noetic Sciences.

Hayflick, L. (1994). *How and why we age.* New York: Ballantine.

Hillman, J. (1975). *Re-visioning psychology.* New York: Harper & Row.

*Hills, C. (1980). *Creative conflict.* Boulder Creek, CA: University of the trees press.

Jung. C.G. (1933). *Modern man in search of a soul.* New York: Harcourt Brace Jovanovich.

*Jung, C. G. (1969). *The archetypes and the collective unconscious.* New York: Princeton University Press.

Kellen, B. (1975). *Muhammad: messenger of god.* New York: Thomas Nelson Publishers.

Keyes, Jr., K. (1975). *Handbook to higher consciousness.* Coos Bay, OR: Love Line Books.

Klimo, J. (1987). *Channeling: Investigations on receiving information from paranormal sources.* Los Angeles, Jeremy Tarcher Inc.

Keyes Jr., K. (1982). *The hundredth monkey.* Coos Bay, OR: Vision Books.

Langley, N. & H. L. Cayce (1967). *Edgar Cayce on reincarnation.* New York: A Kinney Service Co.

Leadbeater, C. W. & A. Besant (1980). *Thought-forms.* Adyar, India: Theosophical Printing House.

Lucas, W.B. (Ed), (1993). *Regression therapy a handbook for professionals.* Crest Park, CA: Deep Forest Press.

*Miller, C.L. (1973). *All about angels.* Glendale, CA: Regal Books.

Moody, R. (1981). *Life after life.* New York: Bantam Books.

Monroe, Robert (1987). *Far journeys.* New York: Bantam Doubleday.

Monroe, Robert (1973). *Journeys out of the body.* New York: Bantam Doubleday.

*Montgomery, R. (1985). *Aliens amongst us.* New York: Ballantine Books.

Parrinder, G. (1971). *World religions.* New York: Random House.

Pelletier, K.R. & Garfield, C. (1976). *Consciousness: east and west.* New York: Harper & Row.

*Percival, H.W. (1946). *Thinking and destiny.* Dallas, TX: Word Foundation.

*Picthall, M. (1919). *The meaning of the glorious koran.* New York: Dorset Press.

Pribram, C. (1976). *Consciousness and the brain.* New York: Plenum.

Priest, S. (1991). *Theories of the mind.* New York: Houghton Mifflin Co.

*Reich, W. (1973) *Either, god and devil & cosmic superimposition.* New York: Farrar, Straus and Giroux.

Reiser, M.F. (1990). *Memory in brain and mind.* New York: Basic Books.

Rieder, M. (1993). Mission to Millboro. Nevada City, CA: Blue Dolphin Publishing.

*Roberts, J. (1970). *The seth material.* New York: Bantam.

Schuchman, H. (1975). *A course in miracles.* Tiburon, CA: Foundation For Inner Peace.

Shafica, K. & Kunz, D.V.G. (1989). *The chakras and the human energy fields.* Wheaton, IL: The Theosophical Publishing House.

Sheldrake, R. (1989). *The Presence of the past - Morphic resonance and the habit of nature.* New York: Random Hourse.

*Spalding, B.T. (1924). *Life and teachings of the masters of the far east.* Los Angeles: DeVorss & Co.

Steiger, B. (1988). *The fellowship.* New York: Doubleday.

Stevenson, I. (1988). *Twenty cases suggestive of reincarnation.* Charlottesville, VA: University Press of Virginia.

*Swedenborg, E. (1980). *The true christian religion.* New York: Swedenborg Foundation.

Tarnas, P. (1991). *Passion of the western mind.* New York: Harmony Books.

Tart, C.T. (1986). *Waking up.* Boston: New Science Library.

Van Dusen, W. (1985). *Hallucinations as the world of spirits.* In White, J. (Ed.), *Frontiers of consciousness.* New York: Julian Press.

Walsh, R. & F. Vaughan (Eds.), (1993). *Paths beyond ego.* Los Angeles, CA: Jeremy P. Tarcher.

Weiss, B. (1988). *Many lives, many masters.* New York: Simon & Schuster.

*Williamson, George H. (1958). *Secret places of the lion.* New York: Warner Books.

Wolf, F.A. (1984). *Star wave.* New York: Macmillan Publishing.

*Yogananda, P. (1981). *Autobiography of a yogi.* Los Angeles, CA: Self Realization Fellowship.